# MASS VIOLENCE IN AMERICA

MASS VIOLENCE IN AMERICA

# PEN AND PENCIL SKETCHES

# OF THE GREAT RIOTS

*J. T. Headley*

ARNO PRESS & THE NEW YORK TIMES

*New York • 1969*

# Editorial Note

NATIONS, LIKE MEN, ARE SOMETIMES INTERESTED IN BURYING THE PAST.

In early 1968, after more than five years marked by political assassinations, racial uprisings, campus disorders, mass demonstrations and the violent suppression of protest, *The New York Times Magazine* asked a group of distinguished scholars to reply to the question, "Is America by nature a violent society?" In answer, University of Chicago anthropologist Clifford Geertz wrote:

> "We do not know very well what kind of society we live in, what kind of history we have had, what kind of people we are. We are just now beginning to find out, the hard way . . ."

The proposition was astonishing but correct: what was least understood about domestic political violence was its role in American history. It was common knowledge that the United States had had a Revolution, a Civil War, some trouble with the Indians and a period of labor-management conflict. But one could search the shelves of the nation's great libraries without discovering more than a handful of works on the subject of violence in American history, and these hopelessly out of date.

Historians had generally ignored or soft-pedaled the history of farmer uprisings, native vigilantism, labor-management struggles, ethnic conflicts and race riots; comparative work in the history of social conflict was particularly weak. Sociologists and political scientists in the grip of "consensus" theory tended to treat episodes of mass violence in America as insignificant or aberrational—temporary exceptions to the norm of peaceful progress. Psychologists and behavioral scientists discussed "mob violence" in terms which suggested that riots, revolts, insurrections and official violence were the products of individual or group pathology. All such interpretations had the effect not only of minimizing group violence in America, but of depriving it of political content—hence, of relevance to the present.

As a result, as late as 1968, the rich, multifarious and often terrifying history of domestic political violence was still largely *terra incognita*. So long as most Americans wished to keep certain skeletons locked away in their closets, few scholars would attempt to open doors. Conversely, once the American people, frightened yet emboldened by the sudden reappearance of intense social conflict, began to ask new questions about the past, so did the scholars.

Our purpose in helping Arno Press and *The New York Times* select and publish significant documents in the history of political violence has not been to compound past errors by overemphasizing the role of conflict in American history. On the contrary, our aim has been to provide materials which will aid in the search for an accurate perspective on the present. MASS VIOLENCE IN AMERICA includes eyewitness reports, government documents and other descriptive and analytic material relating to mass political violence in the United States. These documents not only provide information—they give the "feel" or "flavor" of past eras of civil disorder by evoking the emotional and political context in which revolts took place. Most of them have long been out of print and are obtainable, if at all, only in the nation's largest libraries.

The scope of this series is wide, ranging from accounts of Indian warfare to descriptions of labor-management violence, from narratives of colonial insurrections to reports on modern racial uprisings. It is not, however, limitless, nor were the constituent volumes carelessly selected. The principle of coherence which guided the selections is implicit in the phrase "mass political violence." "Mass" denotes activity engaged in by large groups rather than individuals acting alone; "political" suggests a relationship between such activity and competition among domestic groups for power, property and prestige; and "violence" is narrowly construed as resulting in physical damage to persons or property. In short, the materials reproduced herein are intended to illuminate the resort to violence by American groups seeking to change or to preserve the status quo. Although historical, they are of interest to any who wishes to understand the causes, nature and direction of domestic political violence, whether they be social scientists, historians or just interested Americans.

Of course, we are particularly hopeful that these volumes will prove useful to those now engaged in curriculum-revision and the teaching of high school and college courses in the area of American studies. What Christopher Jencks and David Reisman term "the Academic Revolution" has made difficult demands on all educators, not the least of which is the demand for courses which are both relevant to the condition of modern America and of the highest academic quality. These volumes are meant to provide raw material for such courses— primary source matter which will help both instructors and students to deepen and enrich their views of the American experience.

Most important, the editors and publisher recognize that these volumes appear during a national crisis which is also a crisis of the spirit, a time in which the public response to various manifestations of civil disorder is increasingly governed by anger, fear and hysteria. In such an atmosphere it is important to recognize that one is not alone in time—that such events have taken place before in America and, unless fundamental changes in our social and political life take place, will probably recur in the future. Our fondest hope is that this work, and others like it, will help to keep alive, in a time of growing unreason, the spirit of reasoned inquiry.

RICHARD E. RUBENSTEIN
*The Adlai Stevenson Institute*
*Chicago, Illinois*

ROBERT M. FOGELSON
*Harvard-MIT Joint Center*
*for Urban Studies*
*Cambridge, Massachusetts*

# PEN AND PENCIL SKETCHES

# OF THE GREAT RIOTS

PITTSBURGH—BURNING OF THE UNION DEPOT.

# PEN AND PENCIL SKETCHES

### OF THE

# GREAT RIOTS.

#### AN ILLUSTRATED HISTORY OF THE RAILROAD AND OTHER

## GREAT AMERICAN RIOTS.

### Including all the Riots in the Early History of the Country.

### BY HON. J. T. HEADLEY,

Author of NAPOLEON AND HIS MARSHALS," "WASHINGTON AND HIS GEN-
ERALS," "SACRED MOUNTAINS," "SACRED HEROES AND
MARTYRS," ETC.

### ILLUSTRATED

———— ◆ ————

NEW YORK:
## E. B. TREAT, 757 BROADWAY,
### 1882.

# PREFACE.

THE materials for the descriptions of the Negro and Doctors' Riots were gathered from the Archives of the Historical Society; those of the immediately succeeding ones, from the press of the times.

For the scenes and incidents that occurred on the stage and behind the curtain in the Astor-place Opera Riot, I am indebted to a pamphlet entitled "*Behind the Scenes.*"

The materials for the history of the Draft Riots were obtained in part from the Daily Press, and in part from the City and Military Authorities, especially Commissioner Acton, Seth Hawley, General Brown, and Colonel Frothingham, who succeeded in putting them down.

Mr. David Barnes, who published, some ten years ago, a pamphlet entitled "The Metropolitan Police,"

kindly furnished me facts relating to the Police
Department of great value, and which saved me
much labor and time.

Much difficulty has been encountered in gathering
together, from various quarters, the facts spread over
a century and a half, but it is believed that everything necessary to a complete understanding of the
subjects treated of has been given, consistent with
the continuity and interest of the narrative.

The material for the account of the unparalleled
Railroad Strike, with the Riots connected with it in
various places, are gathered necessarily from the local
press of the country.

Of course some minor riots—a collection of mobs
that were easily dispersed by the police, and were
characterized by no prolonged struggle or striking incidents—are not mentioned.

In addition to the numerous illustrations from
special designs, engraved expressly for this work, the
Publisher is indebted to the courtesy of the Pennsylvania Railroad Company for a number of the
finest illustrations, also to Frank Leslie's Illustrated
Newspaper.

# CONTENTS.

## CHAPTER I.

## CHAPTER II.

### THE NEGRO RIOTS OF 1712-1741.

## CHAPTER III.

### THE STAMP-ACT RIOT OF 1765.

1*

## CHAPTER IV.

### DOCTORS' RIOT, 1788.

## CHAPTER V.

### SPRING ELECTION RIOTS OF 1834.

## CHAPTER VI.

### ABOLITION RIOTS OF 1834 AND 1835.

## CHAPTER VII.

### FLOUR RIOT OF 1837.

# CHAPTER VIII.

### ASTOR-PLACE RIOTS, 1849.

# CHAPTER IX.

### POLICE RIOT—DEAD-RABBITS' RIOT—BREAD RIOT, 1857.

# CHAPTER X.

### DRAFT RIOTS OF 1863.

# CHAPTER XI.

# CHAPTER XII.

# CHAPTER XIII.

# CHAPTER XIV.

# CHAPTER XV.

# CHAPTER XX.

# CHAPTER XXI.

## ORANGE RIOTS OF 1870 AND 1871.

# CHAPTER XXII.

## THE RAILROAD RIOTS OF 1877.

# CHAPTER XXIII.

## THE RAILROAD RIOTS—WEST VIRGINIA.

## CHAPTER XXIV.

### THE RAILROAD RIOTS.—MARYLAND.

## CHAPTER XXV.

### THE RAILROAD RIOTS.—PENNSYLVANIA.

## CHAPTER XXVI.

### THE RAILROAD RIOT—PENNSYLVANIA.

## CHAPTER XXVII

### THE RAILROAD RIOT—PENNSYLVANIA.

## CHAPTER XXVIII.

### THE RAILROAD RIOT.—PENNSYLVANIA.

## CHAPTER XXIX.

## CHAPTER XXX.

### THE RAILROAD RIOTS—NEW YORK.

## CHAPTER XXXI.

### THE RAILROAD RIOTS—OHIO.

## CHAPTER XXXII.

### THE RAILROAD RIOTS--ILLINOIS.

# CHAPTER XXXIII.

### THE STRIKERS AT ST. LOUIS AND LOUISVILLE.

# CHAPTER XXXIV.

# LIST OF ILLUSTRATIONS.

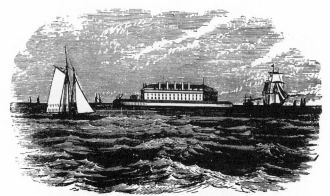

FORT LAFAYETTE, NEW YORK HARBOR, AND

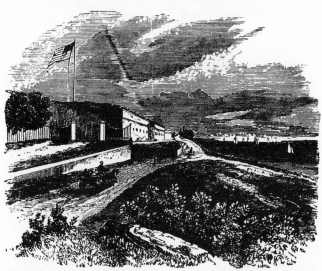

FORT HAMILTON; FROM WHENCE UNITED STATES TROOPS WERE SENT
TO AID IN SUPPRESSING THE DRAFT RIOTS OF 1863.

# THE GREAT RIOTS OF NEW YORK CITY.

## CHAPTER I.

Character of a City illustrated by Riots.—New Material for History of Draft Riots.—History of the Rebellion incomplete without History of them.—The Fate of the Nation resting on the Issues of the Struggle in New York City.—The best Plan to adopt for Protection against Mobs.

THE history of the riots that have taken place in a great city from its foundation, is a curious and unique one, and illustrates the peculiar changes in tone and temper that have come over it in the course of its development and growth. They exhibit also one phase of its moral character—furnish a sort of moral history of that vast, ignorant, turbulent class which is one of the distinguishing features of a great city, and at the same time the chief cause of its solicitude and anxiety, and often of dread.

The immediate cause, however, of my taking up the subject, was a request from some of the chief actors in putting down the Draft Riots of 1863, to write a history of them. It was argued that it had never been written, except in a detached and fragmentary way in the daily press, which, from the hurried manner in which it was done, was necessarily incomplete, and more or less erroneous.

It was also said, and truly, that those who, by their

courage and energy, saved the city, and who now
would aid me not only officially, but by their personal
recollections and private memoranda, would soon pass
away, and thus valuable material be lost.

Besides these valid reasons, it was asserted that the
history of the rebellion was not complete without it,
and yet no historian of that most important event in
our national life had given the riots the prominence
they deserved, but simply referred to them as a side
issue, instead of having a vital bearing on the fate of
the war and the nation.  On no single battle or campaign did the destiny of the country hinge as upon that
short, sharp campaign carried on by General Brown
and the Police Commissioners against the rioters in
the streets of New York, in the second week of July,
1863.  Losses and defeats in the field could be and were
repaired, but defeat in New York would in all probability have ended the war.  It is not necessary to refer
to the immediate direct effects of such a disaster on
the army in the field, although it is scarcely possible
to over-estimate the calamitous results that would have
followed the instantaneous stoppage, even for a short
time, of the vast accumulations of provisions, ammu
nition, and supplies of all kinds, that were on their way
to the army through New York.  Nor is it necessary
to speculate on the effect of the diversion of troops
from the front that such an event would have compelled, in order to recover so vital a point.  Washington had better be uncovered than New York be lost.
One thing only is needed to show how complete and
irreparable the disaster would have been ; namely, the
effect it would have had on the finances of the country.
With the great banking-houses and moneyed institutions

of New York sacked and destroyed, the financial credit of the country would have broken down utterly. The crash of falling houses all over the country that would have followed financial disaster here, would have been like that of falling trees in a forest swept by a hurricane. Had the rioters got complete possession of the city but for a single day, their first dash would have been for the treasures piled up in its moneyed institutions. Once in possession of these, they, like the mobs of Paris, would have fired the city before yielding them up. In the crisis that was then upon us, it would not have required a long stoppage in this financial centre of the country to have effected a second revolution. With no credit abroad and no money at home, the Government would have been completely paralyzed. Not long possession of the city was needed, but only swift destruction.

Doubtless the disastrous effects would have been increased tenfold, if possible, by uprisings in other cities, which events showed were to follow. Even partial success developed hostile elements slumbering in various parts of the country, and running from Boston almost to the extreme West.

In this view of the case, these riots assume a magnitude and importance that one cannot contemplate without a feeling of terror, and the truth of history requires that their proper place should be assigned them, and those who put them down have an honorable position beside our successful commanders and brave soldiers. It is also important, as a lesson for the future, and naturally brings up the question, what are the best measures, and what is the best policy for the city of New York to adopt, in order to protect itself from that which to-day constitutes its greatest danger—*mob violence?* If it ever falls in ruins, the work of destruction will commence and end within its own limits. We have a police and city military which have been thought to be sufficient, but experience has shown that though this provision may be ample to restore law and order in the end, it works slowly, often unwisely, and always with an unnecessary expenditure of life. In conversing with those of largest experience and intelligence in the police department on this subject of such great and growing importance, we are convinced, from their statements and views, a vast improvement in this matter can be made, while the cost to the city, instead of being increased, will be lessened; that is, a cheaper, wiser, and more effectual plan than the present one can be adopted. Of course this does not refer to mere local disturbances, which the police force in the ordinary discharge of its duties can quell, but to those great outbreaks which make it necessary to call out the military. Not that there might not be exigencies in which it would be necessary to resort, not only to the military of the city, but to invoke the aid of neighboring States; for a riot may assume the proportions of a revolution, but for such no local permanent remedy can be furnished.

The objections to relying on the military, as we invariably do in case of a large mob, are many. In the first place, it takes the best part of a day to get the troops together, so that a mob, so far as they are concerned, has time not only to waste and destroy for many hours, but increase in strength and audacity. The members of the various regiments are scattered all over the city, engaged in different occupations and employments, and without previous notice being given, it is a long and tedious process to get them to their respective headquarters and in uniform. This wastes much and most valuable time. Besides, they are compelled to reach the mustering place singly or in small groups, and hence liable to be cut off or driven back by the mob, which in most cases would know the place of rendezvous.

In the second place, the members are taken out from the mass of the people, between whom there might be a strong sympathy in some particular outbreak, which would impair their efficiency, and make them hesitate to shoot down their friends and acquaintances.

In the third place, in ordinary peace times, these uniformed regiments are not the steadiest or most reliable troops, as was witnessed in the riots of 1863, as well as in those of the Astor Place in 1849.

They hesitate, or are apt to become hasty or disorganized in a close, confused fight, and driven back. In the commencement of a riot, a defeat of the military gives increased confidence, and indeed, power to a mob, and makes the sacrifice of life, in the end, far greater.

In the fourth place, clearing the streets does not always dissipate a mob. A whole block of houses may become a fortress, which it is necessary to storm before a permanent victory is gained. Half-disciplined men, unaccustomed, and unskilled to such work, make poor headway with their muskets through narrow halls, up stairways, and through scuttle-holes.

In the fifth place, the military of the city cannot be called away from their work for two or three days, to parade the city, without a heavy expense, and hence the process is a costly one.

In the last place, the firing of these troops at the best is not very judicious, and cannot be discriminating, so that those are shot down often least culpable, and of least influence in the mob—in fact, more lives usually are taken than is necessary.

The simplest, most efficient, and most economical plan would be to select five hundred or more of the most courageous, experienced, and efficient men from the police department, and form them into a separate battalion, and have them drilled in such evolutions, manœuvres, and modes of attack or defence, as would belong to the work they were set apart to do. A battery might be given them in case of certain emergencies, and a portion carefully trained in its use. At a certain signal of the bell, they should be required to hasten, without a moment's delay, to their head-quarters. A mob could hardly be gathered and commence work before this solid body of disciplined, reliable men would be upon them. These five hundred men would scatter five thousand rioters like chaff before them. It would be more efficient than two entire regiments, even if assembled, and would be worth more than the whole military of the city for the first half day.

Besides, clubs are better than guns. They take no time to load—they are never discharged like muskets, leaving their owners for the time at the mercy of the mob. Their volleys are incessant and perpetual, given as long and fast as strong arms can strike. They are also more discriminating than bullets, hitting the guilty ones first. Moreover, they disable rather than kill—which is just as effectual, and far more desirable. In addition to all this, being trained to one purpose, instructed to one duty, a mob would be their natural enemies, and hence sympathy with them in any cause almost impossible.

# CHAPTER II.

## THE NEGRO RIOTS OF 1712–1741.

Almost impossible for the present Generation to comprehend its true
Character and Effect on the People.—Description of New York
at that Time.—The Negro Slaves.—The Negro Riot of 1712.—
Description of it.—The Winter of 1741.—Governor's House
burned down.—Other Fires.—Suspicion of the People.—Arrest
and Imprisonment of the Blacks.—Reward offered for the supposed Conspirators.—Alarm and Flight of the Inhabitants.—Examination and Confession of Mary Burton.—Peggy, the Newfoundland Beauty, and the Hughson Family.—The Conspiracy.
—Executions.—Fast.—Hughson's Hearing.—Hung in Chains.—
The Body, and that of a Negro, left to swing and rot in the Air.
—Strange Change in the Appearances of the Bodies.—The People throng to look at them.—Negroes burned at the Stake.—
Terrific Spectacle.—Bloody Summer.—Execution of a Catholic
Priest.—Strange Scenes.—Upper Classes accused.—Executions
stopped.—Reason of the Panic.

PROBABLY no event of comparatively modern times—
certainly none in our history—has occurred so extraordinary in some of its phases, as the negro riot of 1741.
We cannot fully appreciate it, not merely because of
the incompleteness of some of its details, nor from the
lapse of time, but, because of our inability to place ourselves in the position or state of mind of the inhabitants of New York City at that period. We can no
more throw ourselves into the social condition, and
feel the influences of that time, than we can conceive
the outward physical appearance of the embryo me-

tropolis. It is impossible to stand amid the whirl and
uproar of New York to-day, and imagine men plough-
ing, and sowing grain, and carting hay into barns, where
the City Hall now stands. The conception of nearly
all the city lying below the Park, above it farms
to Canal Street, beyond that clearings where men are
burning brush and logs to clear away the fallow, and
still farther on, towards Central Park, an unbroken
wilderness, is so dim and shadowy, that we can hardly
fix its outlines. Yet it was so in 1741. Where now
stands the Tombs, and cluster the crowded tenements
of Five Points, was a pond or lakelet, nearly two miles
in circumference and fifty feet deep, and encircled by
a dense forest. Its deep, sluggish outlet into the Hudson is now Canal Street. In wet weather there was
another water communication with the East River, near
Peck Slip, cutting off the lower part of the island, leaving another island, containing some eight hundred acres.
Through Broad Street, along which now rolls each day
the stream of business, and swells the tumult of the
Brokers' Board, then swept a deep stream, up which
boatmen rowed their boats to sell oysters. The water
that supplied these streams and ponds is now carried
off through immense sewers, deep under ground, over
which the unconscious population tread. Where Front
and Water Streets on the east side, and West Greenwich and Washington on the west side, now stretch,
were then the East and Hudson Rivers, laving smooth
and pebbly beaches. There was not a single sidewalk
in all the city, and only some half dozen paved streets.
On the Battery stood the fort, in which were the Governor's and secretary's houses, and over which floated the
British flag.

2

But all this outward appearance is no more unlike the New York of to-day than its internal condition.

The population numbered only about ten thousand, one-fifth of which was negroes, who were slaves. Their education being wholly neglected, they were ignorant and debased, and addicted to almost every vice. They were, besides, restive under their bondage and the severe punishments often inflicted on them, which caused their masters a great deal of anxiety. Not isolated as an inland plantation, but packed in a narrow space, they had easy communication with each other, and worse than all, with the reckless and depraved crews of the vessels that came into port. It is true, the most stringent measures were adopted to prevent them from assembling together; yet, in spite of every precaution, there would now and then come to' light some plan or project that would fill the whites with alarm. They felt half the time as though walking on the crust of a volcano, and hence were in a state of mind to exaggerate every danger, and give credit to every sinister rumor.

The experience of the past, as well as the present state of feeling among the slaves, justified this anxiety and dread ; for only thirty years before occurred just such an outbreak as they now feared. On the 7th of April, in 1712, between one and two o'clock in the morning, the house of Peter Van Tilburgh was set on fire by negroes, which was evidently meant as a signal for a general revolt.

The cry of fire roused the neighboring inhabitants, and they rushed out through the unpaved muddy streets, toward the blazing building. As they approached it, they saw, to their amazement, in the red light of the flames, a band of negroes standing in front, armed with guns and long knives.  Before the whites could hardly comprehend what the strange apparition meant, the negroes fired, and then rushed on them with their knives, killing several on the spot.  The rest, leaving the building to the mercy of the flames, ran to the fort on the Battery, and roused the Governor. Springing from his bed, he rushed out and ordered a cannon to be fired from the ramparts to alarm the town.  As the heavy report boomed over the bay and shook the buildings of the town, the inhabitants leaped from their beds, and looking out of the windows, saw the sky lurid with flames.  Their dread and uncertainty were increased, when they heard the heavy splash of soldiers through the mud, and the next moment saw their bayonets gleam out of the gloom, as they hurried forward towards the fire.  In the meantime, other negroes had rushed to the spot, so that soon there were assembled, in proportion to the white population, what in the present population of the city would be fully 10,000 negroes.

The rioters stood firm till they saw the bayonets flashing in the fire-light, and then, giving one volley, fled into the darkness northward, towards what is now Wall Street.  The scattered inhabitants they met, who, roused by the cannon, were hastening to the fire, they attacked with their knives, killing and wounding several.  The soldiers, firing at random into the darkness, followed after them, accompanied by a crowd of people.  The negroes made for the woods and swamps near where the Park now stands, and disappearing in the heavy shadows of the forest, were lost to view. Knowing it would be vain to follow them into the thickets, the soldiers and inhabitants surrounded them and kept watch till morning. Many, of course, got off and buried themselves in the deeper, more extensive woods near Canal Street, but many others were taken prisoners. Some, finding themselves closely pressed and all avenues of escape cut off, deliberately shot themselves, preferring such a death to the one they knew awaited them. How many were killed and captured during the morning, the historian does not tell us. We can only infer that the number must have been great, from the statement he incidentally makes, that " during the day *nineteen more were* taken, tried, and executed—some that turned State's evidence were transported." " Eight or ten whites had been murdered," and many more wounded.

It was a terrible event, and remembered by the present inhabitants with horror and dismay. To the little handful occupying the point of the island, it was a tragedy as great as a riot in New York to-day would be, in which was a loss of 5,000 or more on each side.

Many middle-aged men, in 1741, were young men at that time, and remembered the fearful excitement that prevailed, and it was a common topic of conversation.

The state of things, therefore, which we have described, was natural. This was rendered worse by the arrival, in the winter of 1741, of a Spanish vessel, which had been captured as a prize, the crew of which was composed in part of negroes, who were sold at auction as slaves. These became very intractable, and in spite of the floggings they received, uttered threats that they knew would reach their masters' ears. Still, no evidence of any general plot against the inhabitants was suspected, and things were moving on in their usual

way, when, on the 18th of March, a wild and blustering
day, the Governor's house in the fort was discovered
to be on fire.  Fanned by a fierce south-east wind, the
flames spread to the King's chapel, the secretary's
house, barracks, and stables; and in spite of all efforts
to save them, were totally consumed.  The origin of
the fire was supposed to be accidental, but a few days
after, Captain Warren's house, near the fort, was found
to be on fire.  Two or three days later, the storehouse
of Mr. Van Zandt was discovered on fire.  Still, no
general suspicions were aroused.  Three more days
passed, when a cow-stall was reported on fire, and a
few hours later, the house of Mr. Thompson; the fire
in the latter case originating in the room where a negro
slave slept.  The very next day, live coals were discovered under the stable of John Murray, on Broadway.
This, evidently, was no accident, but the result of design, and the people began to be alarmed.  The day
following, the house of a sergeant near the fort was
seen to be on fire, and soon after, flames arose from the
roof of a dwelling near the Fly Market.  The rumor
now spread like wildfire through the town that it was
the work of incendiaries.  It seems to us a small foundation to base such a belief on, but it must be remembered that the public mind was in a state to believe almost anything.

The alarm was increased by the statement of Mrs.
Earle, who said that on Sunday, as she was looking out
of her window, she saw three negroes swaggering up
Broadway, engaged in earnest conversation.  Suddenly
she heard one of them exclaim, " Fire ! fire !  Scorch !
scorch ! a little d—n by and by!" and then throwing u
his hands, laughed heartily.  Coupled with the numerous

fires that had occurred, and the rumors afloat, it at
once excited her suspicions that this conversation had
something to do with a plot to burn the city. She
therefore immediately reported it to an alderman, and
he, next day, to the justices.

Although the number of buildings thus mysteriously
set on fire was, in reality, small, yet it was as great in
proportion to the town then, as three hundred would
be in New York to-day. Less than that number, we
imagine, would create a panic in the city, especially if
the public mind was in a feverish state, as, for instance,
during the recent civil war.

Some thought the Spanish negroes had set the buildings on fire from revenge, especially as those of the
Government were the first to suffer. Others declared
that it was a plot of the entire negro population to
burn down the city. This belief was strengthened by
the fact that, in one of the last fires, a slave of one of
the most prominent citizens was seen to leap from the
window, and make off over garden fences. A shout
was immediately raised by the spectators, and a pursuit
commenced. The terrified fugitive made desperate
efforts to escape, but being overtaken, he was seized,
and, pale as death, lifted on men's shoulders and carried to jail.

Added to all this, men now remembered it lacked
but a few days of being the anniversary of the bloody
riot of thirty years ago. They began to watch and
question the negroes, and one of the Spanish sailors, on
being interrogated, gave such unsatisfactory, suspicious
answers, that the whole crew were arrested, and thrown
into prison. But that same afternoon, while the magistrates, whom the alarming state of things had called

together, were in consultation about it, the cry of "Fire!" again startled the entire community. The ringing of the alarm-bell had now become almost as terrifying as the sound of the last trumpet, and the panic became general. The first step was to ascertain if there were any strangers in town who might be concealed enemies, and a thorough search was made—the militia being ordered out, and sentries posted at the ends of all the streets, with orders to stop all persons carrying bags and bundles. This was done on the 13th of April. None being found, the conclusion became inevitable that some dark, mysterious plot lay at the bottom of it all, and the inhabitants thought the city was doomed, like Sodom. First, the more timorous packed up their valuable articles and fled into the country, up toward Canal Street. This increased the panic, which swelled until almost the entire population were seen hurrying through the streets, fleeing for their lives. The announcement of an approaching army would not have created a greater stampede. Every cart and vehicle that could be found was engaged at any price, into which whole families were piled, and hurried away to the farms beyond Chambers Street, in the neighborhood of Canal Street. It was a strange spectacle, and the farmers could hardly believe their senses, at this sudden inundation into their quiet houses of the people of the city. The town authorities were also swept away in the general excitement, and negroes of all ages and sexes were arrested by the wholesale, and hurried to prison. The Supreme Court was to sit in the latter part of April, and the interval of a few days was spent in efforts to get at the guilty parties. But nothing definite could be ascertained, as the conspirators, whoever they were, kept their own secret. At length, despairing of getting at the truth in any other way, the authorities offered a reward of a hundred pounds, and a full pardon to any one who would turn State's evidence, and reveal the names of the ringleaders. This was pretty sure to bring out the facts, if there were any to disclose, and almost equally sure to obtain a fabricated story, if there was nothing to tell. A poor, ignorant slave, shaking with terror in his cell, would hardly be proof against such an inducement as a free pardon, and to him or her an almost fabulous sum of money, if he had anything to reveal, while the temptation to invent a tale that would secure both liberty and money was equally strong.

On the 21st of April the court met, Judges Philips and Horsmander presiding. A jury was impanelled, but although there was no lack of prisoners, there was almost a total want of evidence sufficient to put a single man on trial. The reward offered had not borne its legitimate fruits, and no one offered to make any revelations.

Among the first brought up for examination was Mary Burton, a colored servant girl, belonging to John Hughson, the keeper of a low, dirty negro tavern over on the west side of the city, near the Hudson River. This was a place of rendezvous for the worst negroes of the town; and from some hints that Mary had dropped, it was suspected it had been the head-quarters of the conspirators. But when brought before the Grand Jury, she refused to be sworn. They entreated her to take the oath and tell the whole truth, but she only shook her head. They then threatened her, but with no better success; they promised she should be protected

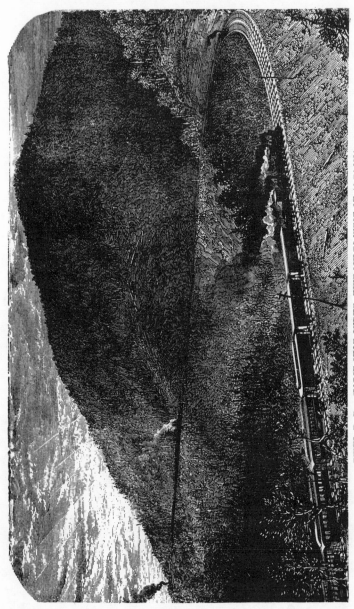

PENN. R. R.—HORSE-SHOE CURVE, FIVE MILES WEST OF ALTOONA.

from danger and shielded from prosecution, but she still maintained an obstinate silence. They then showed her the reward, and attempted to bribe her with the wealth in store for her, but she almost spat on it in her scorn. This poor negro slave showed an independence and stubbornness in the presence of the jury that astonished them. Finding all their efforts vain, they ordered her to be sent to jail. This terrified her, and she consented to be sworn. But after taking the oath, she refused to say anything about the fire. A theft had been traced to Hughson, and she told all she knew about that, but about the fires would neither deny nor affirm anything. They then appealed to her conscience; painted before her the terrors of the final judgment, and the torments of hell, till at last she broke down, and proposed to make a clean breast of it. She commenced by saying that Hughson had threatened to take her life if she told, and then again hesitated. But at length, by persistent efforts, the following facts were wrenched from her by piecemeal She said that three negroes—giving their names—had been in the habit of meeting at the tavern, and talking about burning of the fort and city and murdering the people, and that Hughson and his wife had promised to help them ; after which Hughson was to be governor and Cuff Phillipse king. That the first part of the story was true, there is little doubt. How much, with the imagination and love of the marvellous peculiar to her race, she added to it, it is not easy to say. She said, moreover, that but one white person beside her master and mistress was in the conspiracy, and that was an Irish girl known as Peggy, " the Newfoundland Beauty." She had several *aliases*, and was an abandoned character, being a prostitute to

2*

the negroes, and at this time kept as a mistress by a bold, desperate negro named Cæsar. This revelation of Mary's fell on the Grand Jury like a bombshell. The long-sought secret they now felt was out. They immediately informed the magistrates. Of course the greatest excitement followed. Peggy was next examined, but she denied Mary Burton's story *in toto*—swore that she knew nothing of any conspiracy or of the burning of the stores; that if she should accuse any one it would be a lie, and blacken her own soul.

It is rather a severe reflection on the courts of justice of that period, or we might rather say, perhaps, a striking illustration of the madness that had seized on all, that although the law strictly forbade any slave to testify in a court of justice against a white person, yet this girl Mary Burton was not only allowed to appear as evidence against Peggy, but her oath was permitted to outweigh hers, and cause her to be sentenced to death. The latter, though an abandoned, desperate character, was seized with terror at the near approach of death, and begged to be allowed another examination, which was granted, and she professed to make a full confession. It is a little singular that while she corroborated Mary Burton's statement as to the existence of a conspiracy, she located the seat of it not in Hughson's tavern, but in a miserable shanty near the Battery, kept by John Romme, who, she said, had promised to carry them all to a new country, and give them their liberty, if they would murder the whites and bring him the plunder. Like Mary Burton's confession, if truthful at all, it evidently had a large mixture of falsehood in it.

On Saturday, May 9th, Peggy was again brought in, and underwent a searching examination. Some of her statements seemed improbable, and they therefore tested them in every possible way. It lasted for several hours, and resulted in a long *detailed* confession, in which she asserted, among other things, that it was the same plot that failed in 1712, when the negroes designed to kill all the whites, in fact, exterminate them from the island. She implicated a great many negroes in the conspiracy; and every one that she accused, as they were brought before her, she identified as being present at the meetings of the conspirators in Romme's house. The court seemed anxious to avoid any collusion between the prisoners, and therefore kept them apart, so that each story should rest on its own basis. By this course they thought they would be able to distinguish what was true and what was false.

Either from conscious guilt, or from having got some inkling of the charge to be brought against him, Romme fled before he could be arrested. His wife, however, and the negroes whose names Peggy gave, were sent to jail.

On the 11th of May, or twenty days after the court convened, the executions commenced. On this day, Cæsar and Prince, two of the three negroes Mary Burton testified against, were hung, though not for the conspiracy, but for theft. They were abandoned men, and died recklessly. Peggy and Hughson and his wife were next condemned. The former, finding that her confession did not, as had been promised, secure her pardon, retracted all she had said, and exculpated entirely the parties whose arrest she had caused.

An atmosphere of gloom now rested over the city; every face showed signs of dread. In this state of feeling the Lieutenant-governor issued a proclamation, appointing a day of fasting and humiliation, not only in view of this calamity, but on account also of the want and loss caused by the past severe winter, and the declaration of war by England against Spain. When the day arrived, every shop was closed and business of all kinds suspended, and the silence and repose of the Sabbath rested on the entire community. Without regard to sect, all repaired to the places of worship, where the services were performed amid the deepest solemnity.

The day of execution appointed for Hughson, his wife, and Peggy was a solemn one, and almost the entire population turned out to witness it. The former had declared that some extraordinary appearance would take place at his execution, and every one gazed on him as he passed in a cart from the prison to the gallows. He was a tall, powerful man, being six feet high. He stood erect in the cart all the way, his piercing eye fixed steadily on the distance, and his right hand raised high as his fetters would permit, and beckoning as though he saw help coming from afar. His face was usually pale and colorless, but to-day it was noticed that two bright red spots burned on either cheek, which added to the mystery with which the superstitious spectators invested him. When the sad procession arrived at the place of execution, the prisoners were helped to the ground, and stood exposed to the gaze of the crowd. Hughson was firm and self-possessed; but Peggy, pale, and weeping, and terror-struck, begging for life; while the wife, with the rope round her neck, leaned against a tree, silent and composed, but colorless as marble. One after another they were launched into eternity, and the crowd, solemn and thoughtful, turned their steps homeward.

Hughson was hung in chains; and in a few days a negro was placed beside him, and here they swung, " blind and blackening," in the April air, in full view of the tranquil bay, a ghastly spectacle to the fishermen as they plied their vocation near by. For three weeks they dangled here in sunshine and storm, a terror to the passers-by. At length a rumor passed through the town that Hughson had turned into a negro, and the negro into a white man. This was a new mystery, and day after day crowds would come and gaze on the strange transformation, some thinking it supernatural, and others trying to give an explanation. Hughson had threatened to take poison, and it was thought by many that he had, and it was the effect of this that had wrought the change in his appearance. For ten days the Battery was thronged with spectators, gazing on these bloated, decomposing bodies, many in their superstitious fears expecting some new transformation. Under the increasing heat of the sun, they soon began to drip, till at last the body of Hughson burst asunder, filling the air with such an intolerable stench that the fishermen shunned the locality.

As simple hanging was soon thought not sufficient punishment, and they were left to swing, and slowly rot in chains, so this last was at length thought to be too lenient, and the convicts were condemned to be burned at the stake. Two negroes, named Quack and Cuffee, were the first doomed to this horrible death. The announcement of this sentence created the greatest excitement. It was a new thing to the colonists, this mode of torture being appropriated by the savages for prisoners taken in war. Curious crowds gathered to see the stake erected, or stare at the loads of wood as they passed along the street, and were unloaded at its base.  It was a strange spectacle to behold—the workmen carefully piling up the fagots under the spring sun; the spectators looking on, some horrified, and others fierce as savages; and over all the blue sky bending, while the gentle wind stole up from the bay and whispered in the tree-tops overhead.  On the day of execution an immense crowd assembled. The two negroes were brought forward, pale and terrified, and bound to the stake.  As the men approached with the fire to kindle the pile, they shrieked out in terror, confessed the conspiracy, and promised, if released, to tell all about it.  They were at once taken down.  This was the signal for an outbreak, and shouts of "burn 'em, burn 'em" burst from the multitude. Mr. Moore then asked the sheriff to delay execution till he could see the Governor and get a reprieve.  He hurried off, and soon returned with a conditional one. But, as he met the sheriff on the common, the latter told him that it would be impossible to take the criminals through the crowd without a strong guard, and before that could arrive, they would be murdered by the exasperated populace.  They were then tied up again, and the torch applied.  The flames arose around the unhappy victims.  The curling smoke soon hid their dusky forms from view, while their shrieks and cries for mercy grew fainter and fainter, as the fierce fire shrivelled up their forms, till at last nothing but the crackling of the flames was heard, and the shouting, savage crowd grew still.  As the fire subsided, the two wretched creatures, crisped to a cinder, remained to tell, for the hundredth time, to what barbarous deeds terror and passion may lead men.

Some of the negroes went laughing to the place of execution, indulging in all sorts of buffoonery to the last, and mocking the crowd which surrounded them.

All protested their innocence to the last, and if they had confessed previously, retracted before death their statements and accusations. But this contradiction of themselves, to-morrow denying what to-day they had solemnly sworn on the Bible to be true, instead of causing the authorities to hesitate, and consider how much terror and the hope of pardon had to do with it, convinced them still more of the strength and danger-ous nature of the conspiracy, and they went to work with a determination and recklessness which made that summer the bloodiest and most terrific in the annals of New York. No lawyer was found bold enough to step forward and defend these poor wretches, but all volunteered their services to aid the Government in bringing them to punishment. The weeks now, as they rolled on, were freighted with terror and death, and stamped with scenes that made the blood run cold. This little town on the southern part of Manhattan Island was wholly given to panic, and a nameless dread of some mysterious, awful fate, extended even to the scattered farm-houses near Canal Street. Be-tween this and the last of August, a hundred and fifty-four negroes, exclusive of whites, were thrown into prison, till every cell was crowded and packed to suf-focation with them. For three months, sentence of condemnation was on an average of one a day. The last execution was that of a Catholic priest, or rather of a schoolmaster of the city, who was charged with being one. Mary Burton, after an interval of three months, pretended to remember that he was present with the other conspirators she had first named as being in Hughson's tavern.

His trial was long, and apparently without excitement. He conducted his own case with great ability, and brought many witnesses to prove his good character and orderly conduct; but he, of course, could not disprove the assertion of Mary, that she had some time or other seen him with the conspirators at Hughson's tavern—for the latter, with his wife and Peggy, and the negroes she had before named, had all been executed. Mary Burton alone was left, and her evidence being credited, no amount of testimony could avail him.

Although the proceedings were all dignified and solemn, as became an English court, yet the course the trial took showed how utterly unbalanced and one-sided it had become. To add weight to Mary's evidence, many witnesses were examined to prove that Ury, though a schoolmaster, had performed the duties of a Catholic priest, as though this were an important point to establish. The attorney-general, in opening the case, drew a horrible picture of former persecutions by the Papists, and their cruelties to the Protestants, until it was apparent that all that the jury needed to indorse a verdict of guilty was evidence that he was a Catholic priest. Still it would be unfair to attribute this feeling wholly to religious intolerance or the spirit of persecution. England was at this time at war with Spain, and a report was circulated that the Spanish priests in Florida had formed a conspiracy to murder the English colonists. A letter from Ogilthorpe, in Georgia, confirmed this. Ury, who was an educated

Englishman, but had led an adventurous life in different countries, could not disprove this, and he was convicted and sentenced to be hung. He met his fate with great composure and dignity, asserting his innocence to the last. He made the eighteenth victim hung, while thirteen had been burned at the stake, and seventy-one transported to various countries.

At the average rate of two every week, one hanged and one burned alive, they were hurried into eternity amid prayers, and imprecations, and shrieks of agony. The hauling of wood to the stake, and the preparation of the gallows, kept the inhabitants in a state bordering on insanity. Business was suspended, and every face wore a terrified look. The voice of pity as well as justice was hushed, and one desire, that of swift vengeance, filled every heart. Had the press of to-day, with its system of interviewing, and minuteness of detail and description, existed then, there would have been handed down to us a chapter in human history that could be paralleled only in the dark ages.

A swift massacre, a terrible slaughter, comes and goes like an earthquake or a tornado, and stuns rather than debases ; but this long, steady succession of horrible executions and frightful scenes changed the very nature of the inhabitants, and they became a prey to a spirit demoniacal rather than human. The prayers and tears of those led forth to the stake, their heart-rending cries as they were bound to it, and their shrieks of agony that were wafted out over the still waters of the bay, fell on hard and pitiless hearts. The ashes of the wood that consumed one victim would hardly grow cold before a new fire was kindled upon them, and the charred and blackened posts stood month after month, hideous monuments of what man may become when judgment and reason are surrendered to fear and passion. The spectacle was made still more revolting by the gallows standing near the stake, on which many were hung in chains, and their bodies left to swing, blacken, and rot in the summer air, a ghastly, horrible sight.

Where this madness, that had swept away court, bar, and people together, would have ended, it is impossible to say, had not a new terror seized the inhabitants. Mary Burton, on whose accusation the first victims had been arrested and executed, finding herself a heroine, sought new fields in which to win notoriety. She ceased to implicate the blacks, and turned her attention to the whites, and twenty-four were arrested and thrown into prison. Elated with her success, she began to ascend in the social scale, and criminated some persons of the highest social standing in the city, whose characters were above suspicion. This was turning the tables on them in a manner the upper class did not expect, and they began to reflect what the end might be. The testimony that was sufficient to condemn the slaves was equally conclusive against them. The stake and the gallows which the court had erected for the black man, it could not pull down because a white gentleman stood under their shadow.

Robespierre and his friends cut off the upper-crust of society without hesitation or remorse; but unfortunately the crust next below this became in turn the upper-crust, which also had to be removed, until at last they themselves were reached, when they paused. They had advanced up to their necks in the bloody tide of revolution, and finding that to proceed farther would take them overhead, they attempted to wade back to shore.  So here, so long as the accusations were confined to the lowest class, it was all well enough, but when *they* were being reached, it was high time to stop.  The proceedings were summarily brought to a close, further examinations were deemed unnecessary, and confessions became flat and unprofitable; and this strange episode in American history ended.

That there had been cause for alarm, there can be no doubt.  That threats should be uttered by the slaves, is natural; for this would be in keeping with their whole history in this country.  Nor is it at all improbable that a conspiracy was formed; for this, too, would only be in harmony with the conduct of slaves from time immemorial.  The utter folly and hopelessness of such a one as the blacks testified to, has been urged against its existence altogether.  If the argument is good for anything, it proves that the conspiracy thirty years before never existed, and that the Southampton massacre was a delusion, and John Brown never hatched his utterly insane conspiracy in Harper's Ferry.  There have been a good many servile insurrections plotted in this country, not one of which was a whit more sensible or easier of execution than this, which was said to look to the complete overthrow of the little city.  That the fires which first started the panic were the work of negro incendiaries, there is but little doubt; but how far they were a part of a wide-laid plan, it is impossible to determine.

Unquestionably, success at the outset would have made the movement general, so that nothing but military force could have arrested it.

There is one thing, however, about which there is no doubt—that a panic seized the people and the courts, and made them as unreliable as in the days of the Salem witchcraft. But these striking exhibitions of the weakness of human nature under certain circumstances have been witnessed since the world was made, and probably will continue to the end of time, or until the race enters on a new phase of existence. Panics, even among the most veteran soldiers, sometimes occur, and hence we cannot wonder they take place amid a mixed population. Popular excitements are never characterized by reason and common-sense, and never will be. In this case, there was more reason for a panic than at first sight seems to be.

In the first place, the proportion of slaves to the whites was large. In the second place, they were a turbulent set, and had shown such a dangerous spirit, that the authorities became afraid to let them assemble together in meetings. This restriction they felt sorely, and it made them more restive. All were aware of this hostile state of feeling, and were constantly anticipating some outbreak or act of violence. Besides, it was but a few years since the thing they now feared did actually take place. And then, too, the point first aimed at was significant, and showed a boldness founded on conscious strength. Right inside the fort itself, and to the Governor's house, the torch was applied. It certainly looked ominous. Besides, the very wholesale manner in which the authorities thought it best to go to work increased the panic. In a very short time over a hundred persons were thrown into prison. The same proportion to the population to-day would be over ten thousand. Such a wholesale arrest would, of itself, throw New York into the wildest excitement, and conjure up all sorts of horrible shapes.

Add to this, an average of two hundred burned at the stake, and two hundred hung every week, or more than fifty a day, and nearly three times that number sentenced to transportation, and one can faintly imagine what a frightful state of things would exist in the city. The very atmosphere grew stifling from the smoke of burning men and women, while the gallows groaned under its weight of humanity. Had this been the wild work of a mob it would have been terrible enough, but when it was the result of a deliberate judicial tribunal, which was supposed to do nothing except on the most conclusive evidence, the sense of danger was increased tenfold. The conclusion was inevitable, that the conspiracy embraced every black man in the city, and was thoroughly organized. In short, the whole place was, beyond doubt, resting over a concealed volcano, and the instinct of self-preservation demanded the most summary work. Let the inhabitants of any city become thoroughly possessed of such an idea, and they will act with no more prudence or reason than the people of New York at that time did. An undoubted belief in such a state of things will confuse the perceptions and unbalance the judgment of a community anywhere and everywhere on the globe.

Still, consistent as it is with human history, one can hardly believe it possible, as he stands in New York to-day, that men have there been burned at the stake under the sanction of English law, or left to swing and rot in the winds of heaven, by order of the Supreme Court of the city.

# CHAPTER III.

AT the present day, when personal ambition takes the place of patriotism, and love of principle gives way to love of party; when the success of the latter is placed above constitutional obligations and popular rights, one seems, as he turns back to our early history, to be transported to another age of the world, and another race of beings.

Nothing shows how thoroughly understood by the common people were the principles of liberty, and with what keen penetration they saw through all shams and specious reasoning, than the decided, nay, fierce, stand they took against the stamp act. This was nothing more than our present law requiring a governmental stamp on all public and business paper to make it valid The only difference is, the former was levying a tax without representation—in other words, without the consent of the governed. The colonies assembled in Congress condemned it; hence the open, violent opposition to it by the people rises above the level of a common riot, and partakes more of the nature of a righteous revolution. Still, it was a riot, and exhibited the lawless features of one.

The news of the determination of the English Government to pass a stamp act, raised a storm of indignation throughout the colonies, from Massachusetts to South Carolina, and it was denounced as an oppressive, unrighteous, tyrannical measure From the wayside tavern and the pulpit alike, it was attacked with unsparing severity. The Government, however, thought it a mere ebullition of feeling, that would not dare exhibit itself in open opposition. Nor does this confidence seem strong, when we remember the weakness of the colonies on the one side, and the strength of an organized government, with the law and force both, on the other.

Cadwallader Colden, a Scotchman by birth, and a clergyman by profession, was at that time acting Governor of New York; and to guard against any resort to force on the part of the people when the stamps should arrive, had Fort George, on the Battery, reinforced by a regiment from Crown Point, its magazines replenished, the ramparts strengthened, and its guns trained on the town. The people saw all this, and understood its import; but it had the opposite effect from that which was intended, for, instead of overawing the people, it exasperated them.

At length, in October, 1765, a ship with the British colors flying came sailing up the bay, and anchored off Fort George. In a short time the startling tidings was circulated, that she brought a quantity of stamps. It was like sounding an alarm-bell, and the streets became thronged with excited men, while all the provincial vessels in the harbor lowered their colors to half-mast, in token of mourning. In anticipation of this event, an organization of men had been formed, called "Sons of Liberty." They at once assembled, and resolved at all hazards to get hold of those stamps. They had caused the act itself to be hawked about the streets as "the folly of England and the ruin of America," and now they determined to measure their strength with the Governor of the colony. That night, when the town was wrapped in slumber, they quietly affixed on the doors of every public office and on corners of the streets, the following placard :

PRO PATRIA.

*The first man that either distributes or makes use of stamped paper, let him take care of his house, person, and effects.*

Vox Populi.

"WE DARE."

To the stamp distributors they said, "Assure yourselves, the spirit of Brutus and Cassius is yet alive. We will not submit to the stamp act upon any account or in any instance."

McEvers, the head stamp distributor, frightened by

PENN. R. R.—SAMPLE TRACK AND TRACK TANK FOR SUPPLYING THROUGH TRAINS WITH WATER WHILE IN MOTION.

the bold, determined attitude of the people, refused to receive the stamps, and Colden had them sent for greater safety to Fort George. He had written to the British Secretary, "*I am resolved to have the stamps distributed.*" But the people were equally resolved they should not be. Still, on the 30th day of October, he and all the royal governors took the oath to carry the stamp act into effect; but they soon discovered that they could find no one bold enough to act as distributor. All along the sea-coast, in every part of the colonies, the people were aroused, and either assembling quietly, or called together by the ringing of bells and firing of cannon, presented such a united, determined front, that not one person remained duly commissioned to distribute stamps. On the last day of October, the merchants of New York came together, and bound themselves to "send no new orders for goods or merchandise, to countermand all former orders, and not even receive goods on commission, unless the stamp act be repealed"—that is, give up commerce at once, with all its wealth and benefits, rather than submit to a tax of a few shillings on paper.

Friday, the 1st of November, was the day fixed upon for a public demonstration of the people throughout the colonies against it, and never dawned a morning more pregnant with the fate not only of a nation, but of the world.

From New Hampshire to South Carolina it was ushered in by the tolling of muffled bells, the firing of minute-guns, and flags hung at half-mast. Eulogies were pronounced on liberty, and everywhere people left their shops and fields, and gathered in excited throngs to discuss the great question of taxation.

3

"Even the children at their games, though hardly able to speak, caught up the general chorus, and went along the streets, merrily carolling: 'Liberty, Property, and no Stamps.' " *

In New York the uprising was terrific, for the population rushed together as one man—as Gage, the commander of Fort George said, " by thousands."

The sailors flocked in from the vessels, the farmers from the country, and the shouts, and ringing of bells, and firing of cannon made the city fairly tremble. Colden was terrified at the storm that was raised, and took refuge in the fort.   An old man, bent and bowed with the weight of eighty years, he tottered nervously to the shelter of its guns, and ordered up a detachment of marines from a ship of war in port, for his protection.   In his indignation, he wanted to fire on the people, and the black muzzles of the cannon pointing on the town had an ominous look.   Whether he had threatened to do so by a message, we do not know; at any rate, the people either suspected his determination or got wind of it, for during the day an unknown person handed in at the fort-gate a note, telling him if he did, the people would hang him, like Porteus of Edinburgh, on a sign-post.   He wisely forebore to give the order, for if he had not, his gray hairs would have streamed from a gibbet.

At length the day of turmoil wore away, and night came on, but with it came no diminution of the excitement.   Soon as it was dark, the " Sons of Liberty," numbering thousands, surged tumultuously up around the fort, and demanded that the stamps should be

* Bancroft.

given up that they might be destroyed. Colden bluntly refused, when with loud, defiant shouts they left, and went up Broadway to " the field " (the present Park), where they erected a gibbet, and hanged on it Colden in effigy, and beside him a figure holding a boot ; some said to represent the devil, others Lord Bute, of whom the *boot*, by a pun on his name, showed for whom the effigy was designed.

The demonstration had now become a riot, and the Sons of Liberty degenerated into a mob. The feeling that had been confined to words all day must now have some outlet. A torchlight procession was formed, and the scaffold and images taken down, and borne on men's shoulders along Broadway towards the Battery. The glare of flaring lights on the buildings and faces of the excited crowd, the shouts and hurrahs that made night hideous, called out the entire population, which gazed in amazement on the strange, wild spectacle.

They boldly carried the scaffold and effigies to within a few feet of the gate of the fort, and knocked audaciously for admission. Isaac Sears was the leader of these " Sons of Liberty."

Finding themselves unable to gain admittance, they went to the Governor's carriage-house, and took out his elegant coach, and placing the two effigies in it, dragged it by hand around the streets by the light of torches, amid the jeers and shouts of the multitude. Becoming at last tired of this amusement, they returned towards the fort, and erected a second gallows, on which they hung the effigies the second time.

All this time the cannon, shotted and primed, lay silent on their carriages, while the soldiers from the ramparts looked wonderingly, idly on. General Gage did not dare to fire on the people, fearing they would sweep like an inundation over the ramparts, when he knew a general massacre would follow.

The mob now tore down the wooden fence that surrounded Bowling Green, and piling pickets and boards together, set them on fire. As the flames crackled and roared in the darkness, they pitched on the Governor's coach, with the scaffold and effigies ; then hastening to his carriage-house again, and dragging out a one-horse chaise, two sleighs, and other vehicles, hauled them to the fire, and threw them on, making a conflagration that illumined the waters of the bay and the ships riding at anchor. This was a galling spectacle to the old Governor and the British officers, but they dared not interfere.

What was the particular animosity against those carriages does not appear, though it was the only property of the Governor they destroyed, unless they were a sign of that aristocratic pride which sought to enslave them. There were, at this time, not a half-dozen coaches in the city, and they naturally became the symbols of bloated pride. It is said the feeling was so strong against them, that a wealthy Quaker named Murray, who lived out of town, near where the distributing reservoir now is, kept one to ride down town in, yet dared not call it a coach, but a " *leathern conveni-ence.*"

Although Sears and other leaders of the Sons of Liberty tried to restrain the mob, their blood was now up, and they were bent on destruction. Having witnessed the conflagration of the Governor's carriages, they again marched up Broadway, and some one shouting

" James' house," the crowd took up the shout, and passing out of the city streamed through the open country, to where West Broadway now is, and near the corner of Anthony Street. This James was Major in the Royal Artillery, and had made himself obnoxious to the people by taking a conspicuous part in putting the fort into a state of defence. He had a beautiful residence here, which the mob completely gutted, broke up his elegant furniture, destroyed his library and works of art, and laid waste his ornamented grounds. They then dispersed, and the city became quiet.

The excitement was, however, not quelled—the people had not yet got hold of the stamps, which they were determined to have. Colden, having seen enough of the spirit of the "Sons of Liberty," was afraid to risk another night, even in the fort, unless it was in some way appeased; and so the day after the riot, he had a large placard posted up, stating that he should have nothing more to do with the stamps, but would leave them with Sir Henry Moore, the newly appointed Governor, then on his way from England.

This, however, did not satisfy the Sons of Liberty: they wanted the stamps themselves, and through Sears, their leader, insisted on their being given up—telling him very plainly if he did not they would storm the fort, and they were determined to do it.

The Common Council of the city now became alarmed at the ungovernable, desperate spirit of the mob, which seemed bent on blood, and begged the Governor to let them be deposited in the City Hall. To this he finally though reluctantly consented, but the feeling in the city kept at fever heat, and would remain so until the act itself was repealed.

Moore, the new Governor, soon arrived, and assumed the reigns of government. The corporation offered him the freedom of the city in a gold box, but he refused to receive it, unless upon stamped paper. It was evident he was determined to enforce the stamp act. But on consulting with Colden and others, and ascertaining the true state of things, he wisely abandoned his purpose, and soon made it publicly known. To appease the people still more, he dismantled the fort, which was peculiarly obnoxious to them from the threatening attitude it had been made to assume. Still, the infamous act was unrepealed, and the people refused to buy English manufactures, and commerce languished.

At length, Parliament, finding that further insistance in carrying out the obnoxious act only worked mischief, had repealed it. When the news reached New York, the most unbounded joy was manifested. Bells were rung, cannon fired, and placards posted, calling on a meeting of the citizens the next day to take measures for celebrating properly the great event. At the appointed time, the people came together at Howard's Hotel, and forming a procession, marched gayly to "the field," and right where the City Hall now stands, then an open lot, a salute of twenty-one guns was fired. A grand dinner followed, at which the Sons of Liberty feasted and drank loyal toasts to his Majesty, and all went "merry as a marriage-bell." The city was illuminated, and bonfires turned the night into day. In a few weeks, the King's birthday was celebrated with great display. A huge pile of wood was erected in the Park, and an ox roasted whole for the people. Cart after cart dumped its load of beer on the ground, till

twenty-five barrels, flanked by a huge hogshead of rum,
lay in, a row, presided over by men appointed to deal out
the contents to the populace. A boisterous demonstration followed that almost drowned the roar of the twenty-one cannon that thundered forth a royal salute. As
a fitting wind-up to the bacchanalian scene, at night
twenty-five tar-barrels, fastened on poles, blazed over
the " common," while brilliant fireworks were exhibited
at Bowling Green. The feasting continued late in the
night, and so delighted were the "Sons of Liberty,"
that they erected a mast, inscribed " to his most gra-
cious Majesty, George the Third, Mr. Pitt, and Liberty."
A petition was also signed to erect a statue to Pitt,
and the people seemed determined by this excess of
loyalty to atone for their previous rebellious spirit.
The joy, however, was of short duration—the news of
the riots caused Parliament to pass a "mutiny act," by
which troops were to be quartered in America in sufficient numbers to put down any similar demonstration
in future, a part of the expense of their support to be
paid by the colonists themselves. This exasperated
"the Sons of Liberty," and they met and resolved to
resist this new act of oppression to the last. The
troops arrived in due time, and of course collisions
took place between them and the people. Matters now
continued to grow worse and worse, until the " riot of
the Sons of Liberty " became a revolution, which dis-
membered the British Empire, and established this
great republic, the influence of which on the destiny
of the world no one can predict.

# CHAPTER IV.

Body-snatching.—Bodies dug up by Medical Students.—Excitement of the People.—Effect of the Discovery of a human Limb from the Hospital.—Mob ransack the Building.—Destruction of Anatomical Specimens.—Arrival of Mayor, and Imprisonment of Students.—Second Day.—Examination of Columbia College and Physicians' Houses.—Appeal of the Mayor and distinguished Citizens to the Mob.—Mob attempt to break into Jail and seize the Students.—The Fight.—The Military called out.—Beaten by the Mob.—Larger Military Force called out.—Attacked by the Mob.—Deadly Firing.—Great Excitement.—Flight of Doctors and Students.

In former times "body-snatching," or digging up bodies for dissections, was much more heard of than at present. The fear of it was so great, that often, in the neighborhood where medical students were pursuing their studies, persons who lost friends would have a watch kept over their graves for several nights, to prevent them from being dug up. Neither the high social position of parties nor sex was any barrier to this desecration of graves, and the public mind was often shocked by accounts of the young and beautiful being disinterred, to be cut up by medical students. In the city there was, a few years ago—and perhaps there is now—a regular commercial price for bodies.

Although it was conceded that for thorough instruction in medical science, subjects for dissection were necessary, yet no one outside of the medical profession

could be found to sanction "body-snatching." There
is a sacredness attached to the grave that the most
hardened feel. Whenever the earth is thrown over
the body of a man, no matter how abject or sinful he
may have been, the involuntary exclamation of every
one is " *requiescat in pace.*" When it comes to be one
of our own personal friends, a parent, sister, or child,
to this feeling of sacredness is added that of affection,
and no wrong is like that of invading the tomb of
those we love. Shakespeare left his curse for him
who should disturb his bones ; and all feel like cursing
those who disturb the bones of friends who are linked to
them by blood and affection.

In the winter of 1787 and 1788, medical students of
New York City dug up bodies more frequently than
usual, or were more reckless in their mode of action,
for the inhabitants became greatly excited over the
stories that were told of their conduct. Some of these,
if true, revealed a brutality and indecency, shocking
as it was unnecessary. Usually, the students had contented themselves with ripping open the graves of
strangers and negroes, about whom there was little
feeling; but this winter they dug up respectable
people, even young women, of whom they made an
indecent exposure.

The stories did not lose anything by repetition, and
soon the conduct of physicians and medical students
became a town talk. There seemed to be no remedy
for this state of things ; the graveyards, which were
then in the heart of the city, were easily accessible ;
while plenty of men could be found, who, for a small
sum, would dig up any body that was desired.

A mere accident caused this state of feeling to cul
3*

minate and suddenly break out into action. In the spring, some boys were playing in the rear of the hospital, when a young surgeon, from a mere whim, showed an amputated arm to them. One of them, impelled by curiosity, immediately mounted a ladder that stood against the wall, used in making some repairs, when the surgeon told him to look at his mother's arm. The little fellow's mother had recently died, and filled with terror, he immediately hastened to his father, who was a mason, and working at the time in Broadway. The father at once went to his wife's grave, and had it opened. He found the body gone, and returned to his fellow-workmen with the news. They were filled with rage, and, armed with tools, and gathering a crowd as they marched, they surged up around the hospital.

At first many seemed to be impelled only by curiosity, but as the throng increased, the masons became eager for decisive action. Threats and denunciations began to arise on every side, and then appeals for vengeance, till at length they rushed for the door, and pouring into the building, began the work of destruction. For a while there was a terrible rattling of bones, as they tore down and smashed every anatomical specimen they could lay their hands on. Valuable imported ones shared the common fate. They swarmed through the building, and finally came upon fresh subjects, apparently but just dug up. This kindled their rage tenfold, and the students, who thus far had been unmolested, were in danger of being roughly handled.

The news of the gathering of the crowd and its threatening aspect, had reached the Mayor, who immediately summoned the sheriff, and taking him with several prominent citizens, hastened to the spot. Finding the students in the hands of the infuriated mob, he released them, and to the satisfaction, apparently, of the rioters, sent them to jail for safe-keeping.

There was now nothing left for them to do, and they dispersed, and the matter was thought to be ended.

But, during the evening, knots of men were everywhere discussing the events of the day, and retailing the exciting reports that were now flying thickly around.; and next morning, whether from any concert of action, or impelled by mere curiosity, is not known, crowds began to fill the street and yard in front of the city hospital. The discovery of the bodies the day before had deepened the excitement, and now a more thorough examination of the building was proposed, and also an examination of the physicians' houses. Matters were beginning to wear a serious aspect, and the Governor, Mayor, Chancellor, and some of the prominent citizens of the town, came together to consult on a course of action. It was finally resolved to resort in a body to the spot where the mob was assembled, and make a personal appeal to it. They did so, and presented an imposing appearance as they advanced up Broadway. Although representing the State and city, they did not presume on their authority, but attempted persuasion. Mounting the steps, they in turn addressed the throng, which now kept momentarily increasing, and exhorted them as law-abiding citizens to use no violence. Some made most pathetic appeals to their feelings, their pride and self-respect; indeed, begged them, by every consideration of home and justice, to desist, and retire peacefully to their homes. They solemnly promised that a most thorough investigation should be made, and they should have all the satisfaction the laws could afford. More they ought not to ask. These appeals and promises produced a favorable effect on many of the mob, and they left. But the greater part refused to be pacified. Their blood was up, and they insisted on making the examination themselves. They did not propose to commit any violence, but having begun their investigations they were determined to go through with them.

The Mayor and the Governor seemed to have an unaccountable repugnance to the use of force, and let the mob depart for Columbia College without any resistance. The professors and students were amazed at this sudden inundation of the crowd, who swarmed without opposition through every part of the building. Finding nothing to confirm their suspicions, they left without doing any material injury. Still unsatisfied, however, they repaired to the houses of the neighboring physicians, and the leaders, acting as a delegation of the crowd, went through them with the same result. It was a singularly well-behaved mob, and they received the report of the self-constituted committees with apparently perfect satisfaction, and when they had made the round of the houses, gradually broke up into knots and dispersed.

But the lawless spirit of a mob seldom arrests and controls itself. Having once felt its strength and power, it is never satisfied till it measures them against those of the legal authorities, and yields only when it must. Hence, as a rule, the quicker "it feels the strong hand of power" the better for all parties. Promising legal satisfaction to law-breakers is a very unsatisfactory proceeding. Obedience first and discussion **after-wards** is the proper order to be observed.

The Mayor had hardly time to congratulate himself on having overcome so easily a serious difficulty, before he found that he had not as yet touched it. In the afternoon, the crowd again began to assemble, and this time around the jail, with the avowed purpose of taking vengeance on the students and physicians locked up there for safe-keeping. Having asserted and exercised, against all law, the right of domiciliary visits, it was but a short and easy step to assert the right to punish also contrary to law. As they gathered in front of the jail, it was seen that a different spirit from that which they had hitherto exhibited ruled them. The tiger was unchained, and loud shouts and yells were heard. "Bring out your doctors! bring out your doctors!" arose on every side. They threatened to tear down the building unless they were given up. The inmates became thoroughly alarmed, and barricaded the doors and windows, and armed themselves the best way they could for self-defence. Attempts were made to parley with the crowd, but they would listen to nothing, and answered every appeal with loud shouts for the doctors. What they *intended* to do with them by way of punishment was not so clear, though what their fate would have been, if once at their mercy, there was little doubt. The city authorities now became alarmed, murder was imminent, and having no police force sufficient to cope with such a formidable mob, they decided that the city was in a state of insurrection, and called out the military. About three o'clock, the force marched up the street, and passed quietly through the crowd, which opened as they ad-

vanced.  As they moved past, a shower of dirt and
stones followed them, accompanied with taunts, and
jeers, and mocking laughter.  The whole military
movement was evidently intended only for intimidation—to show the rioters what could be done if they
resorted to violence ; for the soldiers, instead of taking
up their quarters, as they should have done, in the
building, having exhibited themselves, marched away.
But the mob, still retaining its position and threatening attitude, another force, a little later, consisting of
only twelve men, was sent up.  This was worse than
nothing, and as the little handful marched solemnly
up, the crowd broke out into derisive laughter, and all
sorts of contemptuous epithets were heaped upon them.
Instead of waiting for them to come near, they rushed
down the street to meet them, and swarming like bees
around them, snatched away their muskets, and broke
them to pieces on the pavement.*  The soldiers, disarmed, scattered, and hustled about, were glad to escape
with whole bodies.

This first act of open resistance excited the rioters still more—they had passed the Rubicon, and were
now ready for anything, and "to the jail! to the
jail!" arose in wild yells, and the turbulent mass
poured like a tumultuous sea around the building.
They rushed against the doors, and with united shoulders and bodies endeavored to heave them from their
hinges.  But being secured with heavy bolts and bars,
they resisted all their efforts.  They then smashed in
the windows with stones, and attempted to force an

* John Jay and Baron Steuben were both wounded in trying to
allay the mob.

entrance through them; but the handful of men inside took possession of these, and, with such weapons
as they could find, beat them back.  Numbers were of
no avail here, as only a few at a time could approach
a window, while those within, being on the defensive,
knocked them back as often as they attempted to climb
in.  The rioters, baffled in their attempts, would then
fall back, and hurl paving-stones and bricks at the
windows, when those who defended them would step
one side.  But the moment the former advanced
again, the latter would crowd the windows with clubs
and sticks.  The enraged assailants tore off pickets,
and advancing with these, made desperate efforts to
clear the windows.  But those within knew it was a
matter of life and death with them, and stubbornly
held their ground.  The fight was thus kept up till
dark, amid yells and shouts and a pandemonium of
noises, and no efforts apparently were made to put an
end to it, and release the inmates of the jail.  But
steps had been taken to organize and arm a large body
of militia under an experienced officer, and now in the
dim starlight their bayonets were seen gleaming, as
they marched steadily forward on the dark, heaving
mass that filled the street far as the eye could see.
The rioters, however, instead of being intimidated at
the sight, sent up a yell of defiance, and arming
themselves with stones and brick-bats, hurled them in
a blinding volley on the troops.  So fierce was the assault, that before the latter had time to form, many
were knocked down, and some badly wounded.  The
commanding officer, finding the fight thus forced on
him, gave the order in a ringing voice, " Ready, aim,
fire ! "  A flash broad as the street followed, lighting

up the gloom, and revealing the scowling faces of the mob, the battered front of the jail, and the pale faces of those guarding the windows. They had not expected this close, point-blank volley, for the timid action of the authorities had not prepared them for it, and they stopped in amazement and hesitation. The commanding officer understood his business, and instead of waiting to see if they would disperse, poured in another volley. The rioters were confounded as they saw their comrades fall by their side, but still stood at bay; until at last, seeing the dead and wounded on every side, they could stand it no longer, but broke and fled in every direction. In a few minutes the street was clear of all but the dead and wounded, the groans of the latter loading the night air. The poor wretches were carried away, and the troops remained on the spot all night. The next day the city was in a fever of excitement. The number of killed was greatly exaggerated, and the denunciations of the butchery, as it was called, were fierce and loud. On almost every corner groups of excited men were seen in angry discussion—multitudes gathered in front of the jail, and gazed with horror on the blood-stained pavement.

The soldiers who had committed the slaughter were cursed and threatened by turns, but they quietly rested on their arms, ready, it was evident, to repeat the experiment at the first open act of violence. For awhile there was danger of a general outbreak throughout the city; but the authorities had become thoroughly aroused to the danger of the situation, and seeing that the quicker they brought the conflict to a close, the better, made such a display of force, that the riotous spirit

NEW YORK HOSPITAL—SCENE OF THE DOCTORS' RIOT, LOCATED FORMERLY
ON BROADWAY, AT THE HEAD OF PEARL STREET.

NEW YORK—THE COLORED ORPHAN ASYLUM, 143D STREET.   THE FORMER
BUILDING DESTROYED DURING THE DRAFT RIOTS OF 1863.

was overawed.   Still, it was not entirely subdued, and it was evident that it was kept under by fear alone. The physicians of the city came in for almost as large a share of the hatred as the military.   They were the original cause of the disturbance, and threats against them became so open and general, that they were in constant dread of personal violence, and many fled from the city.   They scattered in every direction, and there threatened to be a general Hegira of physicians. All the medical students were secretly stowed into carriages, and hurried off into the country, where they remained till the excitement died away.   It did not, however, subside readily; indeed, the danger of open revolt was so great for several days, that the military continued to keep guard at the jail.

# CHAPTER V.

## SPRING ELECTION RIOTS OF 1834.

Fatal Error in our Naturalization Laws.—Our Experiment of Self-government not a fair one.—Fruit of giving Foreigners the Right to Vote.—Bitter Feeling between Democrats and Whigs.—First Day of Election.—Ships "Constitution" and "Veto."—Whigs driven from the Polls.—Excitement.—Whigs determined to defend themselves.—Meeting called.—Resolutions.—Second Day's Election.—Attack on the Frigate "Constitution."—A Bloody Fight.—Mayor and Officers wounded.—Mob triumphant.—Excitement of the Whigs.—The Streets blocked by fifteen thousand enraged Whigs.—Military called out.—Occupy Arsenal and City Hall all Night.—Result of the Election.—Excitement of the Whigs.—Mass-meeting in Castle Garden.

THIS country never committed a more fatal mistake than in making its naturalization laws so that the immense immigration from foreign countries could, after a brief sojourn, exercise the right of suffrage. Our form of government was an experiment, in the success of which not only we as a nation were interested, but the civilized world. To have it a fair one, we should have been allowed to build and perfect the structure with our own material, not pile into it such ill-formed, incongruous stuff as the despotisms of Europe chose to send us. Growing up by a natural process, educating the people to the proper exercise of their high trust, correcting mistakes, and adjusting difficulties as we progressed, the noble building would have settled into greater compactness as it arose in height, and all its various proportions been in harmony. We should have built slowly but surely. But when there was thrown upon us a mass of material wholly unfit for any political structure, and we were compelled to pile it in hap-hazard, it was not long before the goodly edifice began to show ugly seams, and the despotisms of Europe pointed to them with scorn, and asked tauntingly how the doctrine of self-government worked. They emptied their prisons and poor-houses on our shores, to be rid of a dangerous element at home, and we, with a readiness that bordered on insanity, not only took them into our bosoms, but invited them to aid us in making our laws and electing our rulers. To ask men, the greater part of whom could neither read nor write, who were ignorant of the first principles of true civil liberty, who could be bought and sold like sheep in the shambles, to assist us in founding a model republic, was a folly without a parallel in the history of the world, and one of which we have not yet begun to pay the full penalty. It was a cruel wrong, not only to ourselves, but to the oppressed masses of Europe, who turned their longing eyes on us for encouragement and the moral aid which our success would give them in their struggles against despotism.

If the reason given for endowing this floating population—and dangerous element under any circumstances—with the full rights of citizens had been the true one, namely: to be just to them, and consistent with the great doctrine of equality on which our Government rested, there might be some little comfort in reflecting on the mistake we made. But this was false. The right of suffrage was given them by a party in order to secure their votes, and secure them, too, by appeal-

ing to those very passions that made them dangerous to
the republic, and which the interest of all alike required
should be removed instead of strengthened.

All the good the Democratic party has ever done
this country will hardly compensate for the evil of this
one act.

If our experiment shall finally prove a failure, we
verily believe it will be owing to the extension of the
political franchise to whites and blacks who were unfit
to use it, and cared for it not because of its honor, or
the good use to which it might be put, but as a piece
of merchandise to be sold to the highest bidder or used
as a weapon of assault against good order and righteous laws.

Of course, the first pernicious effect of this transfer
of power to ignorant, reckless men would be felt at the
polls in New York City, where this class was in the
greatest number.  The elections here soon became a
farce, and the boasted glory of a free ballot-box a taunt
and a by-word.  That gross corruption and villany
practised here should eventually result in the open violation of law, as it did in the charter election of 1834,
was natural.

Political animosity was probably more bitter between
the Democrats, under Jackson's administration, and
the Whigs, than between any two political parties since
the time of Federalists and Democrats, in the days of
the elder Adams.

In the spring of 1834 especially, party spirit ran
very high in the city.  As usual, for a month or more
before the election, which took place on the second
Tuesday in April, all kinds of accusations and rumors
were afloat.  There was no registry law, and compara-

tively few places for the polls, so that there could be
little check on voting, no end to repeating, while the
gathering of an immense crowd around each place of
voting became inevitable. At this election, there was
a split in the Democratic party, Mr. Verplanck being
the candidate of the Independent Democrats, and Mr.
Lawrence of the " Tammany."

The most extensive preparations were made on both
sides for the conflict, and it was generally expected
there would be a personal collision in some of the wards.

·Tuesday, the 8th of April, dawned dark and stormy,
and the rain began to fall heavily, at times coming
down in torrents. But to such a fever heat had the
public feeling been carried, that no one seemed to heed
the storm. The stores were closed, business of all
kinds suspended ; while the streets were black with
men hurrying to the polls. At twelve o'clock the
American flag was hoisted on the Exchange, when the
building became deserted, and all gathered at the
places where the voting was going on. Men stood in
long lines, extending clear out into the street, patiently
enduring the pelting rain, waiting till their turn came
to vote.

The famous expression of Jackson, " Perish credit,
perish commerce," had been taken out of the connection in which it was used, and paraded everywhere.
The sailors had been enlisted in the struggle, and rigged
up a beautiful little frigate in complete order, and
named it the " Constitution." Mounting it on wheels,
several hundred of them paraded it through the streets
and past the polls. As they passed through Wall Street,
thundering cheers greeted them, and the excited populace, heedless of the rain, fell into the procession, till

it swelled to thousands, who, with songs and shouts, followed after.    Fearful of the effect of this demonstration on the voters, the Jackson men hastily rigged out a boat, surmounted by a flag on which was painted in large characters, "Veto;" and "Constitution" and "Veto" sailed after each other through the city.    This should have been prevented by the authorities, for it was impossible for these two processions to meet without a fight occurring, while it was equally certain that the Whig one would be attacked, if it attempted to pass the polls in those wards in which the roughs had the control.    But the "Hickory poles" had inaugurated a new mode of carrying on political campaigns.    Appeals were made to the senses, and votes obtained by outward symbols, rather than by the discussion of important political questions.    This mode of electioneering culminated with the log-cabin excitement.

In the Eleventh Ward, the Jackson party had two private doors through which to admit their voters to the polls, while bullies kept back from the main entrance the Independent Republicans.    In most of the strong Jackson wards, where it was all on one side, the voting went on peaceably enough, but in the Sixth, it was soon evident that a storm was inevitable.    Oaths and threats and yells of defiance made the polls here seem more like an object on which a mob was seeking to wreak its vengeance, than a place where freemen were depositing their votes under sanction of law.    The babel of sound continued to grow worse in spite of the rain, and swelled louder and louder, till at last the Jackson roughs, headed by an ex-alderman, made a rush for the committee room where their opponents

were assembled.  Some of them were armed with
clubs, and others with knives, which they brandished
fiercely as they burst into the room.   Before the members could offer any resistance, they were assailed with
such fury, that in a short time nearly twenty were
stretched bleeding and maimed on the floor; one so
badly wounded that he was carried out lifeless, and
apparently dead.   It was a savage onslaught, and
those who escaped injury reached the street hatless,
and with coats half-torn from their backs.   The mob,
now being complete masters of the room, tore down all
the banners, destroyed the ballots, and made a complete
wreck of everything.   The Whig leaders, enraged at
such dastardly, insulting treatment, despatched a messenger in all haste to the Mayor for help, but he replied that he could not furnish it, as all the available
force was away in other sections of the city on duty.
The excitement among the Whigs now became fearful,
and they determined to take the matter in their own
hands.   The election was to last three days, and they
concluded to let the polls, when the mob entered, take
care of themselves the balance of the day, and organize a plan for self-protection on the morrow.

A call was at once issued for a meeting at Masonic
Hall, and that night four thousand Whigs packed the
building, from limit to limit.   General Bogardus was
called to the chair, who, after stating the object of the
meeting, and describing the conduct of the mob in the
Sixth Ward, offered the following resolutions:

" *Whereas*, The authority of the POLICE of the city
has been set at defiance by a band of *hirelings, mer-
cenaries*, and *bullies* in the Sixth Ward, and the LIVES
of our citizens put in jeopardy.   And *whereas* it is

evident that we are in a state of anarchy, which requires the prompt and efficient interposition of every
friend of good order who is disposed to sustain the
constitution and laws, therefore, be it

" *Resolved*, That in order to preserve the *peace* of
the city, and especially of the Sixth Ward, the friends
of the constitution and the liberties of the citizen will
meet at this place (Masonic Hall), to-morrow (Wednesday), at half-past seven o'clock A.M., and repair to
the Sixth Ward poll, for the *purpose of keeping it
open to* ALL VOTERS until such time as the official
authorities may ' procure a sufficient number of special
constables to keep the peace.'

" *Resolved*, That while at the Sixth Ward poll, those
who are not residents thereof will not take part in the
election, but simply act as *conservators of the peace*,
until such times as the MAJESTY OF THE LAWS shall be
acknowledged and respected."

These resolutions were carried with acclamations
and shouts and stamping of feet.

There was no bluster in these resolutions, but their
meaning was apparent enough, and the city authorities understood it. From that hall, next morning,
would march at least five or six thousand determined
men, and if the mob rallied in force, to repeat the
action of the day before, there would be one of the
bloodiest fights that ever disgraced the city. It was
believed that the great mass of the rioters were Irishmen, and the thought that native-born Americans
should be driven from their own ballot-box by a herd
of foreigners, aroused the intensest indignation. It
was an insult that could not and should not be tolerated.

The next morning, at half-past seven, Masonic Hall was filled to repletion. The excitement can be imagined, when such a crowd could be gathered at this early hour.

In the Ninth Ward a meeting was also called, and a resolution passed, tendering a committee of one hundred to the general committee; that, with a committee of the same number from each of the fourteen wards of the city, would make a battalion eighteen hundred strong, to be ready at a moment's notice, to march to any poll "to protect the sacred right of suffrage."

These measures had their desired effect. The presence of large bodies of men at the different polls, for the purpose of protecting them, overawed the unorganized mob, although in some of the wards attempts were made to get up a riot. Stones and clubs were thrown, and one man stabbed; it was thought at the time fatally. The Sixth Ward, "the Bloody Sixth," as it was called, was the point of greatest danger, and thither the Mayor repaired in person, accompanied by the sheriff and a large posse, and remained the greater part of the day. Threats and opprobrious epithets were freely used, and occasionally a paving-stone would be hurled from some one on the outskirts of the crowd; but the passage to the polls was kept open, and by one o'clock the citizens could deposit their votes without fear of personal violence.

The evil of having the election continue three days now became more apparent than ever. The disorderly class, "the roughs," by their protracted drinking, became more and more maddened, and hence riper for more desperate action. This second night was spent by them in carousing, and the next morning

4

they turned out to the polls, not only ready, but eager for a fight. Early in the forenoon, the frigate "Constitution" was again on its voyage through the streets, followed by a crowd. As it passed Masonic Hall, the head-quarters of the Whig Committee, it was saluted with cheers. This was followed by a rush upon it, on the part of the mob, who attempted to destroy it. The Whigs inside of the building, seeing the attack, poured forth with a loud cheer, and fell on the assailants with such fury, that they turned and fled. The news of what was passing, had, in the meantime, reached the Sixth Ward folks, and a shout was raised for followers. Instantly a huge crowd, composed of dirty, ragged, savage-looking men, broke away with discordant yells, and streamed up Duane Street towards the building, picking up paving-stones and brick-bats, and pulling down pickets as they ran. Coming in sight of the little frigate, they raised a shout and dashed on it. The procession had now passed the hall, but the Whigs, informed of what was going on, again sallied forth to the help of the sailors, who were fighting manfully against overwhelming odds. But they were soon overpowered, and again took refuge in the hall. This was now assailed, and stones came crashing through the windows. The Mayor was sent for, and soon appeared with the sheriff, backed by forty watchmen. Mounting the steps, he held up his staff of office, and commanded the peace. But the half-drunken mob had now got beyond the fear of the mere symbol of authority, and answered him with a shower of stones, and then charged on the force that surrounded him. A fierce and bloody fight followed. Citizens rushed out to the help of the Mayor, while the watchmen fell

on the mob with their clubs.  They soon stretched on
the pavement more than their own number, but the
odds against them was too great.  The Mayor received
a wound—ten or fifteen watchmen besides citizens
were wounded—Captains Stewart, Munson, and Flaggs,
badly injured, the latter with his skull horribly fract-
ured, ribs broken, and face cut up.  A few of the
rioters were arrested, but the great mass broke through
all opposition, and streaming into the hall, forced the
committee to creep through back passages and windows.

The news of this high-handed outrage was carried
like the wind to the lower anti-Democratic wards, and
the excited Whigs came streaming up, until Duane, Elm,
Pearl, Cross, Augustus, and Chatham Streets, up to
Broadway, were black with determined, enraged citizens.  Ten or fifteen thousand were in a short time
assembled, and a fearful battle seemed inevitable.  In
this appalling state of things, the Mayor called a consultation, and it was decided to declare the city in a
state of insurrection, and call on the military for help.
A messenger was immediately despatched to the Navy
Yard for a company of marines.  Colonel Gamble,
commanding, replied that he would be glad to comply
with the request, and put himself at their head, but
that he had just sent them on board the "Brandywine"
and "Vincennes."  Application was then made to Com-
modore Ridgely, commander of the station; but he refused, on the ground that he had no authority to interfere.  A messenger was then hurried across to Governor's Island for help, but he met with no better success.  As a last resort, General Sanford was now directed to call out the city military.

All this time the crowd kept increasing, while from out its bosom came an angry murmur like the moaning of the sea before a storm. The polls were deserted, and it seemed impossible that the opposing forces could be long kept apart. At length word passed through the Whigs that the mob were about to take possession of the arsenal. Instantly several hundred citizens made a dash for it, and occupied it. This was a brilliant piece of strategy, and no sooner did the rioters hear of it, than they swarmed around the building with yells and imprecations. The Whigs, however, held it, and some of them passed out arms to their friends.

Three terrible hours had now passed since the first outbreak, and from the Park to Duane Street, Broadway, and the cross streets on the east side of it, were packed with excited men, their shouts, calls, and curses rising over the dwellings in tones that sent terror to the heart. But for the narrow streets, in which but few could come in contact, there would doubtless have been a collision long before.

But at this critical moment a detachment of infantry and two squadrons of cavalry came marching down Broadway, and in close column. The crowd divided as they advanced, and they drew up before the arsenal. The gleaming of the bayonets and the rattle of sabres had a quieting effect on the rioters, and they began to disperse again to the polls, to watch the progress of the voting. In the meantime, the infantry took up their quarters at the arsenal, and the cavalry at the City Hall, for the night.

When the polls closed at evening, the ballot-box of the Sixth Ward was taken under a strong guard to the City Hall, and locked up for 'he night. It was fol-

lowed by four or five thousand excited men, but no
violence was attempted.

The election was over.  For three days the city had
been heaving to the tide of human passion, and trem-
bling on the verge of a great disaster, and all because
a few ruffians, not a fourth part of whom could
probably read or write, chose to deny the right of suffrage to American citizens, and constitute themselves
the proper representatives of the city.

But the excitement did not end with the election.
It was very close, and as the returns came in slowly,
the people assembled in great numbers, to hear them
reported.  The next day, till three o'clock at night, ten
or fifteen thousand people blocked Wall Street, refus-
ing to disperse, till they knew the result.  It was
finally announced that Mr. Lawrence, the Democratic
candidate, was elected by a small majority.

The next thing was to ascertain the character of the
Common Council.  The same mighty throng assembled
next day, forgetting everything else, in the intense
interest they felt in the result.  It would seem impossible to get up such a state of feeling over the election
of a few local officers, but the city shook from limit to
limit as the slow returns came in.  At last, it was announced that the Whigs had carried the Common Council by a small majority.  As the news passed through
the immense concourse, a shout went up that shook
Wall Street from Broadway to the East River.  It
rolled back and forth like redoubled thunder, till every
throat was hoarse.

When the crowd at last dispersed, it was only to
assemble again in separate bodies in different parts of
the city, and talk over the victory.

Even then the excitement was not allowed to die away. The event was too great to be permitted to pass without some especial honor, and a mass-meeting was called in Castle Garden to celebrate it. Webster was sent for to make a speech, the most distinguished speakers of New York were called upon, and a day of general rejoicing followed, great as that which succeeded Lee's surrender.

# CHAPTER VI.

## ABOLITION RIOTS OF 1834 AND 1835.

The Slavery Question agitated.—The End, Civil War.—The Results.—William Lloyd Garrison.—Feeling of the People on the Subject.—First Attempt to call a Meeting of the Abolitionists in New York.—Meeting in Chatham Street Chapel.—A Fight.—Mob take Possession of Bowery Theatre.—Sacking of Lewis Tappan's House.—Fight between Mob and Police.—Mobbing of Dr. Cox's Church, in Laight Street.—His House broken into.—Street Barricaded.—Attack on Arthur Tappan's Store.—Second Attack on Church in Laight Street.—Church sacked in Spring Street.—Arrival of the Military.—Barricades carried.—Mr. Ludlow's House entered.—Mob at Five Points.—Destruction of Houses.—The City Military called out.—Mob overawed, and Peace restored.—Five Points Riot.—Stone-cutters' Riot.

MOST of the riots of New York have grown out of causes more or less local, and wholly transient in their nature. Hence, the object sought to be obtained was at once secured, or abandoned altogether. But those arising from the formation of Abolition societies, and the discussion of the doctrine of immediate emancipation, were of a different character, and confined to no locality or time. The spirit that produced them developed itself in every section of the country, and the question continued to assume vaster proportions, till the Union itself was involved, and what was first only a conflict between the police of the city and a few hundred or thousands of ignorant, reckless men, grew at last into the

most gigantic and terrible civil war that ever cursed
the earth.  The Union was rent asunder, and State
arrayed against State, while the world looked on
aghast at the strange and bloody spectacle.  The final
result has been the emancipation of the slaves, and
their endowment with all the rights and privileges of
American citizens.  But with this has come a frightful national debt, the destruction of that feeling of
common interest and patriotism, which is the strongest
security of a country; a contempt for the Constitution,
the concentration of power in the hands of Congress,
small regard for State rights, while the controlling
power in the South has passed into the hands of an
ignorant, incapable, irresponsible class; and, worse
than all, the people have become accustomed to the
strange spectacle, so fraught with danger in a republic,
of seeing the legislatures and executives of sovereign
States overawed and overborne by the national troops.
That frightful conflict for the slave has sown dangerous seed; what the final harvest will be, the future
historian alone will be able to show.

The inconsistency of having a system of slavery in-
corporated into a republican government was always
felt by good men North and South, as well as its damaging effect on the social and political well-being of
the whole community; and steps had been taken both
in Virginia and Kentucky to do away with it by leg-
islative action.  Whether these incipient steps would
ever have ended in relieving us of the evil, can only
be conjectured.  We only know that a peaceable solution of the question was rendered impossible, by the
action of the Abolitionists, as they were called, who,
governed by the short logic, that slavery being wrong,

PENN. R. R.—COATESVILLE BRIDGE.

it could not exist a moment without sin, and therefore must be abandoned at once without regard to consequences. The system of slavery was no longer a social or political problem, calling for great wisdom, prudence, statesmanship, and patience, but a personal crime, not to be tolerated for a moment. The whole South was divided by them into two classes, the oppressor and oppressed, the kidnapper and kidnapped, the tyrant and the slave—a relationship which liberty, religion, justice, humanity, alike demanded should be severed without a moment's delay.

These views, in the judgment of the press at the time, and of sound statesmen, would eventually end in civil war, if adopted by the entire North, and hence they denounced them. The Abolitionists were considered by all as enemies to the Union, whom the lower classes felt should be put down, if necessary, by violence. This feeling was increased by the action of William Lloyd Garrison, the founder of the society, who went to England, and joined with the antislavery men there in abusing this country for its inconsistency and crime. These causes produced a state of public feeling that would be very apt to exhibit itself on the first opportunity. When, therefore, in the autumn of 1833, after Garrison's return from England, a notice appeared for an antislavery meeting in Clinton Hall, some of the most respectable men in New York determined to attend, and crush out, by the weight of their influence, the dangerous movement. Another class was resolved to effect the same project in another way, and on the 2d of October the following placard was posted in flaming letters all over the city:

4*

NOTICE

*To all persons from the South.*

All persons interested in the subject of the meeting called by

J. Leavitt,     W. Goodell,

W. Green,     J. Rankin,

Lewis Tappan,

At Clinton Hall, this evening, at 7 o'clock, are requested to attend at the same hour and place.

MANY SOUTHERNERS.

NEW YORK, *October* 2d, 1833.

N. B. All citizens who may feel disposed to manifest the *true* feeling of the State on this subject, are requested to attend.

Putting the appeal in the name of the Southerners, was an artful device to call out the people.

At an early hour crowds began to assemble in front of Clinton Hall ; but to their surprise they found a notice nailed on the door, that no meeting would be held. Many, seeing it, returned home ; but still the crowd continued to swell to thousands, who rent the air with shouts and threats against Garrison. Determined not to be disappointed in a meeting of some kind, they forced their way upstairs, till the room in which it was to be held was crammed to suffocation. The meeting was then organized, and waited till quarter past seven, when it was moved to adjourn to Tammany Hall. There it was again organized, and a gentleman was

about to address the crowd, when a man stepped for·
ward to the president, and stated that the meeting announced to be held in Clinton Hall was at that moment under full headway in Chatham Street Chapel.
Instantly several voices shouted, "Let us go there and
rout them!" But the chairman said they had met to
pass certain resolutions, and they should attend to this
business first, and then every one could do as he liked.
The resolutions were read, and after some remarks had
been made upon them, adopted, and the meeting adjourned. A portion of those present, however, were
not satisfied, but resolved to go to the chapel and break
up the meeting there. The little handful assembled
within, apprised of their approach, fled, so that when
the mob arrived, the building, though the doors were
open and the lights burning, was empty. It immediately took possession of the room, and giving a negro
who was foremost in the sport the name of one of the
Abolitionists, made him chairman. The most absurd
resolutions were then offered, and carried, when the
chairman returned thanks for the honor done him amid
the most uproarious laughter, and what had threatened
to be a serious riot ended in a wild, lawless frolic.

This was the beginning of the Abolition riots in
New York City, which afterwards, to a greater or less
extent, prevailed for years in different parts of the
Union.

Next summer the excitement, which during the winter had nothing to call it forth, broke out afresh, end-
ing in destruction of property and bloodshed, and the
calling out of the military. On the evening of the 7th
of July, an assembly of colored persons of both sexes
occupied Chatham Street Chapel, for the purpose of

listening to a sermon from a negro preacher. The New York Sacred Music Society had leased the building for certain evenings in the week, of which it was asserted this was one. Justice Lowndes, of the Police Court, was president, and Dr. Rockwell vice-president of the society, and they repaired to the building during the evening, and finding it occupied, at once claimed their right to it, and demanded that the blacks should leave. But the latter, having hired and paid for it, refused to do so, when a fight ensued, in which lamps and chairs were broken, loaded canes used freely, and some persons seriously injured. The news of the fight spread rapidly, and a dense crowd gathered around the door. But the police soon arrived, and forcing their way in, drove white and black out together, and locked up the church.

The riot, however, continued for some time in the street; but the blacks, finding themselves outnumbered, fled, and peace was restored.

A portion of the crowd, having recognized Lewis Tappan, one of the leading Abolitionists, followed him home with hoots and yells, and even hurled stones at his house after he had entered it.

The next evening, at dusk, the crowd began again to assemble in front of the chapel. But the lessee of it had closed and locked the gates. The multitude determined, however, not to be disappointed of a meeting, and forcing open the gates, obtained entrance. The meeting was then organized, and Mr. William W. Wilder called to the chair. After making a speech, in which he showed the evil effects of a sudden abolition of slavery, by relating his experience in San Domingo, he moved an adjournment until the next meeting of the

Antislavery Society. The motion was carried, and the assembly broke up. This was, however, altogether too quiet a termination for a part of the crowd, and a shout was made for the Bowery Theatre. The attacks on us by the English, for upholding slavery, and their sympathy and aid for Garrison, and co-operation with him in agitating the question of abolition in this country, had rekindled the old slumbering feeling of hostility to that country ; and Mr. Farren, the stage manager of the Bowery, being an Englishman, it was transferred to him, especially as reports had been circulated that he had spoken disrespectfully of the Americans.

This night having been selected to give him a benefit, his enemies had posted placards over the city, stating the fact of his hostility to this country—whether with the intention of causing a thin house, or breaking it up altogether, is not known. At all events, the mob resolved on the latter course, and streaming up the Bowery in one wild, excited mass, gathered with loud shouts in front of the theatre. The doors were closed in their faces, but pressing against them with their immense weight, they gave way, and like a dark, stormy wave, they surged up the aisles toward the footlights. In the garish light, faces grew pale, and turned eagerly toward the doors for a way of escape. But these were jammed with the excited, yelling mob. The play was " Metamora," and was under full headway, when this sudden inundation of the rioters took place. The actors stopped, aghast at the introduction of this new, appalling scene. Messrs. Hamlin and Forrest advanced to the front of the stage, and attempted to address them ; but apologies and entreaties were alike in vain. The thundering shouts and yells that interrupted them were not those of admiration, and spectators and actors were compelled to remain silent, while this strange audience took complete possession of the house, and inaugurated a play of their own.

But the police, having received information of what was going on, now arrived, and forcing their way in, drove the rioters into the street, and restored order. But the demon of lawless violence, that was now fully raised, was not to be thus laid. Some one got hold of a bell, and began to ring it violently. This increased the excitement, and suddenly the shout arose, " to Arthur Tappan's." *   The cry was at once taken up by a thousand voices, and the crowd started down the street. But instead of going to his house, they went to that of his brother, Lewis, in Rose Street, a still more obnoxious Abolitionist. Reaching it, they staved open the doors, and smashed in the windows, and began to pitch the furniture into the street. Chairs, ·sofas, tables, pictures, mirrors, and bedding, went out one after another. But all at once a lull occurred in the work of destruction. In pitching the pictures out, one came across a portrait of Washington. Suddenly the cry arose, " It is Washington ! For God's sake, *don't burn Washington !* " In an instant the spirit of disorder was laid, and the portrait was handed carefully from man to man, till at length the populace, bearing it aloft, carried it with shouts to a neighboring house for safety. It was one of those strange freaks or sudden changes that will sometimes come over the wildest and most brutal men, like a gleam of gentle light across a dark and stormy sea—the good in man

* A silk merchant, and one of the leading Abolitionists.

for a moment making its voice heard above the din and strife of evil passions.

This singular episode being terminated, they returned to their work of destruction. But suddenly the cry of " Watchmen!" was heard, and the next moment the police came charging down the street. The mob recoiled before it, then broke and fled, and the former took possession of the street. But the latter, coming across some piles of brick, filled their arms and hands full, and rallying, returned. Charging the watchmen in turn with a blinding shower of these, they drove them from the ground. They then kindled a fire on the pavement, and as the flames flashed up in the darkness and gained headway, they piled on bedding and furniture, till the whole street was illuminated with the costly bonfire. This caused the fire-bells to be rung, and soon the engines came thundering down the street, before which the crowd gave way. The burning furniture was then extinguished, and the house taken possession of. It was now two o'clock in the morning, and the mob dispersed.

The next day nothing was talked about in the saloons, groggeries, and on the corners of the by-streets, but the events of the night before; and as evening came on, a crowd began to assemble in front of the battered, dilapidated house of Lewis Tappan. Another attack was imminent, when the police came up and dispersed them. They had not, however, abandoned the purpose for which they had assembled.

The little band of Abolitionists, that the year before had been composed mostly of comparatively obscure men, had now increased both in numbers and men of influence. Persecution had produced its usual effects

—advanced the cause it designed to destroy. Among other well-known citizens who had joined their ranks were the two brothers, Dr. Abraham Cox, M.D., and Dr. Samuel Cox, the latter, pastor of Laight Street Church, and one of the most popular preachers of the city. Though opposed by a large majority of his congregation, he had become known as a bold, outspoken man against slavery; and now the mob, bent on mischief, streamed across the city toward his church. It was dark, and as they gathered in a black, dense mass in front of it, suddenly, as if by a common impulse, a loud yell broke forth, and the next moment a shower of stones and brick-bats fell on the windows. Babel was now let loose, and, amid the crashing of window-glass, arose every variety of sound and all kinds of calls, interspersed with oaths and curses on " Abolitionists and niggers."

Shrieks of laughter and obscene epithets helped to swell the uproar. It was evident they would not be satisfied until they left the church a ruin; but at this critical moment, the Mayor, Justice Lowndes, the District Attorney, and a posse of police officers and watchmen arrived on the ground. Expecting trouble, they had arranged to be ready at a moment's warning to hasten to any threatened point. Their unexpected presence frightened the crowd, and fearing arrest, they slunk away in squads, and the danger seemed over. But, evidently by previous arrangement, the broken fragments, arriving by different streets, came together in front of Dr. Cox's house, in Charlton Street.

The doctor, however, was not at home. He had received warnings and threats from various quarters, and knowing, from the fate of Lewis Tappan's house, what that of his own would be, he had, during the day, quietly removed his furniture, and in the afternoon put his family on board of a steamboat, and left the city.

The mob found the door barricaded, but they broke it open, and began to smash the windows and blinds of the lower story. Before, however, they had begun to sack the house, police-officers and watchmen, with two detachments of horse, arrived and dislodged them. They did not, however, disperse. A more dangerous and determined spirit was getting possession of them than they had before evinced. Crowding back on each other, they packed the street east, within four blocks of Broadway. Seizing some carts, they made a hasty barricade of them across the streets, while a neighboring fence supplied them with clubs. A large number were armed with paving-stones, which they would smite loudly together, saying in deep undertones, "*all together.*" As they thus stood savagely at bay, a collision seemed inevitable, and had they been attacked, would doubtless have made a desperate fight. But being let alone they slowly dispersed. A portion, however, though it was now late at night, could not retire without venting a little more spite, and returning to the church, broke in some more windows.

Dr. Cox came back to his house next morning, to see if it was safe. As he left the mutilated building, a crowd of boys, who were looking at the ruins, immediately gave chase to him with yells and derisive laughter, and pressed him so closely, at the same time hurling dirty missiles at him, that he was compelled to take shelter in the house of a parishioner.

The crowd around the house continued to increase all the morning, but a hundred policemen arriving at one o'clock, no disturbance of the peace was attempted. In the afternoon, Mayor Lawrence issued a proclamation, denouncing the rioters, and calling on all good citizens to aid in maintaining the peace, and assuring them that he had taken ample measures to repress all attempts at violence. At the Arsenal, City Hall, and Bazaar, large bodies of troops were assembled, ready to march at a moment's notice; and it was evident that the coming night was to witness a trial of strength between the rioters and the city authorities.

As soon as it was fairly dark, large crowds gathered in front of Arthur Tappan's store, and began to stone the building. Some fifteen or twenty watchmen were stationed here, and endeavored to arrest the ringleaders, when the mob turned on them, and handled them so roughly that they were compelled to take refuge in flight. Alderman Lalagh was severely wounded; but he refused to leave, and standing fiercely at bay, denounced and threatened the maddened wretches, who in turn swore they would take his life. He told them to force open the doors if they dare; that the inside was full of armed men, who were ready to blow their brains out the moment the door gave way. This frightened them, and they had to content themselves with stoning the windows, and cursing the Abolitionist who owned the building. In the meantime, Justice Lowndes came up with a strong police force, when they fled.

While this was going on here, similar scenes were passing in other parts of the city. At dark, some three or four hundred gathered around Dr. Cox's church, in Laight Street, discussing the conduct of the Abolitionists, but making no outward demonstrations calling for the interference of the police, until nine o'clock, when a reinforcement came yelling down Varick Street, armed with stones and brick-bats. These charged, without halting, so furiously on the police-officers, and the few watchmen stationed there, that, bruised and bleeding, they were compelled to flee for their lives. The next moment stones rattled like hail against the church, and, in a few minutes, the remaining windows were smashed in. The police rallied when they reached Beach Street, and hurried off a messenger to the City Hall for the military. In the meantime, loud shouts were heard in the direction of Spring Street, and with answering shouts the mob left the church, and rushed yelling like Indians to the spot. A vast crowd was in front of a church there, under the care of Rev. Mr. Ludlow, another Abolitionist, and had already commenced the work of destruction. They had torn down the fence surrounding it, and were de-molishing the windows. Through them they made an entrance, and tore down the pulpit, ripped up the seats, and made a wreck of everything destructible without the aid of fire. The session-room shared the same fate, and the splintered wreck of both was car-ried in their arms, and on their shoulders, out of doors, and piled into barricades in the street on both sides of the building, to stop the anticipated charge of cavalry. Carts, hauled furiously along by the mob, were drawn up behind this, and chained together, making a formi-dable obstruction. They then rung the bell furiously, in order to bring out the firemen. The watch-house bell in Prince Street gave a few answering strokes, but information being received of what was going on, it ceased, and the firemen did not come out. It was now

near eleven o'clock, when, all at once, an unearthly
yell arose from the immense throng. Word had passed
through it that the military was approaching. Pandemonium seemed suddenly to have broken loose, and
shouts, and yells, and oaths arose from five thousand
throats, as the men sprung behind their barricades.
It was a moonless night, but the stars were shining
brightly, and, in their light, the sheen of nearly a thousand bayonets made the street look like a lane of steel.
The Twenty-seventh Regiment of National Guards, led
by Colonel Stevens, had been sent from the City Hall,
and their regular heavy tramp sounded ominously, as
they came steadily on. The church-bell was set ringing furiously by the mob and there was every appearance of a determined resistance. As Colonel Stevens
approached the first barricade, he halted his regiment,
and ordered his pioneer guard to advance. They
promptly obeyed, armed with their axes. A shower
of stones met them, while clubs were waved frantically in the air, accompanied with oaths and threats.
They, however, moved firmly up to the barricade, and
the shining steel of their axes, as they swung them in
the air, was as terrific as the gleam of the bayonets,
and the crowd retired precipitately behind the second
barricade. The first was now speedily torn down, and
the head of the column advanced. The second was a
more formidable affair, in fact, a regular bastion, behind which were packed in one dense mass an immense body of desperate men, reaching down the
street, till lost in the darkness. It seemed now that
nothing but deadly volleys would answer. One of the
city officers advised Colonel Stevens to retreat, but,
instead of obeying, he ordered the pioneer guard to

advance, and sustained it by a detachment of troops. Amid the raining missiles they moved forward, when the crowd fell back, some fleeing up the side streets. The guard then mounted the barricade, and in a short time it was scattered in every direction; and when the order "Forward" was given, the column marched straight on the mob. At this moment, Justice Lowndes, at the head of a band of watchmen, arrived on the ground, when the two forces moved forward together, clearing the street of the rioters. While the fight was going on, some of the gang remained inside the church, and kept the bell ringing violently, until Colonel Stevens ordered one of his officers to cut the rope.

A portion of the mob now hurried to Thompson Street, where Mr. Ludlow resided. The family had retired for the night, but their repose was suddenly broken by loud yells and the sound of stones dashing in their windows. Jumping up in wild alarm, they saw the doors broken in, through which streamed the shouting, yelling crowd.

Either from fear of the military, which they knew would soon be upon them, or some other cause, they decamped almost as suddenly as they came, and relieved the terror-stricken household of their presence.

About this time, another immense mob had collected at Five Points. The rioters here seemed to be well organized, and to act in concert. Runners were kept passing between the different bodies, keeping each informed of the actions of the other, and giving notice of the approach of the police.

The destruction at Five Points was on a more extensive scale, and the gatherings in this, then dangerous

section of the city—the home of desperadoes and depraved beings of every kind—were of such a character,
that for a time the city authorities seemed to be overawed.   The rioters had it all their own way for several
hours, and the  midnight heavens became lurid with
burning dwellings.   It somehow got round that they
had resolved to attack every house not illuminated with
candles, and these dirty streets soon became brilliant
with the lighted windows.   Five houses of ill-fame were
gutted, and almost entirely demolished.   St. Philip's
Church, in Centre Street, occupied by a colored congregation, was broken into, and for two hours the mob
continued the work of destruction unmolested.   They
left it a complete ruin.   A house adjoining, and three
houses opposite, shared the same fate.   The mob was
everywhere; and although the police made some arrests
and had some fights, they were too weak to effect much.
About one o'clock a shout arose, "away to Anthony
Street!" and thither the yelling wretches repaired.

    The Mayor was at the City Hall all night, doing
what he could; but the mob had arranged their plans
to act in concert, appearing in separate bodies in
different sections of the city at the same time, so
that he hardly knew, with the force at his disposal,
where to strike.   The next morning he issued another
proclamation, calling on the citizens to report to
him and be organized into companies to aid the
police.   He called also on all the volunteer military
companies of the city to rally to the support of the laws.
They did so, and that (Saturday) night they, with most
of the fire companies, who had offered their services,
were stationed in strong bodies all over the city; and
the rioters saw that their rule was ended.   Beside, many

of the most notorious ringleaders had been arrested and put in prison. A short fight occurred in Catharine Street between the police and mob, in which both had some of their men badly hurt; and an attempt was made to get up a riot in Reade Street, but it was promptly put down. The city was rife with rumors of bloody things which the mob had threatened to do; but, with the exception of the military in the streets, the city on Sunday presented its usual appearance. The lawless spirit was crushed out, and a hundred and fifty of the desperadoes who had been instrumental in rousing it were locked up to await their trial.

In June of the summer of 1835 occurred the Five Points riot, which grew out of the feeling between Americans and foreigners. It threatened for a time to be a very serious matter, but was finally quelled by the police without the aid of the military. Dr. W. M. Caffrey was accidentally killed by one of the mob, and Justice Lowndes was dangerously wounded.

In connection with the series of riots of 1834 and 1835, might be mentioned the Stonecutters' riot, though it was promptly suppressed.

## STONECUTTERS' RIOT.

The contractors for the building of the New York University found that they could purchase dressed stone at Sing Sing, the work of the prisoners there, much cheaper than in New York, and so concluded to use it. This, the stonecutters of the city said, was taking the bread out of their mouths, and if allowed to go on would destroy their business. They held excited meetings on the subject, and finally got up a procession

and paraded the streets with placards asserting their
rights and denouncing the contractors.   They even attacked the houses of some of the citizens, and assumed
such a threatening attitude, that the Twenty-seventh
Regiment, Colonel Stevens, was called out.   Their
steady, determined march on the rioters dispersed them
and restored quiet.   Apprehensions were felt, however,
that they would reassemble in the night and vent their
rage on the University building, and so a part of the
regiment encamped in Washington Square in full view
of it.   They remained here four days and nights, until
the excitement subsided, and the work could go on unmolested.

NEW YORK—BURNING OF THE PROVOST MARSHAL'S OFFICE.

# CHAPTER VII.

## FLOUR RIOT OF 1837.

Starvation will always create a Riot.—Foreign Population easily aroused against the Rich.—Severe Winter of 1836.—Scarcity of Flour.—Meeting of Citizens called without Result.—Meeting called in the Park.—Speeches.—Sacking of Hart & Co.'s Flour Store, in Washington Street.—Strange Spectacle.—National Guards called out.—Disperse the Mob.—Attack on Herrick's Flour Store.—Folly of the Riot.

HUNGER will drive any people mad, and once let there be real suffering for want of food among the lower classes, while grain is piled up in the storehouses of the rich, and riots will surely follow. In the French Revolution of 1789, there was a great scarcity of provisions, which caused frightful outbreaks. It will never do to treat with scorn the cry of millions for bread. When, amid the general suffering in Paris, one said to Foulon, the minister of state, the people are starving for bread, he replied, "Let them eat hay." The next day he was hung to a lamp-post. The tumultuous multitude marching on Versailles, shouting wildly for "bread," was a fearful spectacle. One can hardly blame starving men from seizing food by violence, if it can be got in no other way; and if ever a mob could be justifiable, it would be when they see their families suffering and perishing around them, in the very sight of well-stored granaries.

In the old despotisms of Europe, the poor and op-

5

pressed attribute all their want and suffering to the rich and powerful, so that they are not held back from redressing their wrongs by ignorance of their source, but fear of the strong hand of their rulers.

These men, embittered not only by their own sufferings, but by the traditions of the past, when they come to this country are easily roused to commit acts of violence by anything that reminds them of their old oppressions. They have tasted the wormwood and the gall, and refuse to have it pressed to their lips in a country where liberty is the birthright of all. This is what has made, and still makes, the foreign population among us so dangerous. The vast proportion of them are from this very class. Ignorant of everything but their wrongs, they rise in angry rebellion at any attempt, or fancied attempt, to renew them here. Unfortunately there are Americans among us, who, knowing this, work upon this sensitive, suspicious feeling, to accomplish their own ends. The politician does it to secure votes; but the worst class is composed of those who edit papers that circulate only among the scum of society, and embittered by the sight of luxuries beyond their reach, are always ready to denounce the rich and excite the lower classes against what they call the oppression of the aristocracy.

It is doubtful whether the frightful riot of 1863 would ever have taken place, but for this tone assumed by many of the city papers. So of this flour riot, it probably would never have happened, but for demagogues, who lashed the ignorant foreign population into fury against their rich oppressors. Starvation, which as we said may be a justification of violence, did not exist—it was only the high price of provisions,

growing out of scarcity, that caused it, but which scarcity, they were told, was created solely by the cupidity
of the rich.

The year in which the great fire occurred, was a
disastrous one to the crops of the country. The
mighty West, that great granary of the nation, was
not then open as now, and the main supply of grain
came from east of the Alleghanies. Hence the cause
which would create a short crop in one section, would
be apt to prevail more or less over all the grain region.
We imported wheat at this time very largely; not only
from England, but from the Black Sea.

In September, flour was about seven dollars a barrel, but this, as the winter came on, went up to twelve
dollars—a great rise at that time.

From Virginia, a great wheat State, came disastrous
tidings; not only was the crop short and the price of flour
high, but it was said that the latter would probably go up
to fifteen or twenty dollars a barrel. In Troy, a great
depot for State flour, it was stated that there were only
four thousand barrels against thirty thousand at the
same time the previous year. As February came on, a
report circulated in the city that there were only three
or four weeks' supply on hand. This was repeated
in the penny papers, with the information added, that
in certain stores were hoarded vast amounts of grain
and flour, kept out of the market to compel a still greater
advance in the price. This was very probably true,
as it is a rule with merchants, when they have a large
stock of anything on hand, of which there threatens to
be a scarcity, to hold on in order to make the scarcity
greater—thus forcing higher prices. This will always
prove a dangerous experiment in this country in the

article of flour.  It is the prime necessary of life, and
the right to make it scarce for the sake of gain, and at
the expense of human suffering, will always be ques-
tioned by the poorer classes.

Although the stock of grain on hand at this time
was small, there was no danger of starvation, nor was
it to the instinct of self-preservation that demagogues
appealed.  They talked of the rich oppressing the
poor by their extortions—of monopolists, caring only
to increase their gains without regard to the distress
they occasioned.

There was, doubtless, much suffering among the
poorer classes, not only on account of the high price
of flour, but also of all the necessary articles of living.
Meat advanced materially, while from some strange
fatality, coal went up to ten dollars a ton.  There
seemed no reason for this, as the amount sent to market was said to be largely in excess of the previous
year.  In Canada, coal was so scarce, that the line of
steamers between Montreal and Quebec was suspended
before winter set in.

This state of things excited the attention of the people generally, and in the fore-part of this month, a
public meeting was called at the Tabernacle to consider
what could be done.  It amounted to nothing.  Some
speeches were made, resolutions offered, but nothing
practical was proposed.  The temperance people attempted to make a little capital out of it, by asserting
that the high price of grain was owing to the amount
used by the distilleries—rye being sold as high as one
dollar and seventy cents per bushel.

But a different class of people were now discussing
the subject, and in a different spirit.  Their attention

was directed to *men*, not *theories*—the individual oppressors, not the general causes.

Chief among those against whom the popular feeling
was now directed, was Hart & Co., large commission
merchants in Washington Street, between Dey and
Cortlandt Streets. Their store was packed with flour
and wheat, and every day men passed it with sinister
looks. Sometimes a little knot of men would stop
opposite it, and talk of the loads of grain stored up
there, while their own families were pinched for bread.
They would gaze savagely on its heavy iron doors, that
seemed to defy the weak and helpless, and then walk
on, muttering threats and curses. These signs of a
gathering storm were, however, unheeded by the proprietors. Others, better informed, were not so tranquil; and by anonymous letters tried to arouse Mr.
Hart to take precautionary measures. An anonymous
letter addressed to Mr. W. Lenox was picked up in the
Park, in which the writer stated that a conspiracy was
formed for breaking open and plundering Mr. Hart's
store, and gave the following plan of action. On some
dark night, two alarms of fire were to be given, one
near the Battery, and the other up town, in order to
draw off the watchmen and police, when a large crowd
already assembled in the neighborhood would make a
sudden rush for the building, and sack it before help
could arrive. This letter was handed to the High
Constable Hays, who showed it to Hart & Co., but they
seemed to regard it as an attempt to frighten them.
This was followed by anonymous letters from other
parties, that reached the Mayor, insisting on it that
danger was hanging over this house. He sent them to
Hart & Co., but they, thinking it was only a trick to

put down the price of flour, paid no attention to them. They locked their three massive iron doors at night as usual, and went to their homes without fear, and the underground swell kept on increasing in volume.

The first plan of operation, if it ever existed, was either abandoned by the mob or deferred till after other measures were tried.

At length, on the afternoon of the 10th of Febuary, the following placard was posted up all over the city :

### BREAD, MEAT, RENT, FUEL !

*The voice of the people shall be heard and will prevail.*

The people will meet in the PARK, *rain or shine*, at four o'clock on

### MONDAY AFTERNOON,

to inquire into the cause of the present unexampled distress, and to devise a suitable remedy. All friends of humanity, determined to resist monopolists and extortioners, are invited to attend.

| | |
|---|---|
| Moses Jacques. | Daniel Graham. |
| Paulus Hedle. | John Windt. |
| Daniel A. Robertson. | Alexander Ming, Jr. |
| Warden Hayward. | Elijah F. Crane. |

NEW YORK, *Feb.* 10*th*, 1837.

The idle crowd had all day Sunday to talk over this call. Everywhere knots of men were seen gathered before these placards—some spelling out slowly, and with great difficulty, the words for themselves—others

reading the call to those unable to read it.   The groggeries were filled with excited men, talking over the
meeting, and interspersing their oaths with copious
draughts of liquor, and threatening openly to teach
these rich oppressors a lesson they would not soon forget.

There was something ominous in the hour selected
for the meeting; four o'clock in February meant night,
before it would get under full headway.   It was evident that the leaders did not mean the meeting to be
one of mere speech-making.   They knew that under
cover of darkness, men could be incited to do what in
broad daylight they would be afraid to undertake.

Before the time appointed, a crowd began to assemble, the character of which boded no good.   Dirty,
ragged, and rough-looking, as they flowed from different quarters together into the inclosure, those who
composed it were evidently a mob already made to
hand.

At length, four or five thousand shivering wretches
were gathered in front of the City Hall.   Moses
Jacques, a man who would make a good French Communist to-day, was chosen chairman.   But this motley
multitude had no idea or respect for order, or regular
proceedings, and they broke up into different groups,
each pushing forward its favorite orator.

One of the strangest freaks of this meeting, was an
address to a collection of Democrats by Alexander
Ming, Jr.   He forgot all about the object of the meeting, and being a strong Bentonian, launched out into
the currency question, attributing all the evils of the
Republic, past, present, and to come, to the issue of
bank-notes; and advising his hearers to refuse to take

the trash altogether, and receive nothing but specie. This was the more comical, as not one out of ten of the poor wretches he addressed had the chance to refuse either. Half starving, they would have been glad to receive anything in the shape of money that would help them through the hard winter. Yet when Mr. Ming offered a resolution, proposing a memorial to the Legislature, requiring a law to be passed, forbidding any bank to issue a note under the denomination of a hundred dollars, the deluded people, who had been listening with gaping mouths, rent the air with acclamations. It was a curious exhibition of the wisdom of the sovereign people—this verdict of a ragged mob on the currency question. They were so delighted with this lucid exposition of the cause of the scarcity of flour, that they seized the orator bodily, and elevating him on their shoulders, bore him across the street to Tammany Hall, where something beside specie was received from behind the bar to reward their devotion.

There was, however, some excuse for him. He had been several times candidate for city register, and hence was more anxious to secure votes than flour— be a popular demagogue rather than a public benefactor.

But there were other speakers who kept more directly to the point. They launched at once into a bitter tirade against landlords for their high rents, and against monopolists for holding on to flour at the expense of the poor and suffering. Knowing the character of the audience before them, and their bitter hatred of the rich that had grown with their growth, and strengthened with their strength in the old country, it was not difficult to lash them into a tempest of passion.

They depicted the aristocrats around them rolling in wealth, wrung from their necessities—laughing at their sufferings while rioting in luxury—nay, hoarding up the very bread without which they must starve, in order to realize a few dollars more on a barrel of flour. Loud oaths and deep muttered curses followed these appeals, and the excited multitude became agitated with passion. One of the speakers closed his bitter harangue with "Fellow-citizens, Mr. Eli Hart has now 53,000 barrels of flour in his store; let us go and offer him eight dollars a barrel for it, and if he will not take it—" It was not difficult to know how he meant to close the sentence; but just then, a friend shrewder than he, seeing the legal consequences to themselves of an open proposition to resort to violence, touched him on the shoulder, when in a lower tone of voice he concluded: "*we shall depart in peace.*" In the excitement of the moment, he had evidently forgotten the guarded language he intended to use, and was about to utter that which would have consigned him to a prisoner's cell, but checked himself in time. He was willing others should suffer the consequence of violating the law, to which his appeals urged them; but his love for the poor did not prompt him to share their fate.

It was bitterly cold, and it was a wonder that the crowd had listened patiently so long. The proposition to go to Hart's store with a demand for flour, was instantly seized, and those around the speaker started off with a shout, and streaming down Broadway, poured in one dark living stream along Cortlandt Street into Washington Street. The clerks in the store heard the turmoil, and suspecting the object of the rioters,

5*

rushed to the doors and windows, and began to close and bolt them. There were three large iron doors opening on the sidewalk, and they had succeeded in bolting and barring all but one, when the mob arrived. Forcing their way through this middle door, the latter seized the barrels, and began to roll them out into the street. Mr. Hart, who, either from curiosity to hear what the meeting would propose to do, or from his suspicions being aroused from what he had previously heard, was on the spot, and as soon as he saw the crowd stream out of the Park, down Broadway, he hurried to the police, and obtaining a posse of officers, made all haste for his store. But as they were going down Dey Street, the mob, which blocked the farther end, rushed on them with such fury, that before they had time to defend themselves, their clubs, or staves as they were then called, were wrenched from their hands and broken into fragments. The crowd was not yet very great, and the disarmed officers forced their way into Washington Street and into the store. Their presence frightened the few inside, and they hastily decamped. The Mayor, who was in his room at the City Hall, had been speedily notified of the riot, and hurried to the spot. The crowd remaining in the Park had also been informed of what was going on, and dashing madly down Broadway, and through Cortlandt Street, joined with loud shouts their companions in front of the store. The Mayor mounted a flight of steps, and began to harangue the mob, urging them to desist, and warning them of the consequences of their unlawful action. He had not proceeded far, however, before brick-bats, and sticks, and pieces of ice came raining around him in such a dangerous shower, that

he had to give it up, and make his way to a place of
safety. The street was now black with the momentarily
increasing throng, and emboldened by their numbers,
they made a rush at the entrance of the store. Driving the police-officers before them, they wrenched by
main force one of the heavy iron doors from its hinges.
A half a score of men at once seized it, and using it as
a battering-ram, hurled it with such force against the
others, that after a few thundering blows, they one
after another gave way, and the crowd poured in.
The clerks fled, and the rioters went to work without
hindrance. Mounting to the upper lofts, they first broke
in all the doors and windows, and then began to roll
and heave out the flour. The barrels on the ground-
floor were rolled, swift as one could follow another,
into the street, when they were at once seized by those
waiting without, and their heads knocked in, and
their contents strewn over the pavement. On the
upper lofts, they were rolled to the broken windows,
and lifted on to the sill, and tumbled below. Warned
by their descent, the crowd backed to the farther side
of the street. Part would be staved in by their fall;
those that were not, were seized as they rolled off the
sidewalk, and the heads knocked out. One fellow, as
he stood by the window-sill and pitched the barrels below, shouted as each one went with a crash to the flagging: " *Here goes flour at eight dollars a barrel!* "

The scene which now presented itself was a most
strange, extraordinary one. The night was clear and
cold, and the wintry moon was sailing tranquilly
through the blue and starlit heavens, flooding here and
there the sea of upturned faces with its mellow light,
or casting the deep shadow of intervening houses over

the black mass, while the street looked as if a sudden snow-storm had carpeted it with white. The men in the windows and those below were white with flour that had sifted over their garments; while, to give a still wilder aspect to the scene, women, some barehead-ed, some in rags, were roaming around like camp-fol-lowers after plunder. Here a group had seized empty boxes; there others pressed forward with bas-kets on their arms; and others still, empty-handed, pushed along, with their aprons gathered up like a sack. These all knelt amid the flour, and scooped it up with an eagerness that contrasted strangely with the equal eagerness of those who were scattering it like sand over the street. The heavy thud of the barrels as they struck almost momentarily on the sidewalk, could be distinctly heard above the shouts of the men. Some of the mob found their way into Mr. Hart's counting-room, and tore up his papers and scattered them over the floor. It was evident they were bent on utter de-struction; but when about five hundred barrels of flour had been destroyed, together with a thousand bushels of wheat in sacks, a heavy force of police came marching along the street. These were soon after followed by de-tachments of the National Guards from Colonel Smith's and Hele's regiments. The flashing of the moonbeams on the burnished barrels and bayonets of their muskets, struck terror into the hearts of the rioters. The cry of " The soldiers are coming!" flew from lip to lip, caus-ing a sudden cessation of the work of destruction, and each one thought only of self-preservation. Many, however, were arrested, and sent off to Bridewell under the charge of Officer Bowyer, with a squad of police. The latter were assailed, however, on the way, by a portion of the mob that pursued them, and a fierce fight followed. In the struggle, Bowyer and his assistants had their clothes torn from their backs, and some of the prisoners were rescued.

In the meantime, the military paraded the street, clearing it of the mob, and preventing their return. In front of the store, and far beyond it, the flour lay half-knee deep—a sad spectacle, in view of the daily increasing scarcity of grain.

Just before the military and police reached the ground, some one in the crowd shouted "Meeches'." This was another flour store at Coenties Slip, on the other side of the city, nearly opposite. A portion of the mob on the outside, that could not get to the store, and aid in the work of destruction, at once hurried away to this new field of operations. On the way over, they passed Herrick & Co.'s flour store, and stopped to demolish it. They were loaded down with brick-bats, which they hurled at the windows, smashing them in. The doors followed, and the crowd, rushing through, began to roll out the barrels of flour. But when some twenty or thirty were tumbled into the street, and about half of them staved in, they, for some cause or other, stopped. Some said that they ceased because the owner promised, if they did, he would give it all away to the poor the next day. At all events, they would soon have been compelled to abandon the work of destruction, for the police hastened to the spot, accompanied by a large body of citizens, who had volunteered their help. Some were arrested, but most of the ringleaders escaped.

How many of those who attended the meeting in the Park anticipated a mob and its action, it is impossible to say ; but that a great number of them did, there can be no doubt.

By nine o'clock the riot was over, and those who had engaged in it were either arrested or dispersed.

The next day, Mr. Hart issued a card, denying that the exorbitant price of flour was owing to his having purchased a large quantity for the sake of monopolizing it, but to its scarcity alone.

It was certainly a very original way to bring down the price, by attempting to destroy all there was in the city. Complaining of suffering from the want of provisions, they attempted to relieve themselves by putting its possession out of their power altogether. With little to eat, they attempted to make it impossible to eat at all. A better illustration of the insensate character of a mob could not be given.

# CHAPTER VIII.

## ASTOR-PLACE RIOTS, 1849.

Rivalry between Forrest and Macready.—Macready's Arrival in this
Country.—The Announcement of his Appearance at the Astor-
place Opera House, and Forrest at the Broadway Theatre the
same Night posted Side by Side.—Bowery Boys crowd the Opera
House.—Anxiety of the Managers.—Consultations and Dramatic
Scenes behind the Curtain.—Stamping of the People.—Scene on
raising the Curtain.—Stormy Reception of Macready.—Howled
down.—Mrs. Pope driven from the Stage by the Outrageous
Language of the Mob.—Macready not allowed to go on.—His
foolish Anger.—Flees for his Life.—His Appearance the Second
Night.—Preparations to put down the Mob.—Exciting Scene in
the Theatre.—Terrific Scenes without.—Military arrive.—Attacked by the Mob.—Patience of the Troops.—Effort to avoid
Firing.—The Order to Fire.—Terrific Scene.—Strange Conduct
of Forrest.—Unpublished Anecdote of General Scott.

PROBABLY there never was a great and bloody riot,
moving a mighty city to its profoundest depths, that
originated in so absurd, insignificant a cause as the
Astor-place riot. A personal quarrel between two men
growing out of professional jealousy, neither of whom
had any hold on the affections of the people, were able
to create a tumult, that ended only by strewing the
street with the dead and wounded.

Mr. Forrest, it is true, had a certain professional
popularity, but nothing to awaken a personal enthusi-
asm for him. Viewing the matter in this light, some

have thought, there was a mysterious underground influence at work, that has never yet been discovered. But one needs not to go far to find the causes that produced it.

In the first place, ever since our revolt from England, especially since the second war with her, in which the contest for the supremacy of the seas was decided, the spirit of rivalry between the two countries has been intense and often bitter. No matter what the contest was, whether between two boats, or two bullies in the ring, it at once assumed the magnitude of a national one, and no matter how conducted, the winner was always charged with unfairness. It so happened that Forrest and Macready were the two popular tragic actors on either side of the Atlantic. If they had stayed at home, nothing would have been thought of it, but each invaded the domain of the other, and laid claim to his laurels. Of course criticism followed, national prejudices were aroused, and national peculiarities ridiculed. The press took sides, and fanned the excitement. Among other things, it was currently reported that when Forrest was in London, Macready went to see him act, and publicly hissed him. This was generally believed, and of course it alone would insure the latter an unwelcome reception from Forrest's admirers here, should he ever appear on our stage.

Apparently unconscious of this hostility toward him, Macready came over in the spring of 1849, and at once made an engagement at the Astor-place Opera House, corner of Eighth Street and Lafayette Place. He was to appear as Macbeth; and the play was announced sometime beforehand. Forrest at the same time had an engagement at the Broadway Theatre. On the 7th

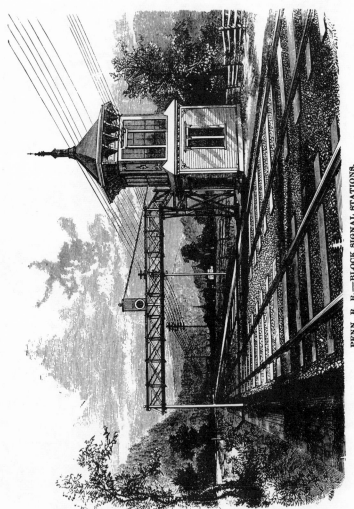

PENN. R. R.—BLOCK SIGNAL STATIONS.

of May, the following two significant placards appeared side by side in all the streets.

ASTOR PLACE OPERA HOUSE.

*This evening will be performed*

MACBETH.

| | | |
|---|---|---|
| MACBETH . . . | | Macready. |
| LADY MACBETH . . | | Mrs. Pope. |

BROADWAY THEATRE.

*This evening will be performed*

MACBETH.

| | | |
|---|---|---|
| MACBETH . . | | Mr. Forrest. |
| LADY MACBETH . . | | Mrs. Wallack. |

This public exhibition of rivalry stimulated the hostility of those opposed to Macready, and there were some fears of disturbance; but nothing serious was anticipated—in fact, it was rather a good advertisement, and promised full houses. Niblo, one of the managers of the Opera House, unwisely gave out tickets for more people than the building would hold, and when, before evening, he found they were taken, he was alarmed. It looked as if they had been so eagerly bought up for other purposes than merely to hear Macready. He therefore went to the Chief of Police, and requested the presence of a force in case any disturbance should be attempted. It was promised, but as it turned out, most of it came too late to be of any service.

A tremendous crowd assembled in front of the building long before dark, and the moment the doors were open, a rush was made, and the human tide poured in, and flowing swiftly over the house, soon filled every part of it, except the boxes. These filled up more slowly; but long before the curtain rose, the house was packed to repletion, while the amphitheatre and parquette were crowded with hard-looking men—a dense mass of bone and muscle. The fashionable portion of the audience in the boxes began to feel anxious, for not only were all the seats occupied, but all the aisles and every foot of standing room. Some were in their shirt-sleeves, others were ragged and dirty, while all had their hats on. Such an audience had never before been seen in the Opera House, and it boded no good. Still, this heterogeneous mass was orderly, but it was noticed that at short intervals telegraphic signals were made by those nearest the stage to those in the wings of the amphitheatre, and answered, indicating a thoroughly arranged plan. The time before the play was to commence passed slowly, but the hard-looking crowd seemed very patient. Occasionally, to vary the monotony, some joke would be passed around, and once a man who was above called out to those below, imitating the English pronunciation : " I say, Jim, come 'hup 'ere! 'ere's some of Macready's hangels—'haint they sweet 'uns ? " If a lorgnette was levelled from one of the boxes, those noticing it below would put their thumbs to their noses and gyrate with their fingers in return. On the whole, however, the strange-looking crowd were orderly, although the quiet had an ominous look.

But at half-past seven, the hour for the play to commence, that regular stamping, common to most theatres, began. But in this case, it did not continue for a little while and then die away, but beginning in a low rumble, every moment gathered strength and grew louder, till it rolled like thunder through the building, shaking the very walls, and making the glasses in the great central chandelier jingle, as though knocked together by invisible hands. As the mighty sound echoed through the recesses and dressing-rooms behind the scenes, Niblo became agitated, and stepping forward on the stage, peered behind the edge of the curtain, and surveyed the strange scene. Turning to Mr. Bowyer, of the chief's bureau, who was by his side, he said: "This looks rather dubious, Mr. Bowyer." "Yes," he replied, "the 'Boy's' are here certainly. What made you sell so many tickets? People are making a tremendous rush at the doors yet, and the house is full; over full already." Niblo then turned to his partner, and said: "What do you think, Mr. Hackett. Is there going to be a disturbance?" "I don't know," he replied; "you must ask Mr. Bowyer."

The latter, putting his eye to the crack, took a careful survey of the audience, and remarked: "There is mischief in the parquette and amphitheatre, but probably no actual violence will be attempted; the 'boys' will make a noise, and endeavor to prevent the play from proceeding, but possibly they will do nothing further; they seem to be patient and good-natured, but Mr. Macready may expect a rough reception."

Macready, who had been dressing, now approached and also took a peep from behind the curtain. His gaze was long and searching. The scrutiny did not satisfy him, and he turned away and began to pace backward and forward in one of the wings, moody and

thoughtful. The stamping had ceased while the or-
chestra was playing, but it now commenced again,
apparently louder than ever. Lady Macbeth in full
dress now came on the stage, pale and agitated. She
also took a peep from behind the curtain. The spectacle frightened her, and turning to Mr. Hackett, she
whispered, rather than exclaimed, "My God! Mr.
Hackett, what is the matter? Are we to be murdered
to-night?" "My dear Madam," he replied, "keep
calm, there is no cause for alarm; everything will go
on smoothly;" but his pale face and anxious look belied
his words. It seemed now as if the house would
come down under the continuous, furious stamping.
Hackett turned to Bowyer, and asked if the chief had
come. The latter replied he did not know; and another
silence followed in the group behind the curtain, while
they stood and listened to the thundering tramp, tramp,
that rose like muffled thunder. At length Hackett
asked: "How many policemen are there in the
house?" "I don't know," replied Bowyer. "But
the chief should have known," retorted the former.
"What do you want the police to do, Mr. Niblo?"
quietly asked Bowyer. The latter hesitated a moment,
when the attaches of the theatre came crowding forward in alarm, and asking by their scared looks what
it all meant.

Macready and Mrs. Pope, in full costume, were at
this time standing apart, talking together, evidently
discussing the best course to be pursued. The uproar
seemed to grow louder, and prudence dictated a suspension of the play; but Macready, after a moment's
hesitation, determined to risk it, and suddenly gave
the signal to raise the curtain. The bell tinkled, and

the curtain slowly rose, revealing the gorgeous scene and the actors standing in a blaze of light. Instantly the tumult ceased, and a deep sudden hush succeeded. Those roughs were evidently taken aback by the dazzling splendor that burst upon them. It was a new revelation to them, and for the moment they seemed to forget the object of their coming, and to be wholly absorbed in the vision before them.

The first scene passed off quietly, and the fears of a disturbance were allayed. In the second, taking Duncan for Macbeth, the crowd began to hiss, but soon finding their mistake ceased. It was evident that some one better posted than the mass had control of this wild element, so eager to be let loose. At length Macbeth came on, and was received with deafening cheers by those in the boxes. As these died away, a hiss ran through the amphitheatre and parquette, followed by cat-calls, cock-crowing, and sounds of every imaginable description. Macready had hardly uttered a single sentence, before his voice was totally drowned in the uproar. Forced to stop; he quietly folded his arms and faced the storm, expecting it would soon blow over. Finding himself mistaken—that if anything it grew louder and fiercer, his disdain turned into foolish anger, and advancing to the footlights, and throwing all the contempt and scorn into his face that he was master of, he deliberately walked the entire breadth of the stage, gazing haughtily as he did so, into the faces of the roughs nearest him, who were bawling their throats hoarse. This did not mend matters any, as he easily could have foreseen, had he known this type of American character better. He then attempted to go on and outbellow, if possible, the audience. But it was like shouting amid the roar of breakers. Nobody heard a word he said, still he stuck to it till he got through that portion of the act. It was now Lady Macbeth's turn, and the appearance of a woman, it was thought, would command that respect which in America is almost always accorded to one. But her reception was worse than that of Macready, for not content with shouts and yells they heaped disgusting epithets on her, and were so vulgar in their ribaldry that she flew in affright from the stage, "blushing," it was said, "even through the rouge on her face." Macready, however, showing, if nothing else, good English pluck, determined to go on. But he had scarcely finished the first sentence, when some potatoes struck the stage at his feet; then rotten eggs, breaking and spattering their sickening contents over his royal robes; while howls that seemed to come from the lower regions arose on every side. It was Pandemonium broke loose, and those in the boxes, thoroughly alarmed, jumped to their feet and stood as if paralyzed, gazing on the strange spectacle below. Macready's passions were now thoroughly aroused, and he stubbornly stood his ground. Suddenly a chair hurled from above, and evidently aimed at his head, struck the stage at his feet and broke into fragments, followed by the shout, "Go off the stage, you English fool! Hoo! Three cheers for Ned Forrest!" which were given with a will. Then came another chair, narrowly missing Macready's head, who, now alarmed for his personal safety, fled from the stage, and the curtain fell. But the bedlam that had been let loose did not stop. Hoots, curses, threats of vengeance, and the confused sounds of a mob given wholly over to passion,

struck terror into all hearts; and Macready, fearing a
rush would be made for him behind the scenes, left the
theatre by a private door, and jumping into a carriage
was rapidly driven to his hotel.    The manager, alarmed
for the safety of the building, attempted to announce
his departure to the audience, but in vain.    They would
not listen to him, and as a last resort he chalked in
large letters on a board, "*Macready has left the theatre*," and hoisted it before the footlights.    This had
the desired effect, and the headlong crowd, with shouts
and laughter, began to tumble out.    Once in the street,
they sent up a loud hurrah, and dispersed in groups to
their various drinking places, to talk over their victory
and damn all Englishmen.

The fact that the mob refrained from damaging the
theatre, shows that they did not desire destruction;
they had only done in their rough way what other men
deemed respectable, and even legislators, have often
done, and almost as boisterously, to prevent an obnoxious
person from being heard.    They certainly had many
respectable precedents for their course, and Mr. Macready should have done what others have been compelled to do—given up the attempt and waited for a
more propitious time.    That a man has a right to play
or speak, is true; but men of all grades have always asserted the right to show their displeasure of the acting
of the one or the sentiments of the other.    Not that
there is any excuse for such conduct as we have described, but it can be hardly called a serious riot, although by whomsoever committed is unquestionably
riotous in its character.

Of this contemptible, disgraceful interference of his
friends in his quarrel, Forrest had nothing to say—he

kept a studied silence. How a man with any self-respect could have refrained from denouncing it, and repudiating all sympathy and connection with it by a public card, it will be difficult for men of ordinary sensibility to imagine.

Macready now determined to throw up his engagement altogether, but after much consultation and deliberation changed his mind. A letter was addressed to him by many of the most wealthy and prominent citizens of the city, in which they expressed their regret at the treatment he had received, and urged him not to yield to such a lawless spirit. They promised that he should be protected in his rights, and hoped he would give the city an opportunity to wipe out the stain that had been put upon its character. This he unwisely consented to do, and the next Thursday was fixed for his appearance in the same play. When the placards announcing it were pasted up, there appeared immediately alongside of them another, announcing the appearance on the same evening of Forrest, in the Broadway Theatre, in the character of the " Gladiator."

In the meantime other posters appeared, and among them the following in startling capitals :

## " WORKINGMEN!

### SHALL AMERICANS OR ENGLISH RULE IN THIS CITY ?

The crew of the British steamer have threatened all Americans who shall dare to offer their opinions this night at the

### ENGLISH ARISTOCRATIC OPERA HOUSE.

**WORKINGMEN! FREEMEN! STAND UP TO YOUR LAWFUL RIGHTS."**

It will be observed, that this artful appeal was like a two-edged sword, cutting both ways. It aimed at the same time to stir up the hatred of the lower classes against the upper, by the word aristocratic; and the national hatred of the English, by calling it the *English aristocratic* Opera House to be guarded by English sailors. Both parties now began active preparations for the eventful night—the rioters by increasing and organizing their forces, and setting on foot plans to get possession of the house ; the friends of Macready, to prevent this from being done, and at the same time secure sufficient aid from the authorities to suppress all open violence. To keep the rowdies from occupying the house, tickets were sold or given away only to those known to be friendly to Macready; while to suppress violence, three hundred police were promised, to be supported if necessary by two regiments of soldiers, who were ordered to be under arms at their quarters, ready to march at a moment's notice.

As the day advertised for the play approached, the excitement deepened, and serious trouble seemed unavoidable. On the appointed evening, a strong body of police was quietly placed inside of the house, with definite instructions how to act. In the meantime, an immense crowd had assembled in front of the building, and, when at last the doors opened, a rush was made for them. But the police kept the crowd back, and only those who had tickets were admitted. When the house was fairly filled, the doors were closed and fastened. In the meantime the windows had been barricaded, with the exception of one, which was overlooked. This the now disappointed rabble assailed with stones, sending them through it, in among the

6

startled audience.   They tried also to break down one
of the doors, but the policemen's clubs stopped them.
Then commenced a series of yells and shouts, mingled
with horrid oaths and threats as the baffled wretches
surged around the building.   Finding nothing else to
vent their rage on, they attacked the lamps in the
neighborhood, breaking them to pieces, and putting
out the lights.

In the meantime, the play inside, with this wild ac-
companiment without, commenced.   Notwithstanding
all the care that had been taken, a large number of
roughs had succeeded in procuring tickets, showing
that some professedly respectable men had been in
collusion with them.   Although the rioters inside were
in a minority, they were not daunted, and being determined that the play should not go on, commenced
stamping and yelling so, that Macready's voice from
the outset was completely drowned.

The police in disguise had mingled all day with the
rioters, and ascertained what the mode of action inside
the house was to be.   At a certain point in the play, a
signal was to be given, on seeing which the entire body
was to make a rush for the stage and seize Macready.
The Chief of Police arranged his plans accordingly,
and imparted them to the force under him.   He therefore made no effort to stop the noise, but waited for the
expected signal.   At length it was given, and the entire
body of rioters rose with a yell and sprang forward.
But at that moment, the chief gave *his* signal, which
was lifting his hat from his head.   Every eye of those
determined policemen had been intently watching it, and
as it now rose, they sprang with a single bound upon the
astonished rowdies, and before they could recover from

their surprise, most of them were outside of the building, while the ringleaders were kept back and caged inside.

The play now went on, but it was a spiritless affair. Every ear was turned to hear the muffled roar of the voices outside, which every moment increased in power as the mighty multitude kept swelling in numbers.

The afterpiece was omitted, and Macready escaping through a private door, hastened to his hotel. It seemed for a time that the building would be torn down; but at length, a regiment of the National Guard, preceded by a body of cavalry, was seen marching steadily up Broadway. The crowd parted as it advanced, and as it turned into Eighth Street, the sharp word of command, "right wheel," rang out distinct and clear over the uproar. The rioters, instead of being intimidated, rushed to a pile of paving-stones that unfortunately happened to be near, and arming themselves with these, began to pelt the horses, which soon became unmanageable, so that the cavalry force had to retire.

The infantry then advanced, but were received with such a deluge of stones that they, too, fell back to Broadway. Here they rallied, and at the order forward, moved steadily on the mob, and forced their way to the front of the Opera House. While forming line here on the sidewalk, they were assailed so fiercely with paving-stones, that the soldiers fell rapidly. The rioters were in close quarters, and the heavy stones, hurled at such a short distance, were almost as deadly as musket-balls. Captain Pond soon fell wounded, when the second in command told the sheriff that if he did not give the order to fire, the troops would be with-

drawn, for they couldn't stand it.   Recorder Talmadge,
unwilling to resort to such a desperate measure, attempted to harangue the mob.   He begged them, in
God's name, to disperse and go home—if they did
not, the soldiers would certainly fire on them, etc.
The only reply was hoots and yells of defiance, and
paving-stones.   The Recorder then forced his way up
to General Hall, standing at the right of the battalion,
and said : " You must order your men to fire ; it is a
terrible alternative, but there is no other."   The General asked for the Mayor, for he was doubtful of his
authority to do so, without his order.   " He won't be
here," replied Talmadge.   General Sandford then
said : " Well, the National Guards will not stand and
be pounded to death with stones ; nearly one-third of
the force is already disabled."   After a little more
hurried conversation, the sheriff said, " If that be so,
you have permission to fire."   The uproar all this time
was deafening, and the order, " Ready ! " of General
Sandford, could hardly be heard ; but the sharp, quick
rattle of steel rose distinctly over the discord.   Still
terribly repugnant to shoot down citizens, General
Hall and Colonel Duryea made another attempt to address the crowd, and begged them to cease these attacks.   " Fire and be d—ned ! " shouted a burly
fellow.   " Fire, if you dare—take the life of a freeborn
American for a bloody British actor !   D—n it, you
dassent fire ! " and he boldly bared his breast to the
levelled muskets.   " Fire, will you ? " yelled another,
as he hurled a paving-stone at General Sandford,
wounding his sword arm.   " Hit 'em again ! " shouted
a third, who saw the well-directed aim.   Still averse to
shedding blood, General Hall told the soldiers to ele-

vate their pieces over the heads of the people, and fire at the blank wall of Mr. Langton's house opposite, hoping thus to frighten the mob. But this only awakened derision, and the leaders shouted, "Come on, boys! they have blank cartridges and leather flints!" In the meantime, the police, who had mingled with the mob, and were making arrests, began to force their way out, in order to escape the fire that now seemed inevitable. The troops moved across the street, and faced toward the Bowery, obeying the word of command promptly, and marching with great steadiness, although the pelting they received was murderous. To retreat would be pusillanimous, to stand there and be pelted to death worse still; and General Hall finally gave the order to fire point blank, but to aim low, so that men would be wounded, rather than killed. The command fell clear and distinct, " Fire!"

A single musket-shot on the extreme left was the only response. They were too near—their muzzles almost touching the hearts of the men, and it seemed terribly murderous to fire. " Fire! " shouted General Sandford.

Three more musket-shots, only, followed. " Fire! " Duryea then cried out, in ringing tones. A swift volley ran along the line, shedding a momentary glare on the wild faces of the mob, the streets, and adjoining houses, and then came the report. This time the dead in their midst told the rioters that it was child's play no longer, and they fell back. But getting a new supply of paving-stones, they rallied, and once more advanced on the troops. A second volley, more murderous than the first, sent them crowding back on each other in terror. The troops now wheeled, and formed line again in front of the Opera House. It had got to be eleven o'clock, and more troops were ordered up, with two cannon. The mob, though dismayed, still refused to retire, and hung sullen and threatening as a thunder-cloud on the skirts of the military, and a third volley was poured into them. The rioters now separated, and fell back into the darkness, when the troops were ordered to fire the fourth time, in different directions—one wing down Eighth Street, and the other into Lafayette Place. This last volley, judging from the testimony of reliable witnesses, was altogether needless. The conflict was over.

A lawyer of Wall Street, noted for his philanthropy and kindness, resided in Fourth Avenue, and being informed by a friend, late in the evening, that men were lying dead and wounded in Astor Place, he hastened down to see if he could be of any assistance to the poor creatures. Reaching Lafayette Place, he saw in the dim light a line of soldiers drawn up, though he saw no mob, only a few scattered men, who seemed to be spectators. Suddenly he heard the order to fire, and the next moment came a flash and report. He could not imagine what they were firing at; but suddenly he felt his arm numb, and the next moment he grew faint and dropped on the sidewalk, his arm broken to shivers. The brother of a well-known banker was shot in Broadway by a random bullet; and a man, while stepping out of a car in Third Avenue, was shot dead. Other innocent persons fell victims, as they always must, if they will hang on the skirts of a mob from curiosity. Men anxious to witness a fight must take the chances of getting hurt.

Great excitement followed; an indignation meeting

was called in the Park, coroners' juries stultified themselves, and a senseless outcry was made generally.
Twenty-two were killed and thirty wounded.  It was
a terrible sacrifice to make for a paltry quarrel between two actors about whom nobody cared; and in
this light alone many viewed it, forgetting that when
the public peace is broken, it matters not how great or
insignificant the cause, it must be preserved; and if
the police or military are called out to do it, and are
attacked, they must defend themselves, and uphold the
laws, or be false to their trust.  The authorities have
to do with riots, not their causes ; put them down, not
deprecate their existence, or argue their justice.

If public indignation had been turned against Forrest, it would have been more sensible.  He knew perfectly well that if his friends persisted in their determination to attack Macready, the second night, blood
would be spilt.  It was *his* quarrel, and yet he deliberately kept his lips closed.  He neither begged them
for their own sake, nor for his, or as good citizens, to
forbear, and let his rival alone ; nor after it was known
that many had been killed, did he express a single
word of regret; apparently having no feeling but
gratification, that even at such a fearful sacrifice his
hated rival had been driven from the field.  But responsibility is not so easily shaken off, and in real
life as well as in tragedy, conscience will force a man
to cry:

" Out! damned blood spot!  Out, I say!"

Macready left the country, and the excitement died
away; but the painful memories of this absurd yet
deadly riot will remain till the present generation has
passed from the stage.

We cannot close this account more fitly than by relating an anecdote of General Scott connected with it,
that has never been made public.  He was living at
the time in Second Avenue, nearly opposite Astor
Place.  He was occupying the upper part of the house
that evening, and his wife the lower.  When the first
volley over the heads of the people was fired, he hastened down, and sent off a servant to ascertain what it
meant.  Before the latter returned, he heard a second
volley.  Hurrying below, he despatched a second servant to find out what was going on, and went back to
his room.  A third volley smote on his ear, and deeply
agitated he hurried below, and began to pace the room
in an excited manner.  His wife, observing how much
he was moved, remarked pleasantly : " Why, General,
you are frightened ! "  This was rather a staggerer to
the old hero, and he turned and exclaimed : " Am I
a man to be frightened, madam ?  It is *volley* firing,
madam—*volley* firing.  They are shooting down American citizens ! "  The old chieftain had heard that firing too often on the field of battle, to be ignorant of
its meaning.  He had seen ranks of living men reel
and fall before it ; nay, stood amid the curling smoke
when his staff was swept down by his side, calm and
unmoved, but here he was unmanned.  Over the
ploughed and blood-stained field, he had moved with
nerves as steady as steel, and pulse beating evenly ; but
now he paced his safe and quiet room with his strong
nature painfully agitated, and all because American
citizens were being shot down by American citizens.
The fact speaks volumes for the nobleness of his nature, and that unsullied patriotism which sheds tenfold
lustre on his well-earned laurels.

NEW YORK—THE FIGHT BETWEEN RIOTERS AND MILITIA.

# CHAPTER IX.

THE year 1857 was a remarkable one in the history
of New York City, and indeed of the whole country.
The year previous had been characterized by intense
political excitement, for the presidential campaign had
been carried on as a sectional fight or a war between the
upholders and enemies of the institution of slavery as it
existed at the South.   Pennsylvania alone by her vote
defeated the antislavery party, and the South, seeing
the danger that threatened it, had already begun to
prepare for that tremendous struggle, that afterwards
tested to the utmost the resources and strength of the
North; while a financial storm overwhelmed the entire
country in disaster.   To these were added local causes,
which affected New York City particularly, and made
it a year of uncommon disturbance.

The Republican party being largely in the ascendant
in the State, determined to revolutionize the municipal
government, and place the Democratic city partially
under Republican rule.   Many bills were passed during
the session of Legislature, peculiarly obnoxious to the

6*

city authorities, but that which excited the most bitter opposition was called the Metropolitan Police Act, by which the counties of New York, Kings, Westchester, and Richmond were made one police district, to be controlled by a board of commissioners, consisting of five members appointed by the Governor and Senate, and to hold office for five years. This board having organized, proceeded to create a police department. Mayor Wood denied the constitutionality of the act and retained the old police—so that there were two police departments existing at the same time in the city. The Mayor resorted to all kinds of legal measures to defeat the action of the board, and the question was finally referred to the Court of Appeals for decision.

In the mean time the death of a street commissioner left a vacancy to be filled. Governor King, acting under the recent law, appointed Daniel D. Conover to fill it, while the Mayor appointed Charles Devlin. A third claimant for the place appeared in the deputy, who asserted his right to act until the decision of the Court of Appeals was rendered. Conover had no idea of waiting for this, and proceeded to assume the duties of his office. The Mayor of course resisted, and so Conover got out a warrant from the Recorder to arrest the former on the charge of inciting a riot, and another on the charge of personal violence. Armed with these papers, and backed by fifty of the new policemen, he proceeded to the City Hall. The Mayor, aware of the movement, had packed the building with his own police, who refused him admittance. The new police attempted to force an entrance, when a fight followed, in which twelve policemen were severely injured. While things were in this critical condition, the Seventh

Regiment passed down Broadway on its way to the boat for Boston, whither it was going to receive an ovation. A request for its interference was promptly granted, and marching into the Park they quickly quelled the riot, and the writs were served on the Mayor.

Intense excitement followed, and so great was the fear of a terrible outbreak, that nine regiments were put under arms, ready to march at a moment's notice.

But on the 1st of July the Court of Appeals decided the act to be constitutional, and the disturbance ended. But of course, while this strife was going on between the police, but little was done to arrest disorder in the city. The lawless became emboldened, and in the evening before the 4th of July a disturbance began, which for a time threatened the most serious consequences.

## DEAD-RABBITS' RIOT.

The origin of the term "Dead Rabbits," which became so well known this year from being identified with a serious riot, is not certainly known. It is said that an organization known as the "Roach Guards," called after a liquor dealer by that name, became split into two factions, and in one of their stormy meetings some one threw a dead rabbit into the room, and one party suddenly proposed to assume the name.

These two factions became bitterly hostile to each other; and on the day before the 4th of July came in collision, but finally separated without doing much damage. They were mostly young men, some of them being mere boys.

The next day, the fight was renewed at Nos. 40 and

42 Bowery Street, and clubs, stones, and even pistols were freely used. The "Dead Rabbits" were beaten and retired, yelling and firing revolvers in the air, and attacking everybody that came in their way. Their uniform was a blue stripe on their pantaloons, while that of the Roach Guards was a red stripe. People in the neighborhood were frightened, and fastened their doors and windows. No serious damage was done, however.

About ten o'clock, a policeman in Worth Street, while endeavoring to clear the sidewalk, was knocked down and severely beaten. At length, breaking away from his assailants, he hastened to the central office in White Street, and reported the state of things. A squad of police was immediately dispatched to arrest the ringleaders. On reaching Centre Street they found a desperate fight going on, and immediately rushed in, to put a stop to it. The belligerents at once made common cause against them. A bloody hand-to-hand conflict followed, but the police at length forced the mob to retreat. The latter, however, did not give up the contest, but mounting to the upper stories and roofs of the tenement-houses, rained down clubs and stones so fiercely, that the police were driven off with only two prisoners.

Comparative quiet was now restored, though the excitement spread in every direction. It lasted, however, only an hour or two, when suddenly a loud yell was heard near the Tombs, accompanied with the report of fire-arms, and crowds of people came pouring down Baxter and Leonard Streets, to get out of the way of bullets. Some wounded men were carried by, and the utmost terror and confusion prevailed. The air was filled with flying missiles and oaths, and shouts of defiance. Now the Dead Rabbits would drive their foes before them, and again be driven back. The bloody fight thus swayed backwards and forwards through the narrow streets for a long time. At length twenty-five Metropolitan Police appeared on the scene, while fifty more were held in reserve. Though assailed at every step with clubs and stones, they marched steadily on, clearing the crowd as they advanced, and forcing the Dead Rabbits into the houses, whither they followed them, mounting even to the roof, and clubbing them at every step. After clearing the houses, they resumed their march, when they were again attacked by the increasing crowd, many of them armed with muskets and pistols. Barricades were now erected, behind which the mob rallied, and the contest assumed the aspect of a regular battle. The notorious Captain Rynders came on the ground, between six and seven o'clock, and attempted to restore quiet. Not succeeding, however, he repaired to the office of the Police Commissioners, and told Commissioner Draper, if he had not police force enough to disperse the mob, he should call out the military. The latter replied that he had made a requisition on Major-General Sandford, for three regiments, and that they would soon be on the ground. But it was nine o'clock before they made their appearance. The police then formed in two bodies of seventy-five men each, and supported, one by the Seventy-first Regiment and the other by the Eighth, marched down White and Worth Streets. This formidable display of force overawed the rioters, and they fled in every direction. This ended the riot, although the military were kept on duty during the night.

At times, the fight was close and deadly, and it

was reported that eight were killed and some thirty wounded.

## BREAD RIOT.

In the autumn there came a financial crisis, that was so wide-spread and disastrous that the lower classes suffered for want of food. Banks suspended specie payment, manufactories were forced to stop work, and paralysis fell on the whole industry of the nation. It was estimated that ten thousand persons were thrown out of employment. These soon used up their earnings, and destitution and suffering of course followed. Their condition grew worse as cold weather came on, and many actually died of starvation. At length they became goaded to desperation, and determined to help themselves to food. Gaunt men and women, clad in tatters, gathered in the Park, and that most fearful of all cries, when raised by a mob, "Bread," arose on every side. Propositions were made to break open the stores, and get what they needed. Flour was hoarded up in them because so little could be got on from the West. The granaries there were groaning with provisions; but there was no money to pay for the transportation. There was money East, but kept locked up in fear. As this became known to the mob, their exasperation increased. To know that there were both food enough and money enough, while they were starving to death, was enough to drive them mad, and there were ominous mutterings. Fortunately, the authorities saw in time the threatened danger, and warded it off. A great many were set to work on the Central Park and other public works, while soup-houses were opened throughout the city, and private associations formed to relieve the suffering; and the winter passed without any outbreak, though more than five thousand business-houses in the country failed, with liabilities reaching three hundred millions of dollars.

# CHAPTER X.

## DRAFT RIOTS OF 1863.

Cause of the Riots.—The London *Times.*—Draft called a despotic Measure.—The despotic Power given to Washington by Congress.—Despotic Action sometimes Necessary, in order to save the Life of the Nation.—The Rights of Government.—Drafting the Legitimate Way to raise an Army—It is not Unequal or Oppressive.

THE ostensible cause of the riots of 1863 was hostility to the draft, because it was a tyrannical, despotic, unjust measure—an act which has distinguished tyrants the world over, and should never be tolerated by a free people. Open hostility to oppression was more than once hinted in a portion of the press—as not only a right, but a duty.

Even the London *Times* said, "It would have been strange, indeed, if the American people had submitted to a measure which is a distinctive mark of the most despotic governments of the Continent." As if the fact that a measure, because resorted to by a despotic government, was therefore necessarily wrong. It might as well be said, that because settling national difficulties by an appeal to arms has always been a distinctive feature of despotic governments, therefore the American people should refuse to sustain the government by declaring or prosecuting any war; or that because it has always been a distinctive feature of despotic governments to have naval and military schools, to train men to the art of war, therefore the American people should not submit to either. It is not of the slightest consequence to us what despotic governments do or not do; the simple question is, whether the measure is necessary for the protection of our own government, and the welfare of the people. To leave this untouched, and talk only about despotism, the right of the people, and all that, is mere demagogism, and shows him who utters it to be unfit to control public opinion. Besides, there is a great difference between measures that are despotic, which are put forth to save the nation's life, or honor, and those put forth to destroy freedom, and for selfish ends. Not that, intrinsically, despotic measures are always not to be deprecated and avoided, if possible; for if tolerated in one case, they may be exacted in another.

Liberty can never be guarded too carefully, or the barriers erected around the rights of every individual respected too scrupulously. But everything in this world is a choice between two evils. The greatest wisdom cannot avoid *all* evils; it can only choose the least. Sound statesmanship regards any stretch of power better than the overthrow of the nation. Probably there never was a more able and wise body of men assembled, or more jealous of any exercise of arbitrary power, than the First Congress of the United States; and yet, almost in the commencement of our struggle for independence, when events wore such a gloomy aspect that failure seemed inevitable, rising above its fears of despotic measures, in its greater fear of total defeat, it conferred on Washington powers that made him to a large extent military dictator. He was authorized to raise sixteen battalions of infantry, three thousand light-horse, three regiments of artillery, together with a corps of engineers, and *appoint the officers himself.* He had, also, full power, when he deemed it necessary, to call on the several States for the militia; to appoint throughout *the entire army all the officers under brigadiers;* fill up all vacancies; to take whatever he wanted for the use of his troops, wherever he could find it, with no other restriction than that he must pay for it, which last was nullified, because he was empowered to *seize and lock up every man who refused to receive in pay Continental money.* It would seem impossible that a body of men who were so extremely sensitive in bestowing power on a military commander, and so watchful of the rights of individuals, could have committed such an act; and yet, who does not see that, under the circumstances, it was wise. Now, granting that conscription is a despotic measure, no truthful, candid man will deny that, in case of a war, where men must be had, and can be got in no other way, that it would be the duty of government to enforce it. It is idle to reply that the supposition is absurd—that in this country such a thing can never happen; for what has been in the world can be again. Besides, this does meet the question of the *right* of the Government, that must be settled before the emergency comes. Now, we do not believe there is sounder principle, or one that every unbiassed mind does not concede with the readiness that it does an axiom, that, if necessary to protect and save itself, a government may not only order a draft, but call out *every* able-bodied man in the nation. If this right does not inhere in our government, it is built on a foundation of sand, and the sooner it is abandoned the better.

But we go farther, and deny that a draft is a despotic measure at all, but is a just and equitable mode of raising an army. True, if troops enough can be raised on a reasonable bounty, it is more expedient to do so; but the moment that bounty becomes so exorbitant as to tempt the cupidity of those in whom neither patriotism nor sense of duty have any power, volunteering becomes an evil. We found it so in our recent war. The bounty was a little fortune to a certain class, the benefit of which they had no idea of losing by being shot, and hence they deserted, or shammed sickness, so that scarce half the men ever got to the front, while those who did being influenced by no motive higher than cupidity, became worthless soldiers. A draft takes in enough men of a higher stamp to leaven the mass. The first Napoleon, when asked what made his first "army of Italy" so resistless, replied that almost every man in it was intelligent enough to act as a clerk. The objection that a rich man, if drafted, can buy a substitute, while the poor man, with a large family depending upon him, must go, if of any weight at all, lies against the whole structure of society, which gives the rich man at every step immunities over the poor man. When pestilence sweeps through a city, the rich man can flee to a healthy locality, while the poor man must stay and die; and when the pestilence of war sweeps over the land, must one attempt to reverse all this relation between wealth and poverty?

When society gets in that happy state, that the rich man has no advantages over the poor, there will be no need either of drafting or volunteering. Yet, after all, it is not so unequal as it at first sight appears. War must have money as well as men, and the former the rich have to furnish ; and if they do this, it is but fair that they should be allowed to furnish with it also the men to do their fighting. Besides, there must be some rule that would exempt the men that carry on the business of the country.

We have said this much, because the riots in New York, which might have ended in national destruction, were brought about by preaching views directly the opposite of these.

The military spirit is so prevalent in the nation, that in any ordinary war the Government can get all the troops it wants by giving a moderate bounty, and wages but a little greater than can be secured at any ordinary business or occupation. Still, the right to raise them differently should never be denied it.

When the old militia system was given up in the State, and a certain number of regiments were raised and equipped and drilled for active duty, and for which the people paid taxes, it was thought they would furnish all the quota that would ever be called for from the State—and in any ordinary war will. The crisis, however, in which we found ourselves had never been anticipated, and hence not provided against, and when Congress attempted to do it in what seemed to it the best way, an outcry was raised of injustice and oppression. It was hard, doubtless, but there are a great many hard things in the world that have been and have to be borne. The feeling of hostility unquestionably would have been less intense, had not so many of those to be drafted been bitterly opposed to the war. Believing it to have been brought about by the reckless demagogism and fanaticism of their political opponents, and levied as it was against those who had been their warm political friends, indeed, chief dependence for political success, it was asking a good deal, to require them to step to the front, and fight in such a war. Whether this feeling was right or wrong, had nothing to do with the influence it actually exerted.

On this feeling was based, in fact, the real hostility to the draft, in which a portion of the press shared. But, as we said before, we having nothing to do with the justice or injustice of this belief or feeling ; we only state the fact, with our denial that it furnished any excuse for the denunciations uttered against the draft as a wrong use of power, or the refusal to submit to it on that account. The Government, whether wrong or right, must be supported, or abandoned and given over to revolution. In ordinary times, denunciation of its measures, and the most strenuous opposition to them, is the right and often the duty of every conscientious man. This right, exercised by the press, is one of the most effectual checks against abuses, and the most powerful lever to work reform and changes. But in a great crisis, to set one's self against a measure on which the fate of the nation hangs, is a flagrant abuse of that right; for the effort, if successful, will not work change and an improved condition of things, but immediate, irretrievable ruin, and put the nation beyond the reach of reform.

# CHAPTER XI.

THE rights of municipalities have been conceded from the first dawn of constitutional liberty—indeed municipal freedom may be said to be the first step in the onward progress of the race toward the full recognition of its rights. To interfere with a great commercial city like New York, except by general laws, is as a rule unwise, impolitic, and, indeed, unjust. Like a separate State, it had better suffer many and great evils, than to admit the right of outward power to regulate its internal affairs. To do so, in any way, is fraught with mischief; but to do so as a political party, is infinitely more pernicious. It leaves a great metropolis, on which the welfare of the commercial business of the nation mainly depends, a foot-ball for ambitious or selfish politicians to play with. But as there are exceptions to all rules, so there may be to this—still they should always be exceptions, and not claimed as a settled policy.

We mention this, because the interference of the Legislature, or rather the dominant part of it, in the internal policy of New York, about the time the war commenced, was in itself a mischievous and tyrannical act, while, under the circumstances that soon after occurred, it proved of incalculable benefit.

With the city stripped of its military, and the forts in the harbor of their garrisons, the police, under the old régime, during the draft riots, would have been trustless and powerless, even if the city government had attempted to uphold the national authority, which is doubtful. The Republicans established a Board of Police Commissioners, the majority of which were of their own political faith, who had the entire control of the department. Uuder their hands, an entire different set of men from those formerly selected, composed the force, and a regular system of drills, in fact, a thorough organization, adopted.

But in 1862 the Democrats elected their governor, though they failed to secure the Legislature. Mr. Seymour, immediately on his inauguration, summoned the Commissioners to appear before him, the object of which was to change the character of the board. The latter understood it, and refused to appear. Legal proceedings were then commenced against them, but they were staved off, and in the meantime the Legislature had got to work, and took the matter in hand ; and Messrs. Bowen, Acton, and Bergen, were made to constitute the board—John A. Kennedy being superintendent of police. Mr. Bowen, the president of the board, having been appointed brigadier-general, resigned, and Mr. Acton, under the law, became president. This political character of the board, so diametrically opposed to the feelings and wishes of the vast majority of the citizens, tested by the ordinary rules and principles of a Republican Government, was unjust; a palpable, deliberate encroachment on the right of self-government. But as we remarked, just now, it was fortunate for the country that such a state of things existed. In the extraordinary, not anticipated, and perilous condition in which we found ourselves, everything was changed. Neither constitutions nor laws had been framed to meet such an emergency, and both, in many cases, had to be suspended. What was right before, often became wrong now, and vice versa. The article inserted in the Constitution of the State, that the moment a bank refused specie payment, it became bankrupt, was a wise and just provision, but to enforce it now, would be financial ruin, and it was not done.

This usurpation of the government of New York by the Republican party, which seemed so unjust, was, doubtless, under the circumstances, the salvation of the city. It was, moreover, highly important to the whole country, in the anomalous war which threatened our very existence, that the controlling power of the city should be in sympathy with the General Government, but it was especially, vitally so, when the latter put its provost marshals in it to enforce the draft. That this *mode* of enforcing the draft by provost marshals, was an encroachment on the rights and powers of the separate States, there can be no doubt. It is equally clear that the proper way was to call on the separate governors for their quota, and let *them* enforce the draft. If they refused to do it, then it was time for the General Government to take the matter in its own hand. This, however, was no encroachment on *individual* rights. The oppressive nature of the act and the result were the same to the person, whether en-

NEW YORK—THE ATTACK ON THE TRIBUNE BUILDING.

forced by the State or General Government. Still it was a total departure from the practice of the General Government since its first organization, and it moreover established a dangerous precedent, which the sooner it is abandoned the better. But this had nothing to do with the opposition to the draft. That was a personal objection.

With the Police Department in sympathy with the rioters, it is not difficult to see what the end would have been. We do not mean by that, that the heads of the department would not have endeavored to do their duty, but it would have been impossible to control the kind of element they would inevitably have to deal with. This even the long-tried, trusted leaders of the Democratic party acknowledged. In fact, the police force would not have been in a condition, with ever so good a will, to have acted with the skill and promptness it did.

The draft riots, as they are called, were supposed by some to be the result of a deep-laid conspiracy on the part of those opposed to the war, and that the successful issue of Lee's invasion of Pennsylvania was to be the signal for open action. Whether this be so or not, it is evident that the outbreak in New York City on the 13th of July, not only from the manner of its commencement, the absence of proper organization, and almost total absence of leadership, was not the result of a general well-understood plot. It would seem from the facts that those who started the movement had no idea at the outset of proceeding to the length they did. They simply desired to break up the draft in some of the upper districts of the city, and destroy the registers in which certain names were enrolled.

7

A general provost marshal had been appointed over the whole city, which was subdivided into various districts, in each of which was an assistant provost marshall. Although there had been no provision for a general assistant provost marshal or aid, yet Colonel Nugent acted in this capacity. The drafting was to take place in the separate districts, under the direction of the assistant provost marshals.

Although there had been some rumors of resistance to it, they received very little credence, and no special provision was made for such an emergency. The city was almost denuded of the military; the regiments having been called to Pennsylvania to repel Lee's invasion; yet so little fear was entertained, that even the police department was not requested to make any special preparation. The Invalid Corps, as it was called, composed of the maimed and crippled soldiers who could no longer keep the field, were thought to be quite sufficient to preserve the peace.

The draft commenced on Saturday in the Eleventh and Ninth Districts, and passed off quietly; and it was thought the same order would be maintained throughout, and if any force were necessary to repress violence, it would be when the conscripts were required to take their place in the ranks.

Still Superintendent Kennedy of the Police Department feared there might be some difficulty experienced by the officers in charge of the draft, even if no serious resistance should be offered. Some of the enrolling officers, a short time previous, while taking the names of those subject to draft, had been assailed with very abusive language, or their questions received in sullen silence or answered falsely; fictitious names often being given instead of the true ones. In the Ninth District, embracing the lower part of the city, the provost marshal, Captain Joel T. Erhardt, came near losing his life in the performance of this duty. At the corner of Liberty Street and Broadway a building was being torn down, preparatory to the erection of another, and the workmen engaged in it threatened the enrolling officer who came to take down their names, with violence, and drove him off.

Captain Erhardt, on the report being made to him, repaired to head-quarters, and requested of Colonel Nugent a force of soldiers to protect the officer in the discharge of his duty. But this the latter declined to do, fearing it would exasperate the men and bring on a collision, and requested the Captain to go himself, saying, if he did, there would be no difficulty. Captain Erhardt declined, on the ground that he was not an enrolling officer. But Colonel Nugent persisting, the Captain finally told him, if he ordered him, as his superior officer, to go, he would. Nugent replied that he might so consider it. Erhardt then said he would go, but only on one condition, that if he got in trouble and asked for help, he would send him troops. To this he agreed, and Captain Erhardt proceeded to the building on the corner of Broadway and Liberty Street, and stepping on a plank that led from the sidewalk to the floor, asked a man on a ladder for his name. The fellow refused to answer, when an altercation ensuing, he stepped down, and seizing an iron bar advanced on the provost marshal. The latter had nothing but a light Malacca cane in his hand, but as he saw the man meant murder he drew a pistol from his pocket, and levelled it full at his breast. This brought him to a halt; and after looking at Erhardt for awhile he dropped his bar. Erhardt then put up his pistol, and went on with his enrolling. The man was dogged and angry, and watching his opportunity, suddenly made a rush at the provost marshal. The latter had only time to deal him, as he sprang forward, one heavy blow with his cane, when they closed. In a moment both reeled from the plank and fell to the cellar beneath, the provost marshal on top. Covered with dirt, he arose and drew his pistol, and mounted to the sidewalk.

The foreman sympathized with the workmen, and Erhardt could do nothing. Determined to arrest them for resisting the draft, he despatched a messenger to Colonel Nugent for the promised force. None, however, was sent. He, in the meantime, stood with drawn pistol facing the men, who dared not advance on him. Aid not arriving, he sent again, and still later a third time. He stood thus facing the workmen with his pistol for three hours, and finally had to leave without making any arrests. This failure of Colonel Nugent to fulfil his promise and perform his duty came near costing Erhardt his life, and then and there starting the riot. The next day he had the foreman arrested, and completed his work of enrolling.

The time selected for commencing the draft was unfortunate. Saturday, of all days in the week, was the worst. It was a new thing, and one under any circumstances calculated to attract universal attention among the lower classes, and provoke great and angry discussion. Hence, to have the draft commence on Saturday, and allow the names to be published in the papers on Sunday morning, so that all could read them, and spend the day in talking the matter over, and lay

plans for future action, was a most unwise, thoughtless
procedure.   If there had been any choice as to the day,
one, if possible, should have been chosen that preceded
the busiest day of the week.   To have the list of
twelve hundred names that had been drawn read
over and commented on all day by men who enlivened
their discussion with copious draughts of bad whiskey,
especially when most of those drawn were laboring-
men or poor mechanics, who were unable to hire a
substitute, was like applying fire to gunpowder.   If a
well-known name, that of a man of wealth, was among
the number, it only increased the exasperation, for the
law exempted every one drawn who would pay three
hundred dollars towards a substitute.   This was taking
practically the whole number of soldiers called for
out of the laboring classes.   A great proportion of
these being Irish, it naturally became an Irish question,
and eventually an Irish riot.   It was in their eyes the
game of hated England over again—oppression of
Irishmen.   This state of feeling could not be wholly
concealed.   Kennedy, aware of it, felt it necessary, on
Monday morning, to take some precautionary measures.   Still, in the main, only small squads of policemen were sent to the various points where the drafting
was to take place, and merely to keep back the crowd
and maintain order, in case a few disorderly persons
should attempt to create disturbance.   It was true, a
rumor had been put in circulation that a body of men
had planned to seize the arsenal, and Kennedy, as a
matter of precaution, sent fifty policemen to occupy it.
But during the morning, word was brought him that
the street-contractor's men in the Nineteenth Ward
were not at work.   This looked ominous, and he be-

gan to fear trouble. Thinking that Provost Marshal Maniere's office, 1190 Broadway, and that of Marshal Jenkins, corner of Forty-sixth Street and Third Avenue, would be more likely to be the points attacked, he hurried off the following telegrams :

July 13, 8.35 A.M. From Central Office to Seventeenth, Eighteenth, and Twenty-first Precincts : Send ten men and a sergeant forthwith to No. 677 Third Avenue, and report to Captain Porter of Nineteenth Precinct for duty.                 J. A. KENNEDY.

July 13, 8.50 A.M. To Twenty-ninth Precinct : Place a squad of ten of your men, with a competent sergeant, at No. 1190 Broadway, during the draft—if you want more, inform me.                 J. A. K.

8.55 A.M. To Sixteenth and Twentieth Precincts : Send your reserve to Seventh Avenue Arsenal forthwith.                 J. A. K.

Telegrams were now pouring in from different quarters, showing that mischief was afoot, and at nine o'clock he sent the following despatch :

" To all platoons, New York and Brooklyn : Call in your reserve platoons, and hold them at the stations subject to further orders."

It should be noted, that ordinarily one-half of the police of the Metropolitan District, which took in Brooklyn, is relieved from both patrol and reserve duty, from six o'clock in the morning till six in the evening. The other half is divided into two sections, which alternately perform patrol and reserve duty during the day. A relief from patrol duty of one of these sections takes place at eight o'clock A.M., when it goes to breakfast. Hence, the orders issued by the Superinténdent to call in these could not reach them without a considerable delay.

It now being about ten o'clock, Mr. Kennedy, having despatched an additional body of men to the Twenty-ninth Precinct, got into his light wagon, to take a drive through the districts reported to be most dangerous. He went up far as the arsenal, and giving such directions as he thought necessary, started across the town to visit Marshal Jenkins' quarters in the Twenty-ninth Precinct.

# CHAPTER XII.

MEANWHILE, events were assuming an alarming aspect in the western part of the city. Early in the morning men began to assemble here in separate groups, as if in accordance with a previous arrangement, and at last moved quietly north along the various avenues. Women, also, like camp followers, took the same direction in crowds. They were thus divided into separate gangs, apparently to take each avenue in their progress, and make a clean sweep. The factories and workshops were visited, and the men compelled to knock off work and join them, while the proprietors were threatened with the destruction of their property, if they made any opposition. The separate crowds were thus swelled at almost every step, and armed with sticks, and clubs, and every conceivable weapon they could lay hands on, they moved north towards some point which had evidently been selected as a place of rendezvous. This proved to be a vacant lot near Central Park, and soon the living streams began

to flow into it, and a more wild, savage, and heteroge-
neous-looking mass could not be imagined. After a
short consultation they again took up the line of
march, and in two separate bodies, moved down Fifth
and Sixth Avenues, until they reached Forty-sixth and
Forty-seventh Streets, when they turned directly east.

The number composing this first mob has been so
differently estimated, that it would be impossible from
reports merely, to approximate the truth. A pretty
accurate idea, however, can be gained of its immense
size, from a statement made by Mr. King, son of
President King, of Columbia College. Struck by its
magnitude, he had the curiosity to get some estimate
of it by timing its progress, and he found that although
it filled the broad street from curbstone to curbstone,
and was moving rapidly, it took between twenty and
twenty-five minutes for it to pass a single point.

A ragged, coatless, heterogeneously weaponed army,
it heaved tumultuously along toward Third Avenue.
Tearing down the telegraph poles as it crossed the
Harlem & New Haven Railroad track, it surged an-
grily up around the building where the drafting was
going on. The small squad of police stationed there
to repress disorder looked on bewildered, feeling they
were powerless in the presence of such a host. Soon
a stone went crashing through a window, which was
the signal for a general assault on the doors. These
giving way before the immense pressure, the foremost
rushed in, followed by shouts and yells from those behind, and began to break up the furniture. The
drafting officers, in an adjoining room, alarmed, fled
precipitately through the rear of the building. The
mob seized the wheel in which were the names, and

7*

what books, papers, and lists were left, and tore them up, and scattered them in every direction. A safe stood on one side, which was supposed to contain important papers, and on this they fell with clubs and stones, but in vain. Enraged at being thwarted, they set fire to the building, and hurried out of it. As the smoke began to ascend, the onlooking multitude without sent up a loud cheer. Though the upper part of the building was occupied by families, the rioters, thinking that the officers were concealed there, rained stones and brick-bats against the windows, sending terror into the hearts of the inmates. Deputy Provost Marshal Vanderpoel, who had mingled in the crowd, fearing for the lives of the women and children, boldly stepped to the front, and tried to appease the mob, telling them the papers were all destroyed, and begged them to fall back, and let others help the inmates of the building, or take hold themselves. The reply was a heavy blow in the face. Vanderpoel shoved the man who gave it aside, when he was assailed with a shower of blows and curses. Fearing for his life, he broke through the crowd, and hastened to the spot where the police were standing, wholly powerless in the midst of this vast, excited throng.

In the meantime, the flames, unarrested, made rapid way, and communicating to the adjoining building, set it on fire. The volumes of smoke, rolling heavenward, and the crackling and roaring of the flames, seemed for a moment to awe the mob, and it looked silently on the ravaging of a power more terrible and destructive than its own.

At this time Superintendent Kennedy was quietly making his way across the town toward the office of the provost marshal, Jenkins. But noticing a fire as he approached, he left his wagon at the corner of Forty-sixth Street and Lexington Avenue, and walked over toward Third Avenue. The street was blocked with people, but they seemed quiet and orderly as any gathering in presence of a fire, and differed from it only in that the countenances of all seemed to wear a pleased, gratified look. As he unsuspiciously edged his way forward toward the fire, he heard some one cry out, "There's Kennedy!" "Which is him?" asked a second; and he was pointed out.

Kennedy was dressed in ordinary citizen's clothes, and carried only a slight bamboo cane. Thinking the allusion to him was prompted only by curiosity, he kept on, when suddenly he felt himself violently pushed against. Turning around, he encountered a man in a soldier's old uniform, and sternly demanded whàt he meant by that. The words had hardly escaped his lips, when a heavy blow was planted full in his face. Instantly the crowd closed around him, and rained blows in rapid succession on him, until he fell over and down the graded street, some six feet, into a vacant lot. The crowd, with yells, poured after him. Kennedy, springing to his feet, started on a run across the lot towards Forty-seventh Street, distancing his pursuers. But as he reached Forty-seventh Street, and attempted to ascend the embankment, another crowd, which had witnessed the pursuit, rushed upon him, and knocked him back again in front of his pursuers. He quickly sprang up, though bleeding and stunned, for he knew his only chance for life was in keeping his feet. But the crowd closing around on both sides gave him no chance to run. One huge fellow, armed with a heavy club, endeavored to break in his skull, but Kennedy dodged his blows. Careful only for his head, he let them beat his body, while he made desperate efforts to break through the mass, whose demoniacal yells and oaths showed that they intended to take his life. In the struggle the whole crowd, swaying to and fro, slowly advanced toward Lexington Avenue, coming, as they did so, upon a wide mud-hole. "Drown him! drown him!" arose at once on every side, and the next moment a heavy blow, planted under his ear, sent him headforemost into the water.

Falling with his face amid the stones, he was kicked and trampled on, and pounded, till he was a mass of gore. Still struggling desperately for life, he managed to get to his feet again, and made a dash for the middle of the pond. The water was deep, and his murderers, disliking to get wet, did not follow him, but ran around to the other side, to meet him as he came out. But Kennedy was ahead of them, and springing up the bank into Lexington Avenue, saw a man whom he knew, and called out: "John Eagan, come here and save my life!" Mr. Eagan, who was a well-known and influential resident of that vicinity, immediately rushed forward to his assistance, and arrested his pursuers. But the Superintendent was so terribly bruised and mangled, that Eagan did not recognize him. He, however, succeeded in keeping the mob back, who, seeing the horrible condition their victim was in, doubtless thought they had finished him. Other citizens now coming forward, a passing feed wagon was secured, into which Kennedy was lifted, and driven to police head-quarters. Acton, who was in the street as the wagon approached, saw the mangled body within,

but did not dream who it was. The driver inquired
where he should take him. " Around to the station,"
carelessly replied Acton. The driver hesitated, and
inquired again, " Where to ? " Acton, supposing it
was some drunkard, bruised in a brawl, replied rather
petulantly, " Around to the station." The man then
told him it was Kennedy. Acton, scanning the features more closely, saw that it indeed was the Superintendent himself in this horrible condition. As the
officers gathered around the bleeding, almost unconscious form, a murmur of wrath was heard, a sure pre-
monition what work would be done when the hour of
vengeance should come.

Kennedy was carried into head-quarters, and a surgeon immediately sent for. After an examination had
shown that no bones were broken, he was taken to the
house of a friend, and, before the week closed, was on
his feet again.

Acton, now the legal head of the police force, soon
showed he was the right man in the right place. Of a
nervous temperament, he was quick and prompt, yet
cool and decided, and relentless as death in the discharge of his duty. Holding the views of the first
Napoleon respecting mobs, he did not believe in speech-
making to them. His addresses were to be locust
clubs and grape-shot. Taking in at once the gravity of
the situation, he, after despatching such force as was
immediately available to the scene of the riot, telegraphed to the different precincts to have the entire
reserve force concentrated at head-quarters, which were
in Mulberry Street, near Bleecker.

He saw at once, to have his force effective it must
be well in hand, so that he could send it out in any

direction in sufficient strength to bear down all opposition.  Subsequent events proved the wisdom of his
policy, for we shall see, after it had been accomplished,
the police never lost a battle.

There being thirty-two precincts in the limits of the
Metropolitan Police, a vast territory was covered.
These were reached by a system of telegraph wires,
called the Telegraph Bureau, of which James Crowley
was superintendent and Eldred Polhamus deputy.
There were three operators—Chapin, Duvall, and Lucas.
A telegraph station was in each precinct—thus making
thirty-two, all coming to a focus at head-quarters.
These are also divided into five sections—north, south,
east, west, and central.  The Commissioners, therefore,
sitting in the central office, can send messages almost
instantaneously to every precinct of the city, and receive immediate answers.  Hence, Mr. Acton was a
huge Briareus, reaching out his arms to Fort Washington in the north, and Brooklyn in the south, and at the
same time touching the banks of both rivers.  No
other system could be devised giving such tremendous
power to the police—the power of instant information
and rapid concentration at any desired point.  That it
proved itself the strong right arm of the Commissioners, it needs only to state, that during the four days of
the riot, between five and six thousand messages passed
over the wires, showing that they were worked to their
utmost capacity, day and night.  The more intelligent
of the mob understood this, and hence at the outset
attempted to break up this communication, by cutting
down the poles on Third Avenue.  This stopped all
messages to and from the precincts at Fort Washing-

ton, Manhattanville, Harlem, Yorkville, and Blooming-
dale, as well as with the Nineteenth Precinct.

But fortunately, the orders to these had passed
over the wires before the work was completed.   Subsequently, the rioters cut down the poles in First
Avenue, in Twenty-second Street, and Ninth Avenue,
destroying communication between several other precincts.

Mr. Crowley, the Superintendent of the Telegraph
Bureau, was made acquainted early, Monday, by mere
accident with this plan of the rioters.   Coming to town
in the Third Avenue cars from Yorkville, where he resided, he suddenly found the car arrested by a mob,
and getting out with the other passengers, discovered
men chopping furiously away at the telegraph poles;
and without stopping to think, rushed up to them and
ordered them to desist.   One of the ruffians, looking
up, cried out, " he is one of the d—d operators."   Instantly yells arose, " Smash him," " Kill him," when
those nearest seized him.   By great adroitness he disarmed their suspicions sufficiently to prevent further
violence, though they held him prisoner for an hour.
At last, seeing an opportunity when more important objects attracted their attention, he quietly worked his
way out and escaped.

# CHAPTER XIII.

IN the meantime, the mob that stood watching the
spreading conflagration in Third Avenue increased
rapidly, fed by tributaries from the tenement-houses,
slums, and workshops in that vicinity. But they were
soon startled from their state of comparative quietness,
by the cry of "the soldiers are coming." The Invalid
Corps, a small body sent from the Park, was approaching. As it came up, the soldiers fired, either blank
cartridges, or over the heads of the crowd, doubtless
thinking a single discharge would disperse it. The
folly of such a course was instantly shown, for the mob,
roused into sudden fury, dashed on the small body of
soldiers before they could reload, and snatching away
their muskets, pounded them over the head, and
chased them like sheep for ten blocks. One soldier
was left for dead on the pavement, beaten to a jelly.
Another, breaking from the crowd, attempted to climb
some rocks near Forty-second Street, when his pursu-

NEW YORK—THE RIOTERS DRAGGING COL. O'BRIEN'S BODY THROUGH THE STREET.

ers grabbed him and dragged him to the top, where they tore off his uniform, and beat him till he was senseless, and then threw him down to the bottom and left him.

In the meantime, Sergeant McCredie, "fighting Mac," as he was called, from the Fifteenth Precinct, Captain C. W. Caffrey, arrived on the scene with a few men. Marching down Forty-third street to Third Avenue, they looked up two blocks, and to their amazement beheld the broad avenue, as far as they could see, blocked with the mob, while before it, bearing swiftly down on them, and running for life, came the terror-stricken Invalid Corps. At this juncture, other squads sent from various precincts arrived, swelling this force to forty-four. It was a mere handful among these enraged thousands; but McCredie, who at once took command, determined to stand his ground, and meet as best he could the overwhelming numbers that came driving down like a storm, filling the air with yells and oaths, and brandishing their clubs over their heads. He thought that another police force was beyond the mob, on the north, and if he could press through and form a junction with it, the two combined would be strong enough to hold their own. He therefore quickly formed his men in line across the street, and awaited the shock. As the disorderly mass following up the fugitives drew near, McCredie ordered a charge, and this mere handful of men moved swiftly and steadily upon it. The rioters, stunned by the suddenness and strength of the blow, recoiled, and the police, following up their advantage, drove them back, step by step, as far as Forty-sixth street. Here the sergeant, instead of meeting another body of police, as he

expected, met a heavier body of rioters that were blocking up Forty-sixth Street on both sides of the avenue.
Backed by these, the main body rallied and charged
on the exhausted police force in turn, and almost surrounded them.   To render their already desperate situation hopeless, another mob suddenly closed in behind
them from Forty-fifth street.

Thus attacked in front and rear with clubs, iron
bars, guns and pistols, and rained upon with stones
and brick-bats from the roofs of the houses, they were
unable longer to keep together, and broke and fled—
part up the side streets, and some down the avenue—
bruised, torn, and bleeding.

The desperate nature of this first conflict can be imagined, when, out of the fourteen men composing
Sergeant McCredie's original force, only five were left
unwounded.   At the very outset of the charge, the
sergeant himself was struck with an iron bar on the
wrist, which rendered the arm almost useless.   In the
retreat, four men assailed him at once.   Knocking
down two, he took refuge in the house of a German,
when a young woman told him to jump between two
mattresses.   He did so, and she covered him up just
as his pursuers forced their way in.   Streaming
through the house from cellar to garret, they came
back, and demanded of the young woman where the
man was hid.   She quietly said he had escaped by the
rear of the house.   Believing she told the truth, they
took their departure.   Officer Bennett was knocked
down three times before he ceased fighting.   The last
time he was supposed to be dead, when the wretches
began to rob him even of his clothing, stripping him
of every article except his drawers.   He was soon

after taken up and carried to St. Luke's Hospital, and placed in the dead-house, where he lay for several hours. When the sad news was brought to his wife, she hastened to the hospital, and fell weeping on the lifeless form of her husband. She could not believe he was dead, and laying her hand on his heart, found to her joy that it pulsated. She immediately flew to the officials of the hospital, and had him brought in, and restoratives applied. He revived, but remained unconscious for three days, while the riot raged around him. Officer Travis, in the flight down the avenue, saw, as he looked back, that his foremost pursuer had a pistol. Wheeling, he knocked him down, and seized the pistol, but before he could use it, a dozen clubs were raining blows upon him, which brought him to the ground. The infuriated men then jumped upon him, knocking out his teeth, breaking his jaw-bone and right hand, and terribly mutilating his whole body. Supposing him to be dead, they then stripped him stark naked and left him on the pavement, a ghastly spectacle to the passers-by. Officer Phillips ran the gauntlet almost unharmed, but was pursued block after block by a portion of the mob, till he reached Thirty-ninth street. Here he attempted to enter a house, but it was closed against him. As he turned down the steps, one of the pursuers, in soldier's clothes, levelled his musket at him and fired. Missing his aim, he clubbed his weapon, and dealt him a deadly blow. Phillips caught the musket as it descended, and wrenching it from his grasp, knocked the fellow down with it, and started and ran across some vacant lots to Fortieth Street. But here he was headed off by another portion of the mob, in which was a woman, who made a lunge at him with a shoemaker's knife. The knife missed his throat, but passed through his ear. Drawing it back, she made another stab, piercing his arm. He was now bleeding profusely, and his death seemed inevitable, when a stranger, seeing his condition, sprang forward, and covering his body, declared he would kill the first man that advanced. Awed by his determined manner, the fiends sullenly withdrew. Officers Sutherland and Mingay were also badly beaten. Officer Kiernan, receiving a blow on his head with a stone, another on the back of his neck with a hay-bale rung, and two more on the knees, fell insensible, and would doubtless have been killed outright, but for the wife of Eagan, who saved Kennedy. Throwing herself over his body, she exclaimed, " for God's sake do not kill him." Seeing that they had got to attack this lady to get at Kiernan, they passed on.

The scene in Third Avenue at this time was fearful and appalling. It was now noon, but the hot July sun was obscured by heavy clouds, that hung in ominous shadows over the city, while from near Cooper Institute to Forty-sixth Street, or about thirty blocks, the avenue was black with human beings,—sidewalks, house-tops, windows, and stoops all filled with rioters or spectators. Dividing it like a stream, horse-cars arrested in their course lay strung along as far as the eye could reach. As the glance ran along this mighty mass of men and women north, it rested at length on huge columns of smoke rolling heavenward from burning buildings, giving a still more fearful aspect to the scene. Many estimated the number at this time in the street at fifty thousand.

In the meantime the fire-bell had brought the fire-men on the ground, but the mob would not let them approach the burning houses. The flames had communicated with the adjoining block and were now making fearful headway. At length Engineer Decker addressed the mob, which by this time had grown thinner by the main mass moving farther down town, who told them that everything relating to the provost marshal's office was destroyed, and now the fire was destroying private property, some of which doubtless belonged to persons friendly to them, and finally persuaded them to let the engines work. Water was soon deluging the buildings, and the fire at length arrested, but not until four were consumed with all their contents.

The drawing commenced in the Eighth District, 1190 Broadway, Captain Maniere provost marshal, on the same morning, and continued quietly until about 12 o'clock, when it was adjourned, and policemen who had been stationed there to guard it were sent over to the Ninth District, where the mob was carrying everything before it. But coming in small bodies, they were easily overcome and scattered. Sergeant Ellison, especially, got badly beaten; and Sergeant Wade, who came up soon after, and charged gallantly on the mob, shared the same fate, and had to be taken to St. Luke's Hospital. The work of destruction having commenced, it went on after this with the wild irregularity characteristic of mobs. The news of the uprising and destruction of property, as it spread through those portions of the city where the low Irish dwelt, stirred up all the inmates, and they came thronging forth, till there were incipient mobs on almost every corner. From this time no consecutive narrative can be given of the after doings.

This immense mass seemed to split up into three or four sections, as different objects attracted their attention ; and they came together and separated apparently without any concert of action.  A shout and a cry in one direction would call off a throng, while a similar shout in another would attract a portion thither. Some feeling the need of arms, and remembering that a gun factory was at the corner of Second Avenue and Twentieth Street, called out to the crowd, and soon a large body was rushing in that direction.   The Police Commissioners had also thought of this, and hastily sent off the Broadway squad to occupy it, and they succeeded, by going singly and in pairs, in reaching it— thirty-five all told.   These men, selected for their size, being all six feet or upward, were ordered to hold the place at all hazards.

In the meantime the mob endeavored to gain admittance, but warned off by Sergeant Burdick, left.   But scarcely a quarter of an hour had elapsed, when they returned heavily reinforced, armed with all kinds of weapons, and yelling and hooting like fiends.   Stones and bricks came crashing through the windows, but still the squad, though every man was armed with a carbine, did not fire.

The mob then tried to set the factory on fire, but failed.   Enraged at being baffled, a powerful man advanced on the door with a sledge-hammer, and began to pound against it.   At length one of the panels gave way, and as a shout arose from those looking on, he boldly attempted to crawl through.   The report of a solitary carbine was heard, and the brains of the man lay scattered on the floor.   This staggered the mob for a moment, but soon fear gave way to rage, and shots and stones were rained against the building, smashing in the windows, and rapidly making a clean breach through the door. Burdick sent to Captain Cameron for aid, but he replied that he could not reach him.

At 3.45 the following telegram was sent from the Eighteenth Precinct:

" The mob have attacked the armory, Second Avenue and Twenty-first Street. There is danger of firing the building."

Fifteen minutes later came: " It is impossible for us to protect the armory at Second Avenue and Twenty-first Street."

*Answer*—" Draw your men off.       D. C."

The squad, in evacuating the building, found themselves cut off both in front and at the sides.

The only mode of escape was through a hole in the rear wall, some eighteen feet from the ground, and scarcely a foot and a half in diameter. Piling up boxes to reach this aperture, these large men squeezed themselves through one by one, feet foremost, and swinging to a gutter-trough, dropped into the yard below. Climbing from thence over a wall into a stone-yard, they sped across it to the Eighteenth Precinct Station in Twenty-second Street. Here taking off their uniforms, they made their way singly, or in groups of two or three, back to the central office.

No sooner did they leave the building than the mob entered it, and the work of pillage commenced. Every man armed himself with a musket. The stacks of weapons left, after they had taken all they wanted, were broken up or rendered useless. One thrown out of the window fell on a man's head in the street and killed him.

While the armory was being attacked, another mob was sacking and burning houses on Lexington Avenue, near Forty-seventh Street. Within five minutes from the announcement of this fact, came from the Sixth Precinct the following dispatch: " A mob of about seven hundred attacked some colored people in Baxter Street, and then went to the saloon of Samuel Crook, in Chatham Street, and beat some colored waiters there."

A few minutes later from Sixteenth came: " A crowd of about three hundred men have gone to the foot of Twenty-fourth Street, to stop men in the foundry from working."

At the same time the following was received from the Twenty-first Precinct: " The mob avow their determination of burning this station. Our connection by telegram may be interrupted at any moment."

Another from the Twentieth said: " A very large crowd is now going down Fifth Avenue, to attack the *Tribune* building."

As fast as the wires could work, followed " from the Twenty-fourth Precinct:"

" The mob have fired the buildings corner of Broadway and Twenty-fourth Street."

All this time, while new notes of alarm were sounded, and the police department was struggling to get its force in hand, the work of destruction was going on in the upper part of the city. Bull's Head Tavern, in Forty-sixth Street, attracted the attention of the mob. The sales of the immense herds of cattle in the adjoining yard had been suspended, and the hotel closed. The crowd, however, forgetting the draft, and intent only on pillage, streamed up around it, and shouted,

NEW YORK—BURNING OF THE SECOND AVENUE ARMORY.

" Fire it ! fire it ! " While some were calling for axes
and crowbars, ten powerful men jumped on the stoop,
and with a few heavy blows sent the hall door flying from its hinges. The yelling crowd then rushed in,
and after helping themselves to what they wanted, applied the torch, and soon the entire building was a
mass of flame.

At this time another mob was sacking houses in Lexington Avenue. Elegant furniture and silver plate
were borne away by the crowd, while the ladies, with
their children and servants, fled in terror from the
scene. The provost marshal's head-quarters were also set
on fire, and the whole block on Broadway, between
Twenty-eighth and Twenty-ninth Streets, was burned
down, while jewelry stores and shops of all kinds were
plundered and their contents carried off. A vast horde
followed the rioters for the sole purpose of plunder,
and loaded down with their spoils, could be seen hastening home in every direction.

While these fires were under full headway, a new idea
seemed to strike the mob, or at least a portion of it.
Having stopped the draft in two districts, sacked and
set on fire nearly a score of houses, and half killed as
many men, it now, impelled by a strange logic, sought
to destroy the Colored Orphan Asylum on Fifth Avenue, extending from Forty-third to Forty-fourth Street.
There would have been no draft but for the war—
there would have been no war but for slavery. But
the slaves were black, ergo, all blacks are responsible
for the war. This seemed to be the logic of the mob,
and having reached the sage conclusion to which it
conducted, they did not stop to consider how poor
helpless orphans could be held responsible, but pro-

8

ceeded at once to wreak their vengeance on them. The building was four stories high, and besides the matrons and officers, contained over two hundred children, from mere infants up to twelve years of age. Around this building the rioters gathered with loud cries and oaths, sending terror into the hearts of the inmates. Superintendent William E. Davis hurriedly fastened the doors; but knowing they would furnish but a momentary resistance to the armed multitude, he, with others, collected hastily the terrified children, and carrying some in their arms, and leading others, hurried them in a confused crowd out at the rear of the building, just as the ruffians effected an entrance in front. Then the work of pillage commenced, and everything carried off that could be, even to the dresses and trinkets of the children, while heavy furniture was smashed and chopped up in the blind desire of destruction. Not satisfied with this, they piled the fragments in the different rooms, and set fire to them. At this juncture Chief Engineer Decker arrived, and determined, if possible, to save the building, addressed the crowd, as he had in the morning, hoping to induce them to forbear further violence, and let him extinguish the flames. But they had now got beyond argument of any kind, and knocking him down twice, pitched him into the street. But ten brave firemen at this juncture rushed to his side, and together fought their way through the crowd into the building, where they were joined by two assistant engineers, Lamb and Lewis. They at once began to scatter and extinguish the burning fragments, keeping back for a while, by their bold bearing, the rioters. The latter, however, soon rallied in force, and some mounting to the loft, set it on fire in every part. Decker and his few gallant allies, finding it impossible to save the building, retreated into the street, and soon the massive structure was a sheet of flame.

The crowd now proceeded to Mayor Opdyke's house, and gathering in front of it, sent up shouts and calls for the Mayor. They were, however, deterred at that time from accomplishing their purpose by an appeal from Judge Barnard, who addressed them from the steps of an adjoining house.

Soon after, an immense mob was reported coming down Broadway, for the purpose, some thought, of attacking the negro waiters in the Lafarge House, between Amity and Bleecker Streets, but in fact to attack police head-quarters in Mulberry Street, and break up the very centre of operations. It was a bold stroke, but the ringleaders had been drinking all day, and now, maddened by liquor, were ready for the most desperate attempts. When the news of this movement reached head-quarters, the commissioners saw that a crisis had come. The mob numbered at least five thousand, while they could not muster at that moment two hundred men. The clerk, Mr. Hawley, went to the commissioners' room, and said: "Gentlemen, the crisis has come. A battle has got to be *fought now, and won too*, or all is lost." They agreed with him. "But who," they asked, "will lead the comparatively small force in this fight?" He replied that he thought that Sergeant Carpenter should be selected, as one of the oldest and most experienced officers on the force. "Well," they said, "will you go down to his room and see what he says about it?" He went, and laid before him the perilous condition of things, and that an immediate and successful battle *must* be fought.

Carpenter heard him through, and taking in fully the perilous condition of things, paused a moment, and then rising to his full height and lifting his hand, said, with a terrible oath, " I'll go, and I'll win that fight, or *Daniel Carpenter will never come back a live man.*" He walked out and summoned the little force, and as " Fall in, men; fall in," was repeated, they fell into line along the street. When all was ready, Acton turned to Carpenter, every lineament of whose face showed the stern purpose that mastered him, and quietly said, " *Sergeant, make no arrests.*"

It was to be a battle in which no prisoners were to be taken. " All *right*," replied Carpenter, as he buttoned up his coat and shouted " Forward." Solid, and silent save their heavy, measured tread on the pavement, they moved down Bleecker Street towards Broadway. As they turned into the latter street, only a block and a half away, they saw the mob, which filled the entire street far as the eye could reach, moving tumultuously forward. Armed with clubs, pitchforks, iron bars, and some with guns and pistols, and most of them in their shirt-sleeves and shouting as they came, they presented a wild and savage appearance. Pedestrians fled down the side streets, stores were hastily closed, stages vanished, and they had the street to themselves. A huge board, on which was inscribed " No Draft," was borne aloft as a banner, and beside it waved the Stars and Stripes.

The less than two hundred policemen, compact and firm, now halted, while Carpenter detached two companies of fifty each up the parallel streets to the right and left, as far as Fourth Street. Coming down this street from both directions, they were to strike the mob on both flanks at the same time he charged them in front. He waited till they had reached their positions, and then shouted, "*By.the right flank Company front, double-quick*, CHARGE." Instantaneously every club was swung in air, and solid as a wall and swift as a wave they swept full on the astonished multitude; while at the same time, to cut the monster in two, the two companies charged in flank. Carpenter, striding several steps in advance, his face fairly blazing with excitement, dealt the first blow, stretching on the pavement a powerful ruffian, who was rushing on him with a huge club. For a few minutes nothing was heard but the heavy thud of clubs falling on human skulls, thick and fast as hailstones on windows. The mob, just before so confident and bold, quailed in terror and would have broke and fled at once, but for the mass behind which kept bearing down on them. This, however, soon gave way before the side attacks and the panic that followed. Then the confusion and uproar became terrible, and the mass surged hither and thither, now rolling up Broadway, and again borne back or shoved up against the stores, seeking madly for a way of escape. At length, breaking into fragments, they rushed down the side streets, hotly pursued by the police, whose remorseless clubs never ceased to fall as long as a fugitive was within reach. Broadway looked like a field of battle, for the pavement was strewn thick with bleeding, prostrate forms. It was a great victory and decisive of all future contests.

Having effectually dispersed them, Carpenter, with the captured flag, marched up to Mayor Opdyke's house, when, finding everything quiet, he returned to head-quarters. This successful attack of the police was received with cheers by those spectators who had witnessed it.

# CHAPTER XIV.

THE terrible punishment the rioters received at the hands of Carpenter had, however, only checked their movements for a time; and, as the sun began to hang low in the summer heavens, men looked forward to the coming night with apprehension.

In the meantime, however, the authorities, conscious of the perilous condition of the city, had resorted to every means of defence in their power. Unfortunately, as mentioned before, nearly the whole of its military force, on which it depended in any great emergency, was absent. Lee's brilliant flank movement around Hooker and Washington, terminating in the invasion of Pennsylvania, had filled the country with consternation. His mighty columns were moving straight on Philadelphia, and the Government at Washington, roused to the imminent danger, had called for all the troops within reach, and New York had sent forward nearly every one of her regiments. Ordinary prudence would have dictated that the draft should be postponed for a few days, till these regiments, now on their way back, or preparing to return, should arrive. It was running a needless risk to urge it in such a crisis—indeed, one of the follies of which the Administration at this time was so needlessly guilty.

General Wool, at this juncture, commanded the Eastern Department, with his head-quarters at the corner of Bleecker and Greene Streets. Mayor Opdyke immediately called on him for help, and also on Major-general Sandford, commanding the few troops that were left in the city. The latter immediately issued an order requesting the Seventh Regiment to meet that evening, at their drill-rooms, at eight o'clock, to consult on the measures necessary to be taken in the present unexpected crisis, and another to the late two-years' volunteers then in the city, to report at the same hour in Grand Street, to Colonel William H. Allen, for temporary duty.

General Wool, also, during the afternoon, while the rioters were having it all their own way, sent an officer to the adjutant-general of General Brown, commanding the troops in garrison in New York harbor, ordering up a force of about eighty men immediately.

General Brown, on his way from his office to Fort Hamilton, was informed by Colonel Stinson, chief clerk, that a serious riot was raging in the city, and that General Wool had sent to Fort Hamilton for a detachment of some eighty men, and that a tug had gone for them. Surprised at the smallness of the number sent (he was, by special orders of the War Department, commandant of the city, and commander of all the forts and troops in the harbor except Fort

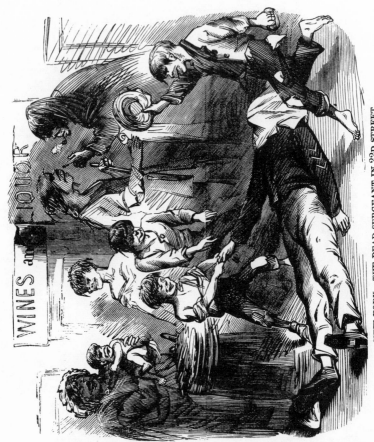

NEW YORK—THE DEAD SERGEANT IN 22D STREET.

Columbus), he immediately ordered the company at Fort Wood to the city, and sent a tug for it. He then made a requisition on the quartermaster for transportation of all the other companies, and proceeded without delay to Fort Hamilton. General Brown's office was close to General Wool's; but he did not think proper to consult him on the movement.

General Brown, immediately on his arrival at Fort Hamilton, directed that all the troops there, as well as at Forts Lafayette and Richmond, be got in readiness to move at a moment's notice, and also that a section of artillery be organized, in case it should be wanted. Having taken these wise precautions he hastened up to the city, and reported to General Wool. The result proved the wisdom of his forecast. A new order was at once dispatched for the remaining troops, and just at twilight, Lieut. McElrath saw two steamers making directly for the fort. They were hardly fastened to the dock, when an officer stepped ashore and handed him an order from General Brown to send up at once all the efficient troops in the forts, and have their places supplied as best he could with some volunteer artillery companies.

The reports coming in to police head-quarters had shown that it was no common uprising of a few disaffected men to be put down by a few squads of police or a handful of soldiers. The Mayor, after consulting with the Police Commissioners, felt that it was the beginning of a general outbreak in every part of the city, and by his representations persuaded General Wool to apply to Rear-admiral Paulding, commanding the Navy Yard, for a force of marines, and eventually to Colonel Bowman, Superintendent of West Point, and

8*

also to the authorities of Newark, and Governors of New York, New Jersey, Massachusetts, Connecticut, and Rhode Island for troops.

General Brown, after reporting to General Wool, repaired to police head-quarters, which he adopted as his own, and issued the following order:

"HEAD-QUARTERS, NEW YORK, July 13, 1863.

"In obedience to the orders of the Major-general commanding the Eastern Department, the undersigned assumes command of the United States troops in this city.

"Lieutenant-colonel Frothingham and Captain Revolle are of the staff of the undersigned, and will be obeyed accordingly.

"HARVEY BROWN,
"*Brevet Brigadier-general.*"

He also sent a dispatch to General Sandford, at the arsenal, notifying him of his action, and requesting him to come down and consult with him on the course to be pursued. General Sandford, after awhile, did come down, and, to General Brown's amazement, insisted that all the troops should be sent up to the arsenal. General Brown, seeing the utter madness of such a disposition of his force, refused decidedly to permit it to be done. This was of course denying Sandford's claim to be his superior officer. It was well for the city that he took this ground.

Mayor Opdyke also issued a proclamation, calling on the rioters to disperse.

But while these measures were being set on foot, the rioters were not idle.

All day long a crowd had been gathering in the Park around the City Hall, growing more restless as night came on. The railroad-cars passing it were searched, to see if any negroes were on board, while eyes glowered savagely on the *Tribune* building. They had sought in an eating-house for the editor, to wreak their vengeance on him. Not finding him, they determined that the building, from which was issued the nefarious paper, should come down, but were evidently waiting for help to arrive before commencing the work of destruction. The mob, which Carpenter had so terribly punished in Broadway, were marching for it, designing to burn it after they had demolished police head-quarters. Their dispersion delayed the attack, and doubtless broke its force, by the reduction of numbers it caused. There seemed enough, however, if properly led, to effect their purpose, for the Park and Printing-house Square were black with men, who, as the darkness increased, grew more restless; and " Down with it! burn it!" mingled with oaths and curses, were heard on every side.

At last came the crash of a window, as a stone went through it. Another and another followed, when suddenly a reinforcing crowd came rushing down Chatham Street. This was the signal for a general assault, and, with shouts, the rabble poured into the lower part of the building, and began to destroy everything within reach. Captain Warlow, of the First Precinct, No. 29 Broad Street, who, with his command, was in the gallant fight in Broadway, after some subsequent fighting and marching, had at length reached his head-quarters in Broad Street, where a despatch met him, to proceed at once to the *Tribune* building. He immediately started off on the double-quick. On reaching the upper end of Nassau Street, he came to a halt, and gave the club signal on the pavement, to form column. Captain Thorne, of the City Hall, in the meantime, had joined his force to him, with the gallant Sergeant Devoursney. Everything being ready, the order to "Charge" was given, and the entire force, perhaps a hundred and fifty strong, fell in one solid mass on the mob, knocking men over right and left, and laying heads open at every blow. The panic-stricken crowd fled up Chatham Street, across the Park, and down Spruce and Frankfort Streets, punished terribly at every step. The space around the building being cleared, a portion of the police rushed inside, where the work of destruction was going on. The sight of the blue-coats in their midst, with their uplifted clubs, took the rioters by surprise, and they rushed frantically for the doors and windows, and escaped the best way they could. In the meantime, those who had taken refuge in the Park found themselves in the lion's jaws. Carpenter had hardly rested from his march up Fifth Avenue to Mayor Opdyke's house, when he, too, received orders to hasten to the protection of the *Tribune* building. Taking one hundred of his own men, and one hundred under Inspector Folk, of Brooklyn, who had been early ordered over, and been doing good service in the city, he marched down Broadway, and was just entering the Park, when the frightened crowd came rushing pell-mell across it. Immediately forming "company front," he swept the Park like a storm, clearing everything before him. Order being restored, Folk returned with his force to Brooklyn, where things began to wear a threatening aspect, and Carpenter took up his station at City Hall for the night.

This ended the heavy fighting of the day, though minor disturbances occurred at various points during the evening. Negroes had been hunted down all day, as though they were so many wild beasts, and one, after dark, was caught, and after being severely beaten and hanged to a tree, left suspended there till Acton sent a force to take the body down. Many had sought refuge in police-stations and elsewhere, and all were filled with terror.

The demonstrations in the lower part of the city excited the greatest anxiety about the Government buildings in that section—the Custom House and Sub-treasury were tempting prizes to the rioters. General Sandford, commanding the city military, had sent such force as he could collect early in the day to the arsenal, to defend it; for, should the mob once get possession of the arms and ammunition stored there, no one could tell what the end would be. United States troops also were placed in Government buildings to protect them. Almost the last act of the mob this evening was the burning of Postmaster Wakeman's house, in Eighty-sixth Street. Mrs. Wakeman was noted for her kindness to the poor and wretched, who now repaid her by sacking and burning her house. The precinct station near by was also destroyed.

In the meanwhile, an event happened which threatened to disarrange all the plans that had been laid. Military etiquette often overrides the public good, and here, at this critical moment, General Wool chose to consider that, as General Sandford was Major-general, though not in the United States service, he, therefore, ranked Brigadier-general Brown of the regular army, and required him to act under the other's orders. This, Brown promptly refused to do, and asked to be relieved, telling General Wool that such a proceeding was an unheard-of thing. That he was right the order below will show* that his troops must be under his own command, as he was responsible for their action to the Government, and Sandford was not. Wool, however, continued obstinate, and a total disruption seemed inevitable. Mayor Opdyke, President Acton, Governor Seymour, with several prominent American citizens, were present, and witnessed this disagreement with painful feelings. They knew that it would work mischief, if not paralyze the combined action they hoped to put forth in the morning. General Brown, finding Wool inflexible, turned away, determined to retire altogether. The Mayor and others followed him, and begged him not to abandon them in the desperate strait they were in—to think of nothing but saving the city. General Brown had been too hasty, sticking on a point of mere etiquette, with, perhaps, too much tenacity. True, an officer must insist on his rank as a rule, but there are emergencies when everything of a personal nature must be forgotten—crises where it may

---

* [GENERAL ORDER No. 36.]        WAR DEPARTMENT,
        *Adjutant-general's Office, Washington*, April 7th, 1863.
6. The military commander's duties in reference to all troops and enlisted men who happen to serve within the limits of his command will be *precisely those of a commanding officer of a military post.*

The duties of military commanders above defined, will devolve in the *City of New York, and the military posts in that vicinity*, on Brevet Brigadier-general H. Brown, Colonel Fifth U. S. Artillery.
        By order of the Secretary of War,
            (Signed)   L. THOMAS, *Adjutant-general.*

be an officer's duty to serve in any capacity, however subordinate, and trust to being righted afterwards. Luckily, General Brown, on a sober second thought, took the proper view, and returned to General Wool, and asked to be reinstated in his command, but giving him to understand that, though he would co-operate in every possible way with General Sandford, he still must retain distinct and separate command of his own troops. This was right, and whether General Wool perfectly understood the arrangement, or seeing how deeply the gentlemen present felt on the subject, chose not to press a mere point of etiquette, does not appear. We only know that if General Brown had given up the command of his troops, the results to the city would have been disastrous.

While these events were passing in the St. Nicholas Hotel, the streets were comparatively quiet. It had been a hard day for the rioters, as well as for the police, and they were glad of a little rest. Besides, they had become more or less scattered by a terrific thunderstorm that broke over the city, deluging the streets with water. In the midst of it, there came a telegraphic dispatch to the commissioners, calling for assistance. The tired police were stretched around on the floor or boxes, seeking a little rest, when they were aroused, and summoned to fall in; and the next moment they plunged into the darkness and rain. They were drenched to the skin before they had gone a block, but they did not heed it—and then, as to the end, and under all circumstances, answered promptly and nobly to every call.

Acton had now gathered a large force at head-quarters, and felt ready to strike at any moment.

While the men flung themselves on the hard floor, like soldiers on the field of battle, ready to start on duty at the first call, Acting Superintendent Acton and his assistants never closed their eyes, but spent the night in telegraphing, organizing, and preparing for the fiercer fights of next day.   Much was to be done to cover and protect a district that reached from Brooklyn to Westchester, and it was an anxious night. They had one consolation, however : though taken unawares, they had at the close of the day come out victors, which gave them confidence in the future, especially as now Brown and his trained soldiers were with them.

Some fifteen or twenty policemen had been more or less severely injured, while the number of the killed and wounded of the mob was wholly unknown.   Both the dead and maimed were left by the police where they fell, and were almost immediately hurried away by their friends.

The destruction of property on this first day, consisted of four buildings on Third Avenue burned, also a block on Broadway between Twenty-eighth and Twenty-ninth Streets ; two brown-stone dwellings in Lexington Avenue ; Allerton's Hotel near Bull's Head ; a cottage, corner of Forty-fifth Street and Fifth Avenue ; the Colored Orphan Asylum, and the armory corner of Twenty-first Street and Second Avenue.

PENN. R. R.—CONESTOGA BRIDGE.

# CHAPTER XV.

ONE thing Commissioners Acton and Bergen in
their consultation settled must be done at all hazards
—telegraphic communication must be kept open with
the different precincts. Otherwise it would be impossible to concentrate men at any given point, quick
enough to arrest the mob before they spread devastation and conflagration far and wide. Every hour
gained by a mob in accumulating or organizing its
forces, increases the difficulty of dispersing it. The
rioters understood this partially, and had acted accordingly; but the rich spoils they had come across during
the day, had driven, for the time being, all other
thoughts but plunder out of their heads. Some com-
munications had already been destroyed, and the rioters
would evidently by morning have their eyes open to the
importance of doing this everywhere, and their efforts
must be foiled, no matter what the risk or sacrifice
might be. They had already cut down over sixty
poles, and rendered upwards of twelve miles of wire
useless; and how much more would share the same
fate the next day, no one could tell.

The superintendent and deputy of the Telegraph

Bureau, Messrs. Crowley and Polhamus, with the operators mentioned before, were, therefore, set at work this very evening in the storm to restore the broken lines.

This was a perilous undertaking, for if once discovered, their lives would be instantly sacrificed.

The details of their operations, their disguises, ingenious contrivances, deceptions, and boldness in carrying out their object, would make an attractive chapter in itself. Often compelled to mingle with the mob, always obliged to conceal what they were about, not daring to raise a pole or handle a wire unless cautiously or secretly, they yet restored the lines in the north section by morning, and those in the south by Wednesday evening. Sometimes they were compelled to carry a wire over the top of a house, sometimes round it, through a back-yard; in short, every device and expedient was resorted to by these daring, sharp-witted men. Once Polhamus had his boots burned off in tramping through the burning ruins of a building after the wires. Once he and Mr. Crowley came near being clubbed to death by the police, who mistook them for rioters, so ingeniously and like them were they at work among the ruins. Captain Brower rescued them, or their services might have ended on the spot.

This work was kept steadily up during the continuation of the riots. On one occasion, Mr. Crowley, hearing that the wires were down in the Ninth and Tenth Avenues, hastened thither alone, when he encountered a large mob. Fearing to pass through it he hesitated a moment, when he noticed a carriage driving in the direction he wished to go, in which was a Catholic priest. He immediately hailed it and was taken in. As the carriage entered the mob, the latter surrounded it, and supposing the inmates were reporters, began to yell "Down with the d—d reporters;" but the moment they recognized the priest, they allowed it to pass. Often the two would take a hack; and passing themselves off as drivers, go through infected districts, and search points to which they otherwise could not have gone. One time they were returning from an expedition through Third Avenue, and had reached Houston Street, when they were hailed by a gang of rioters, who demanded to be taken downtown. They had to comply, for the men were armed with pistols, and so took them in and kept along Houston Street, under the pretence of going down through Broadway, knowing that when they reached Mulberry Street they would be in hailing distance of the head-quarters of the police. It was just after daybreak, and Crowley and Polhamus urged on the horses, expecting in a few minutes to have their load safely locked up. The fellows evidently not liking the vicinity to which the drivers were taking them, ordered them to wheel about, which they were compelled to do, and drive under their direction to an old house in the Tenth Ward. There they got out, and offering the drivers a drink and fifty cents, let them go. On one occasion, Crowley, while examining the wires in Second Avenue, was suspected by the mob, who fell upon him, and it was only by the greatest coolness and adroitness he convinced them he was a rioter himself, and so escaped. At another time they were going along in a common wagon, when they were hemmed in by a crowd, and escaped by passing themselves off as farmers from Westchester. Had they been discovered, they would have been killed on the spot.

## DETECTIVE FORCE.

The duties of this force are well known, but during the riots they had something more important to do than to work up individual cases. The force, with John Young as chief, and M. B. Morse as clerk, consisted in all of seventeen persons. These men are selected for their superior intelligence, shrewdness, sagacity, and undoubted courage. Full of resources, they must also be cool, collected, and fearless. During the riots they were kept at work day and night, obtaining knowledge of facts that no others could get, and thus supplying the different precincts and head-quarters with invaluable information. Their duty was a most perilous one, for it called them to go into the very heart of the turbulent districts ; nay, into the very midst of the mob, where detection would have been followed by death, and that of the most horrible kind. Chief Young, with his clerk, was engaged at head-quarters, so that fifteen men had to perform the required work for the whole city. Sometimes alone, sometimes two or three together, they seemed omnipresent. In all sorts of disguises, feigning all sorts of employments and characters, sometimes on horseback and again driving an old cart or a hack, they pressed with the most imperturbable effrontery into the very vortex of danger. Ever on the watch, and accustomed to notice every expression of the countenance, they would discover at a single glance when they were suspected, and remove the suspicion at once by some clever device. Sometimes one of them, seeing himself watched, would quietly ascend the steps of a residence, and ringing the bell, make some inquiry as though he were on business, and then deliberately walk off; or if he thought it would not do to have his face too closely scanned, he would step inside and wait till the crowd moved on. Sometimes, with a stone or club in their hands, they would shout with the loudest, and engaging in conversation with the ringleaders themselves, ascertain their next move; then quietly slip away to the nearest station, and telegraph to head-quarters the information. When the telegraph had been cut off, they had to take the place of the wires, and carry through the very heart of the crowd their news to the department.

On their ears again and again would ring the fearful cry, "There goes Kennedy's spies;" and it required the most consummate acting and self-possession to allay the suspicion. Often on a single word or act hinged their very lives. Some of these men were in the mob that made the first attack on Mayor Opdyke's house, and while apparently acting with it, learned of the intended movement down to police head-quarters, and at once telegraphed the fact, which enabled Carpenter to prepare for them, and give them the terrible beating we have described. At the burning and sacking of different buildings they were present, and often would follow unnoticed the ringleaders for hours, tracking them with the tireless tenacity of a sleuth hound, until they got them separate from the crowd, and then pounce suddenly upon them, and run them into the nearest station. The lawlessness that prevailed not only let loose all the thieves and burglars of the city, but attracted those from other places, who practised their vocation with impunity. To lessen this evil, the detectives one night quietly made visits to some half a dozen "lushing cribs," as they are called, in Eighth and Fourteenth Streets, and seized about thirty noted thieves, burglars, and garroters, and locked them up for safe-keeping. They also warned the negroes of threatened danger, and directed them to places of safety; and in case of emergency acted as guides to the military in their operations. In short, they were ubiquitous, indefatigable, and of immense service. They played the part of unerring pointers to the commissioners, telling them when and where to strike; yet strange to say, such was their skill, their ingenuity, and exhaustless resources, that they all escaped being assaulted, save one named Slowly. He was passing through the very heart of the riotous district, in Second Avenue, when some one who had evidently been once in his clutches, recognized him, and pointing him out, shouted "Detective!" Instantly a rush was made for him, and he was knocked down, and kicked and stamped upon. Regaining, with a desperate effort, his feet, he sprang up the steps of a house, and fought his assailants fiercely, till the lady of the house, seeing his perilous situation, courageously opened the door and let him in, and then bolted and barred it in the face of the mob. Through some strange apprehension, the baffled wretches, though they howled, and swore, and threatened, did not force an entrance, and he escaped.

In this connection, while speaking of those whose duties were uniform and running through the whole period of the riots, might be mentioned Seth C. Hawley, the chief clerk. Like Acton, he has a nervous, wiry temperament. This often makes a man rash and headlong, and hence not reliable ; but when combined, as in him, with perfect self-possession and self-control, imparts enormous power. It matters not how nervous and excitable a man is, if danger and responsibility instead of confusing and unsettling him, only winds him up to a higher tension, till he becomes like a tightly-drawn steel spring. Excitement then not only steadies him, but it quickens his perceptions, clears his judgment, gives rapidity to his decisions, and terrible force to his blow. Mr. Hawley's duties were of a various and exhausting kind, so that during all the riots, he allowed himself only one hours' rest out of every twenty-four. Besides his ordinary supervisory duties over the clerks, etc., he had to see to the execution of the almost incessant orders of the commissioners, provide and issue arms, see to the refugees and prisoners, and act as commissary to over four thousand men on duty in and around head-quarters. Two men more perfectly fitted to work together in such a crisis as this, than he and Acton, could not well be found.

# CHAPTER XVI.

## SECOND DAY.

THE early July morning broke tranquilly over the great city, and the rattling of vehicles was heard in some of the streets, where men were going to their places of business. In a large portion of it everything wore its usual air of tranquillity, yet a close observer would notice an uneasiness resting on the countenances of men. Furtive glances were cast down side streets, and people seemed on the watch, as though in expectation of something to come, and the very atmosphere appeared laden with evil omens. Around police head-quarters, and inside the building, were large bodies of policemen and the U. S. troops under General Brown.

NEW YORK—HANGING AND BURNING A NEGRO IN CLARKSON STREET.

But uptown, in the vicinity of Thirteenth Street and Second and Third Avenues, crowds of men began early to assemble, though perfectly quiet in their demeanor, while smaller knots in the adjoining wards could be seen discussing the events of the day before. In the meantime, exciting reports came from Harlem and York-ville—as early as five o'clock, the following telegram was sent to the Twentieth Precinct: "Notify General Sandford to go immediately to Eighty-sixth Street and Harlem—mob burning." Indeed the air was charged with electricity, but the commissioners now felt ready to meet the storm whenever and wherever it should burst. A large force of special policemen had been sworn in, while General Brown had over seven hundred troops, ready to co-operate with the police. The public build-ings were all well guarded—Sandford had a strong force in the arsenal, and the military and civil authori-ties stood waiting the next movement of the mob. Telegrams arriving, showed that the northern part of the city was alive with gathering crowds, while from Sixth Avenue on the west nearly to Second Avenue in the east, and down almost to Broome Street, the streets were black with excited men. Stores were closed, fac-tories emptied of their hands, who voluntarily joined the rioters, or were forced into their ranks, and there was evidently a gathering of the elements in those directions for a fearful storm. Soon immense crowds began to patrol the streets in different wards, showing that sim-ultaneous action would be required at various points. The troops were called out and marshalled in Mulberry Street, and those companies selected for immediate ac-tion drawn up in line. Colonel Frothingham, after an earnest conversation with the officers, addressed the

9

soldiers. He told them that the fate of the city was in their hands, and everything depended on their good conduct. Knowing the temptations to disorderly conduct in the midst of the great city, he urged on them especially to obey implicitly their officers under all circumstances. His manner and words were earnest, and listened to with profound attention. Soon a company headed by Sergeant Carpenter, with a police force two hundred and fifty strong, started for Second and Third Avenues, where the greatest gatherings were reported to be.

At this time the rioters seemed hesitating about their course of action. There was apparently no recognized leader, no common understanding and purpose, though all were engaged in animated discussions of some topic. Dirty, ferocious-looking women were scattered through the crowd; some of the men were armed, while all looked defiant and determined.

There were doubtless many who had come from mere curiosity, and a few attempted to allay the excitement, among them a Catholic priest, who harangued them, urging them to maintain peace. His address seemed to have considerable influence on those immediately around him; but as soon as he left, his words were forgotten, and the mighty throng, estimated by some at ten thousand, began to be agitated by passion. What would have been the first act of violence, it is impossible to say, had they been left undisturbed. But at the cry of "the police and soldiers are coming," everything else was forgotten.

Inspector Carpenter, coming down Twenty-first Street, struck Second Avenue, and wheeling, moved in solid column through the crowd up to Thirty-second

Street. The force was assailed with hoots and yells, and all kinds of opprobrious epithets, but no violence was shown, until it had crossed Thirty-second Street. The mob not only filled the street, but numbers, with piles of stones and brick-bats, had climbed to the roofs of the houses. These deeming themselves secure, suddenly, with one accord, rained their missiles on the rear of the column.

The men fell rapidly, and two were dangerously hurt. Carpenter immediately halted his command, and ordered fifty men to enter the houses, and mounting to the roof, clear them of the assailants. Barricaded doors were at once broken in, and every one that opposed their progress clubbed without mercy, as they made their way to the upper floors. Captain Mount of the Eleventh Precinct, led this storming party. Officers Watson and Cole distinguished themselves by being the first on the roof, fighting their way through a narrow scuttle. As the police, one by one, stepped on to the roof, they rushed on the desperadoes with their clubs, and felled them rapidly. Those who attempted to escape through the scuttles were met by the police in the rooms below ; or if one chanced to reach the street, he was knocked down by those keeping guard there. Some dropped from second and third story windows, and met with a worse fate than those who staid behind. One huge fellow received such a tremendous blow, that he was knocked off his feet and over the edge of the roof, and fell headlong down a height of four stories to the pavement beneath. Crushed to death by the force of the fall, he lay a mangled heap at the feet of his companions.

The fight was sharp and fierce, and kept up for

nearly an hour, and bodies scattered around showed with what deadly force the club had been wielded. But with the clearing of the houses there came a lull in the conflict, and the immense crowd looked on in sullen silence, as the police reformed in the street, and recommenced their march. The military force that had accompanied the police, had formed on the avenue, about a block and a half above where the latter were stationed, while the detachment was clearing the houses. Two howitzers were placed in position commanding the avenue. Colonel O'Brien, of the Eleventh New York Volunteers, who was raising a regiment for the war, had gathered together, apparently on his own responsibility, about fifty men, and appearing on the field, from his superior rank, assumed command. For a short time the rioters remained quiet, but as the police marched away, they suddenly awoke out of their apparent indifference. Maddened at the sight of the mangled bodies of their friends stretched on the pavement, and enraged at their defeat by the police, they now turned on the soldiers, and began to pelt them with stones and brick-bats. O'Brien rode up and down the centre of the street a few times, evidently thinking his fearless bearing would awe the mob. But they only jeered him, and finding the attack growing hotter and more determined, he finally gave the order to fire. The howitzers belched forth on the crowd, the soldiers levelled their pieces, and the whistling of minie-balls was heard on every side. Men and women reeled and fell on the sidewalk and in the street. One woman, with her child in her arms, fell, pierced with a bullet. The utmost consternation followed. The crowd knew from sad experience that the police would use their clubs, but they seemed to think it hardly possible that the troops would fire point-blank into their midst. But the deadly effect of the fire convinced them of their error, and they began to jostle and crowd each other in the effort to get out of its range. In a few minutes the avenue was cleared of the living, when the wounded and dead were cared for by their friends. Order had been restored, and O'Brien, with some twenty or thirty men, marched down to police head-quarters, and offered his services to General Brown. Colonel Frothingham thanked him, but soon saw that the Colonel was not in a fit state to have command of troops, and so reported to General Brown. O'Brien appeared to comprehend the state of things, and asked to be excused on the plea of sickness. He was excused, and rode away. Whether he disbanded his handful of men, or they disbanded themselves, was not stated, but *he* was soon back again at the scene of the riot. His residence was close by, but had been deserted that morning by the family, which had fled in alarm to Brooklyn. Scowling visages lowered on the colonel, as he rode slowly back among the crowd, and low muttered threats were heard. Although an Irishman, and well-known in that neighborhood, his sympathy with the Government had awakened more or less hostile feeling against him, which his conduct to-day kindled into deadly hate. Apparently unconscious or reckless of this, he dismounted, and entered a neighboring drug-store or saloon. After remaining a few moments, he came out, and paused as he beheld the crowd that had assembled around the door. There was little said, but dark and angry countenances were bent on him from every side, and he saw that mischief was intended. Drawing his sword, and taking a revolver in the other hand, he deliberately walked out into the street. He had taken but a few steps, when a powerful blow on the back of his head made him stagger forward. In an instant a rush was made for him, and blows were rained so fast and fierce upon him, that he was unable to defend himself. Knocked down and terribly mangled, he was dragged with savage brutality over the rough pavement, and swung from side to side like a billet of wood, till the large, powerful body was a mass of gore, and the face beaten to a pumice. The helpless but still animate form would then be left awhile in the street, while the crowd, as it swayed to and fro, gazed on it with cool indifference or curses. At length a Catholic priest, who had either been sent for, or came along to offer his services wherever they might be needed, approached the dying man and read the service of the Catholic Church over him, the crowd in the meantime remaining silent. After he had finished, he told them to leave the poor man alone, as he was fast sinking. But as soon as he had disappeared, determined to make sure work with their victim, they again began to pound and trample on the body. In the intervals of the attack, the still living man would feebly lift his head, or roll it from side to side on the stones, or heave a faint groan.

The whole afternoon was spent in this fiendish work, and no attempt was made to rescue him. Towards sundown the body was dragged into his own back-yard, his regimentals all torn from him, except his pantaloons, leaving the naked body, from the waist up, a mass of mangled flesh clotted with blood.

But the dying man could not be left alone in his own

yard. A crowd followed him thither, among which were women, who committed the most atrocious violence on the body, until at last, with one convulsive movement of the head, and a deep groan, the strong man yielded up his life.

While this tragedy was being enacted here, similar scenes were occurring all over the city. Mobs were everywhere, the spirit of pandemonium was abroad, and havoc and revenge let loose.

Lieutenant Wood, whom General Brown had sent off, with a company of regulars, came in conflict with a mob, two thousand strong, in Pitt and Delancey Streets. Marching along Houston to the Bowery, he turned down the latter, and kept on to Grand. On reaching Pitt Street, he beheld the hooting, yelling crowd coming straight towards him. He immediately formed his little force of one hundred and fifty men in line across the street, and brought them to "shoulder arms." One of the ringleaders stepped forward to speak to him, when Lieutenant Wood waved him off. This was the signal for the attack, and immediately a shower of stones fell among the soldiers. The officer ordered the men to fire—it was said over the heads of the rioters—in order to disperse them. The result was scattering shots in return from the latter. Wood then ordered a point-blank volley, when men tumbled over right and left. The crowd did not wait for a second, but fled in every direction. Wood then marched back to headquarters, but on the way slipped and sprained his ankle, which caused a report that he had been wounded.

A bloody conflict also took place between the police and mob in the same avenue where Colonel O'Brien fell, below Thirtieth Street. There was a wire fac-

tory here, in which several thousand carbines were
stored.  Of this, some of the rioters were aware, and
communicated the fact to others, and a plan was formed
to capture them.  Having discovered from the morning's experience that the military had been called in
to aid the police, arms became imperatively necessary,
if they hoped to make a successful resistance.  All
public depositories of arms they knew were guarded,
but this factory was not, and hence they resolved to
capture it without delay.  Swarming around it, they
forced the entrance, and began to throw out the carbines to their friends.  The attack, however, had been
telegraphed to head-quarters, and Inspector Dilks was
despatched with two hundred men to save the building,
and recover any arms that might be captured.  He
marched rapidly up to Twenty-first Street, and down
it to the avenue.  Here he came suddenly upon the
mob, that blocked the entire street.  As the head of the
force appeared, the rioters, instead of being frightened,
greeted it with jeers and curses.  It was two hundred
against a thousand; but the inspector did not hesitate a
moment on account of the inequality of numbers, but
instantly formed his men and ordered a charge.  The
mob, instead of recoiling, closed desperately on the
police, and a fierce hand-to-hand encounter took place.
The clubs, however, mowed a clean swath along the
street, and the compact little force pushed like a
wedge into the throng, and cleared a bloody space for itself.  The orders were to recapture all the arms; for this
was of more vital importance than the capture of men.
Wherever, therefore, a musket was seen, a man would
dash for it, and, seizing it, fight his way back into line.
On the pavement, the sidewalk, and in the gutters, men

PENN. R. R.—ALLEGHENY MOUNTAIN TUNNEL, TWELVE MILES WEST OF ALTOONA.

lay bleeding and dying, until at last, the more resolute having been knocked on the head, the vast crowd, like a herd of buffalo, broke and tore madly down the street. One of the leaders was a man of desperate courage, and led on the mob with reckless fury, though bleeding freely from the terrible punishment he received. As his comrades turned to flee, leaving him alone, a fearful blow sent him reeling and staggering towards the sidewalk. As he reached it, he fell heavily over against the iron railing, and his chin striking one of the iron pickets, the sharp point entered it and penetrated through to the roof of his mouth. No one noticed him, or if they did, paid no attention to him in the headlong flight on the one hand, and swift pursuit on the other. Thus horridly impaled, his body hanging down along the sidewalk, the wretched man was left to die. At length Captain Hedden noticed him, and lifting up the corpse, laid it down on the sidewalk. It was found, to the surprise of all, to be that of a young man of delicate features and white, fair skin. " Although dressed as a laborer, in dirty overalls and filthy shirt, underneath these were fine cassimere pants, handsome, rich vest, and fine linen shirt."* He was evidently a man in position far above the rough villains he led on, but had disguised himself so as not to be known. He never was known. The corpse, during the fight that followed, disappeared with the bodies of many others.

The street being cleared, Dilks turned his attention to the factory, which was filled with armed rioters, who were determined to defend it to the last. Detaching a portion of his force, he ordered it to take the building by storm. Dashing over all obstacles, the men won the

* D. M. Barnes.

9*

stairway step by step, and entering the main room on the second story, felled a man at almost every blow. Those who succeeded in escaping down-stairs were knocked on the head by the force in the street, and soon no rioters were left but the dead and dying. How many fell in this fight it is impossible to tell; but one physician alone dressed the wounds of twenty-one desperately wounded men. Taking what guns they could find and had captured in the street, the force marched triumphantly back, cheered on their way by the spectators.

In the meantime, Mayor Opdyke's house in Fifth Avenue had again been attacked and partially sacked. Captain Maniere, one of the provost marshals, however, assembled a small force, and drove out the rioters, who were mostly young men and boys, before the work of destruction was complete. The news of this attack had been telegraphed to head-quarters of the police, and Captain Helme, of the Twenty-seventh Precinct, despatched to its defence. At his approach the rioters dispersed. Soon after, he was ordered with his command over to the Second Avenue, accompanied by a detachment of troops under Captain Franklin. This was in the afternoon—the mob had reassembled, and reinforced by those who had been dispersed at Thirty-fourth Street, where Colonel O'Brien fell, had overcome the small body of police at the wire factory, and again taken possession of it. They had found some boxes of guns that had been overlooked by Dilks, and having armed themselves, determined to hold it. Even women joined in the defence. As the force approached, it was greeted with shouts of defiance and missiles of every kind. An immense crowd was gathered outside, while the windows of the five-story building were filled

with angry, excited faces, and arms wildly gesticulating. Charging on this dense mass, and clubbing their
way to the building, the police entered it, and streaming
up the stairways, cleared it floor by floor, some being
knocked senseless, others leaping from windows, to be
killed by the fall, and others escaping down-stairs, to
be met by the force in the street. A thorough
search was now made for arms, and the building
emptied of them. Taking possession of these, the
police and military took up their line of march for
head-quarters. They had not proceeded far, however,
before the mob that had scattered in every direction
began to pour back again into the avenue, and close on
the military that were bringing up the rear. Following
them with hoots and yells that were unheeded, they
became emboldened, and pressing nearer, began to hurl
stones and bricks, and everything they could lay their
hands on, against the soldiers. The latter bore it for
awhile patiently; but this only made the wretches
more fierce and daring. Seeing there was but one way
to end this, Captain Franklin ordered his men to
" About face; " and " ready, aim, fire," fell in quick
succession. The yelling, shouting crowd were in point-
blank range, and the volley told with deadly effect.
The street was strewed with dead and dying, while the
living fled down the avenue.

In the meantime, mobs had sprung up in every part
of the city; some larger and some smaller; some after
negroes, others firing buildings or sacking them.

Some idea of the pressure on the Police Commissioners during this forenoon, and the condition the city was
in, may be gathered from the following despatches,

which are only a small portion of those received and answered in two hours:

10.20. From Thirteenth. Send military here immediately.

10.22. To Seventh. Find military and send them to Thirteenth Street forthwith.

10.45. From Sixteenth. A mob has just attacked Jones' soap factory ; stores all closed.

10.50. To Twenty-sixth. Tell Inspector Leonard to send one hundred men here forthwith.

10.55. To Twentieth. From General Brown. Send to arsenal and say a heavy battle is going on. Captain Wilkins and company of regulars will report to me here at once.

11.18. From Sixteenth. Mob is coming down to station-house; we have no men.

11.20. From Eighteenth. The mob is very wild, corner Twenty-second Street and Second Avenue. They have attacked the Union steam factory.

11.35. To Twenty-sixth. Send another one hundred men here forthwith.

11.35. From Twentieth. Send one hundred men to disperse mob assailing Mayor Opdyke's house.

11.38. To Twenty-first. Can you send a few men here?

11.40. From Twenty-second. The mob has gone to Mr. Higgins' factory, foot of Forty-third Street, to burn it.

11.45. From Eighteenth. What shall we do? The mob is about 4,500 strong.

*Answer.* Clear them down, if you can.

11.50. From Eighteenth. We must leave; the mob is here with guns.

11.50. From Twentieth. Mob tearing up track on Eleventh Avenue.

11.58. The mob have just sacked a large gun-store in Grand Street, and are armed, and are on the way to attack us.

12.10. To Fifteenth. Send your men here forthwith.

12.35. From Twentieth. Send two hundred men forthwith to Thirty-fifth Street arsenal.

12.36. From Twenty-first. The mob have just broken open a gun-store on Third Avenue, between Thirty-sixth and Thirty-seventh Streets, and are arming.

12.40. From Twenty-first. Send help—the crowd is desperate.

And so on.

Between these rapid telegrams asking for help, were others making and answering inquiries. And so it was kept up from daylight till midnight for three days in succession. These urgent calls for help coming from every quarter at the same time, would have thrown into inextricable confusion a less clear head than Acton's. It was a terrible strain on him, and had it continued a little longer, would have cost him his life. In the midst of it all he received anonymous letters, telling him he had but one more day to live.

But while the police head-quarters were thus crowded with business, and the commissioners were straining every nerve to meet the frightful state of things in the city, other means were being taken to add to their efficiency.

Governor Seymour had reached the city, and after being closeted with Mayor Opdyke, had issued a proclamation, calling on the rioters to disperse, and saying that they would be put down at all hazards.

At a meeting of the merchants and bankers in Wall Street, it was resolved to close up business, and form volunteer companies of a hundred men each, to serve under the military. General Wetmore was one of the first to offer his services. The high-spirited citizen, William E. Dodge, was among the most prominent advocates of the measure, and soon found himself a captain under orders. The steamboat of the harbor police was busy in bringing troops and cannon from Riker's and Governor's Island, and rapidly steaming from point to point on the river, to prevent destruction around the docks. Around the arsenal cannon were placed. At the city armory, corner of White and Elm Streets, were a company of the Eighty-fourth New York Militia, and some of the Zouaves and other troops. The Sub-treasury and Custom House were defended by the Tenth National Zouaves and a hundred and fifty armed citizens. In front of the Government stores in Worth and White streets, the Invalid Corps and a company of marines patrolled, while howitzers loaded with grape and canister stood on the corner of the street. Nearly four hundred citizens had been sworn in at police head-quarters as special policemen, and had been furnished with clubs and badges. All this time the fight was going on in every direction, while the fire-bells continually ringing increased the terror that every hour became more wide-spread. Especially was this true of the negro population. From the out-set, they had felt they were to be objects of vengeance, and all day Monday and to-day those who could leave, fled into the country. They crowded the ferry-

boats in every direction, fleeing for life.   But old men
and women, and poor families, were compelled to stay
behind, and meet the fury of the mob, and to-day it became a regular hunt for them.   A sight of one in the
streets would call forth a halloo, as when a fox breaks
cover, and away would dash a half a dozen men in
pursuit.   Sometimes a whole crowd streamed after
with shouts and curses, that struck deadly terror to
the heart of the fugitive.   If overtaken, he was
pounded to death at once ; if he escaped into a negro
house for safety, it was set on fire, and the inmates
made to share a common fate.   Deeds were done and
sights witnessed that one would not have dreamed of,
except among savage tribes.

    At one time there lay at the corner of Twenty-
seventh Street and Seventh Avenue the dead body of
a negro, stripped nearly naked, and around it a collection of Irishmen, absolutely dancing or shouting like
wild Indians.   Sullivan and Roosevelt Streets are
great negro quarters, and here a negro was afraid to
be seen in the street.   If in want of something from a
grocery, he would carefully open the door, and look up
and down to see if any one was watching, and then
steal cautiously forth, and hurry home on his errand.
Two boarding-houses here were surrounded by a mob,
but the lodgers, seeing the coming storm, fled.   The desperadoes, finding only the owner left behind, wreaked
their vengeance on him, and after beating him unmercifully, broke up the furniture, and then fired the buildings.   A German store near by, because it was patron-
ized extensively by negroes, shared the same fate,
after its contents had been distributed among themselves.   A negro barber's shop was next attacked, and

the torch applied to it. A negro lodging-house in the same street next received the visit of these furies, and was soon a mass of ruins. Old men, seventy years of age, and young children, too young to comprehend what it all meant, were cruelly beaten and killed. The spirit of hell seemed to have entered the hearts of these men, and helpless womanhood was no protection against their rage. Sometimes a stalwart negro would break away from his murderers, and run for his life. With no place of safety to which he could flee, he would be headed off in every direction, and forced towards the river. Driven at last to the end of a pier, he would leap off, preferring to take his chances in the water rather than among these bloody men. If bruised and beaten in his desperate struggle for life, he would soon sink exhausted with his efforts. Sometimes he would strike out for a ship, but more often dive under the piers, and hold on to a timber for safety, until his yelling pursuers had disappeared, when he would crawl stealthily out, and with terrified face peer in every direction to see if they had gone. Two were thus run off together into the East River. It was a strange spectacle to see a hundred Irishmen pour along the streets after a poor negro. If he could reach a police station he felt safe; but, alas! if the force happened to be away on duty, he could not stay even there. Whenever the police could strike the track of the mad hunt, they stopped it summarily, and the pursuers became the pursued, and received the punishment they had designed for the negro. All this was in the nineteenth century, and in the metropolis of the freest and most enlightened nation on earth.

The hunt for these poor creatures became so fearful,

NEW YORK.—THE RIOT IN LEXINGTON AVENUE.

NEW YORK—THE RIOT IN LEXINGTON AVENUE.

and the utter impossibility to protect them in their scattered localities so apparent, that they were received into the police stations. But these soon proved inadequate, and they were taken to Head-quarters and the arsenal, where they could be protected against the mob. Here the poor creatures were gathered by hundreds, and slept on the floor, and were regularly fed by the authorities.

It is impossible to give a detailed account of what transpired in every part of the city. If there had been a single band of rioters, no matter how large, a force of military and police, properly armed, could have been concentrated to have dispersed it. But bodies of men, larger or smaller, bent on violence and devastation, were everywhere; even out at Harlem eight buildings were burned, and the lower end of Westchester was in a state of agitation and alarm. A mob of thousands would be scattered, only to come together at other points. A body of police and military plunging through the heaving multitude, acted often only as a stone flung into the water, making but a momentary vacuum. Or, if they did not come together again, they swung off only to fall in, and be absorbed by a crowd collected in another part of the city. The alarm of Monday had only been partial, but to-day it culminated. Families, husbands, and sons left their business, and with arms patrolled the streets. Stores were shut up, stages and cars stopped running, and all business was suspended.

The blood flowing through the thousand arteries of this great mart seemed suddenly frozen in its channels, and its mighty pulsations to stop at the mandate of lawless men. The city held its breath in dread, but there were firm hearts at police head-quarters. Acton never flinched, and in General Brown he found a soldier that knew his duty, and would do it at all hazards. Still, the uprising kept swelling into vaster proportions, embracing a still larger territory.

Broadway was deserted. A few hacks could be seen, but with very different occupants than those which they ordinarily contained. The iron shutters were closed on the Fifth Avenue Hotel, and a stack of arms stood in the hall-way. Crowds of respectable citizens, not on duty, were making all haste toward railroad depots and steamboat landings. Every boat, as it swung from the dock, was loaded to its utmost capacity with people leaving a city that seemed doomed to destruction; going, many knew not where, only out of New York. Cars were packed, and long trains were made up to carry the crowds in haste to get away. But travel on the Hudson River Road was soon stopped by the mob, that tore up the track to prevent communication with other parts of the State, and the arrival of troops.

The Harlem and Third Avenue tracks were also torn up, as the rioters were determined to isolate the great city, which they had doomed to destruction. Passing from one object to another, now acting as if from plan, and now intent only on destruction and plunder, the crowd streamed from point to point with shouts and yells, that sent terror through the adjoining streets. Suddenly, some one remembered that they were in the vicinity of Colonel Nugent's house, in Yorkville, the assistant provost marshal general, and shouting out the news, a rush was made for it, and it was sacked from top to bottom.

As the police were gathered together either at the precinct stations or head-quarters, ordinary patrol duty was out of the question; hence, many isolated acts of violence could be committed with impunity. This freedom from close surveillance, coupled with the contagion of the lawless spirit which was abroad, made every section of the city where the lower classes lived more or less restless. It was impossible for the police to divide itself up so to furnish protection in individual cases, and yet be in sufficient force to cope with the mobs, that numbered by thousands. Although the whole city was heaving like a troubled sea, yet the main gathering this day had been in the upper part and on both sides of it. The terrific contests we described farther back were in the Second Avenue, on the east side, but, nearly opposite, in the Sixth Avenue, crowds had been gathering since early in the forenoon.

For a long time they swayed backward and forward, apparently without any definite purpose, and moved only by the spirit of disorder that had taken possession of the city. But about two o'clock, these various bodies began by mutual attraction to flow together, and soon became one immense mass, and impelled by some information or other, gathered threateningly around a large mansion on the corner of Forty-sixth Street and Fifth Avenue. They had supplied themselves with all sorts of weapons, revolvers, old muskets, stones, clubs, barrel-staves—in short, everything that could be found, that might be of service in a fight—and soon commenced plundering the residence. But their movements had been telegraphed to head-quarters, and Captain Walling, of the Twentieth Precinct, was dis-

patched thither, with a company of regulars under
Captain Putnam, a descendant of "Old Put." The report soon spread through the crowd, that bayonets could
be seen coming up the avenue. Marching up to Forty-
sixth Street, the force turned into it, towards the Fifth
Avenue; and breaking into the charge step, with the
order "no prisoners" ringing in their ears, struck the
mob almost in the centre, cutting it in two, like a mighty
cleaver. There was no need of bayonets—the police, at
the head of the military, went right through it, and
scattered the men in every direction. The force then
divided into squads, and each one taking a section of
the mob, followed it up on a swift run, and smote them
right and left for several blocks. The larger portion
went down Sixth Avenue, and seeing only a portion of
the police pursuing, turned and showed fight, when the
leader received a bullet in the head and fell. Seeing
their leader fall, the mob wheeled and took to their
heels.

Captain Walling in one instance saw a crowd with
fire-arms standing in an alley-way. Just then a fire-
engine and company came down the street, and he with
his small force got behind it, and kept concealed until
opposite the unsuspecting crowd, when, with a shout,
they dashed on it. A volley received them,—with
answering volley, the police charged into the narrow
opening. The rioters fled into a tenement-house, from
which came yells and screams of terrified women and
children. Walling had some sharpshooters with him,
to pick off those beyond the reach of the clubs. One
fellow, armed, was seen astraddle of the ridge pole of
a house. The next moment a sharpshooter covered
him, and he tumbled headlong to the ground. The

same afternoon he saw some twenty or thirty men attempting to stave in a hardware store, evidently after pistols. Walling charged on them alone, and with one terrible blow, his club sent the leader to the pavement with his brains oozing out.

Although the draft was almost forgotten by the rioters, in the thirst for plunder and blood, still men in the streets and some of the papers talked of its being unconstitutional, and to be contested in the courts—others that it had been and would be suspended, as though any disposal of it now could affect the conduct of the rioters. Force was the only argument they would listen to. The riot had almost ceased to wear any political aspect since the attack on the *Tribune* office, the day before, had been defeated. An occasional shout or the sight of a negro might now and then remind one of its origin, but devastation and plunder were the great objects that urged on the excited masses. The sacking of Opdyke's house was done chiefly by a few youngsters, who were simply following the example set them the day before; while the burning of negro buildings, the chasing and killing of negroes, seemed to have only a remote connection with the draft, and was simply the indulgence of a hatred they were hitherto afraid to gratify. So the setting fire to the Weehawken ferry afterwards, could be made to grow out of politics only so far as a man who kept a liquor saloon there was a known Republican. This seemed a weak inducement to draw a crowd so far, when more distinguished victims were all around them. It is more probable that some personal enemy of parties in the vicinity, finding the mob ready to follow any cry, led them thither; for one man seemed to be the leader, who, mounted on a fine cavalry horse, and brandishing a sword, galloped backwards and forwards through the crowd, giving his orders like a field officer. Mobs springing up everywhere, and flowing together often apparently by accident, each pursuing a different object: one chasing negroes and firing their dwellings; others only sacking a house, and others still, wreaking their vengeance on station-houses, while scores, the moment they got loaded down with plunder, hastened away to conceal it—all showed that the original cause of the uprising had been forgotten. A strong uncertainty seemed at times to keep them swaying backwards and forwards, as though seeking a definite object, or waiting for an appointed signal to move, and then at some shout would rush for a building, a negro, or station-house. The mob was a huge monster—frightful both in proportions and appearance, yet not knowing where or how to use its strength. The attack on Mr. Gibbon's house at Twenty-ninth Street and Eighth Avenue, during this afternoon, was attributed to the fact that he was Mr. Greeley's cousin, and that the former sometimes slept there—rather a far-fetched inference, as though a mob would be aware of a fact that probably not a dozen immediate neighbors knew.

Some one person might have raised a cry of "Greeley's house," which would have been sufficient to insure its destruction. The police being notified of this attack, sent a squad of men with a military force to disperse the mob. Captain Ryer formed his troops in front of the house, and Sergeant Devoursney did the same with a part of his men, while the other portion was sent into the building, that was filled with men, women, and children, loading them-

selves down with the spoils. The appearance of the
caps and clubs in the rooms created a consternation
that would have been ludicrous, but for the serious
work that followed. No defence was made, except by
a few persons singly. One fellow advanced to the
door with a pistol in his hand, and fired, sending a ball
through Officer Hill's thigh. The next instant the latter
felled him to the floor with his club, and before he
could even attempt to rise he was riddled with balls.
Some of the women fell on their knees, and shrieked
for mercy; while one strong Irish woman refused to
yield her plunder, and fought like a tigress. She seized
an officer by the throat, and trying to strangle and bite
him, would not let go till a blow sobered her into
submission.

Some were loaded with shawls and dresses, and one
burly, ferocious-looking Irishman carried under his
arm a huge bundle of select music. As the police
chased the plunderers down-stairs, and out into the
street, in some unaccountable way the troops got so confused that they fired a volley that swept the police as
well as the rioters. Officer Dipple was so severely
wounded that he died the following Sunday, while
Officers Hodson and Robinson both received flesh
wounds.

In the upper part of the city, few buildings, except
those too near police and army head-quarters, or too
well defended, offered much spoil except private
houses, and these had been the chief objects of attack.
But Brooks and Brothers' clothing store in Catharine
Street, situated in a part of the city thickly pop-
ulated with the very class mobs are made of, became toward evening an object of great attraction

to groups of hard-looking men and women. As night settled down, the heavens being overcast, it became very dark; for in all the neighboring houses the lights were extinguished by the inmates, who were terribly alarmed at the rapidly increasing crowd in the street. To deepen and complete the gloom the rioters turned off the gas. Officer Bryan, of the Fourth Ward, telegraphed to head-quarters the threatening appearance of things, and a force of fifty or sixty men were at once despatched to the spot. In the mean time Sergeant Finney, with Platt and Kennedy, stood at the entrance to defend the building till the police could arrive.

For awhile the three determined police officers, standing silent in the darkness, overawed the leaders. But soon from the crowd arose shouts, amid which were heard the shrill voices of women, crying, "Break open the store." This was full of choice goods, and contained clothing enough to keep the mob supplied for years. As the shouts increased, those behind began to push forward those in front, till the vast multitude swung heavily towards the three police officers. Seeing this movement, the latter advanced with their clubs to keep them back. At this, the shouts and yells redoubled, and the crowd rushed forward, crushing down the officers by mere weight. They fought gallantly for a few minutes; but, overborne by numbers, they soon became nearly helpless, and were terribly beaten and wounded, and with the utmost exertions were barely able to escape, and make their way back to the station. The mob now had it all its own way, and rushing against the doors, burst bolts and bars asunder, and streamed in. But it was dark as midnight

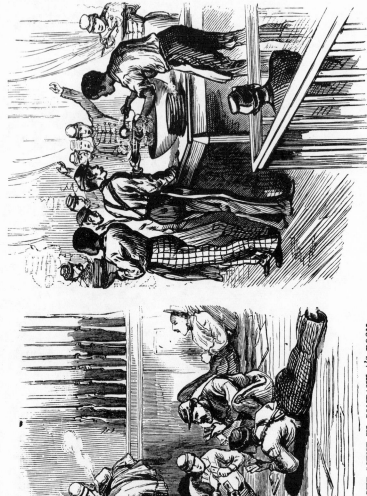

NEW YORK—A NIGHT SCENE IN COMPANY A's ROOM.

NEW YORK—SERVING CHOWDER TO THE SOLDIERS.

inside, and they could not distinguish one thing from
another; not even the passage-ways to the upper rooms
of the building, which was five stories high.   They
therefore lighted the gas, and broke out the windows.
In a few minutes the vast edifice was a blaze of light,
looking more brilliant from the midnight blackness
that surrounded it.   The upturned faces of the excited,
squalid throng below presented a wild and savage spectacle in the flickering. light.   Men and women kept
pouring in and out, the latter loaded with booty, making their way home into the adjacent streets, and the
former rushing after their portion of the spoils.   Coats
and pantaloons, and clothing of every description, were
rapidly borne away; and it was evident, give them
time enough, the crowd would all disappear, and there
would be scarcely enough left to finish the work of destruction.   Thinking only of the rich prize they had
gained, they seemed to forget that retribution was possible, when suddenly the cry of "Police! police!"
sent a thrill of terror through them.   Sergeant De-
laney, at the head of his command, marched swiftly
down the street, until close upon the mob, when the
order, "Double-quick," was given, and they burst with
a run upon them.   For a moment, the solid mass, by mere
weight, bore up against the shock; but the clubs soon
made a lane through it broad as the street.   Just then
a pistol-shot rung from a house, almost over their heads.
Many of the rioters were armed with muskets, and
the comparatively small police force, seeing that fire-
arms were to be used, now drew their revolvers, and
poured a deadly volley right into their midst.   Several
fell at the first discharge; and immediately terror
seized that portion of the multitude nearest the police,

10

especially the women, and many fell on their knees, crying for mercy. Others forced their way recklessly over their companions, to get out of reach. As the police made their way to the front of the store, they formed line, while Sergeant Matthew, of the First Precinct, with his men, entered the building. The scene here became more frightful than the one without. The rioters on the first floor made but little resistance, and, thinking only of escape, leaped from the windows, and rushed out of doors like mad creatures. But as they attempted to flee, those without knocked them over with their clubs. Having cleared this story, the police mounted to the second, where the rioters, being more closely penned, showed fight. Pistol-shots rang out, and some of the police officers had narrow escapes. One powerful bully fought like a tiger, till two policemen fell upon him with their clubs, and soon left him stark and stiff. At last they drove the whole crowd into a rear building, and kept them there till they had time to secure them.

Just as the store was cleared, Sergeant Carpenter, who had been sent as a reinforcement in case of need, came up with a hundred and fifty men, and charging on the crowd, sent them flying down the narrow streets. After quiet had been restored, a military force arrived and took possession of the building.

Just previous to this, another attempt was made to burn the *Tribune* building, but was easily repelled. The *Times* office, near by, warned by the fate of its neighbor the night before, had established a regular garrison inside, while it brilliantly illuminated the open space all around it, in the circle of which the rioters did not care to come.

The invaluable service of the telegraph was tested to-day, not merely in enabling General Brown and the commissioners to despatch men quickly to a threatened point, but to keep a force moving from one ward to another, as messages came in, announcing the incipient gathering in different districts. Word sent to the station in the neighborhood where they were acting, would instantly change their route ; and knots of men, which if left alone would soon have swelled into formidable mobs, were broken up, for they found military and police force marching down on them before they could form a plan of action. Nor was this all. A force sent to a certain point, after dispersing the mob, would be directed to make a tour through the disaffected districts—all the time keeping up its communication with head-quarters, so that if any serious demonstration was made in that section of the city, it could be ordered there at once, thus saving half the time it would take to march from head-quarters. Thus, for instance, Captain Petty was ordered this morning to head-quarters from the City Hall, where he had passed the night, and directed to take two hundred men (including his own precinct force), and go to the protection of a soap factory in Sixteenth Street, Eighth and Ninth Avenues. He moved off his command, marching rapidly up Broadway and down Sixteenth Street. The mob saw it coming two blocks off, and immediately scattered in every direction, which awakened the supreme contempt of the captain. He now marched backward and forward, and through the cross streets, up as far as Nineteenth Street, scattering every fragment of the mob that attempted to hold together, and finally returned to head-quarters. This

was a long march, but the men had scarcely rested,
when the captain was hurried off to aid in the protection at the wire factory in Second Avenue. In the
fierce fight that followed, he, with ten men at his back,
charged up the broad stairway, fighting his way step
by step to the fifth story. Caught up here at the top
of the building, the rioters were clubbed without
mercy. Some, to escape the terrible punishment,
plunged down the hatchway; others attempted to dash
past the men, and escape down the stairs. At one
time eight bodies lay in the door-way, blocking it up.
He then marched back to head-quarters. He had
been marching and fighting all day. Similar exhausting duties were performed by other commands, both
police and military. Inspector Dilks, with his force
gathered from various precincts, passed the entire day
in marching and fighting. The men, weary and hungry, would reach head-quarters or certain points, hoping to get a little rest and refreshment, when the
hurried order would come to repair to a point a mile
off, where the mob was firing and sacking houses, and
off they would start on the double-quick. Uncom-
plaining and fearless of danger, and never counting
numbers, both police and soldiers were everywhere
all this day, and proved themselves as reliable, gallant,
and noble a set of men as ever formed or acted as the
police force of any city in the world.

In the meantime, Governor Seymour and the Mayor
of the city were not idle. The latter at the City Hall,
fearing an attack, asked Acton for a guard of protection, and fifty men were sent him. Report of the mob
assembled there, reached Governor Seymour, at the
St. Nicholas, and he immediately hastened thither, and

addressed the crowd from the steps, which allayed excitement for the time.   This speech was variously commented upon.   Some of the criticisms were frivolous, and revealed the partisan, rather than the honest man. If the Governor had not previously issued a proclamation to the whole city, in which he declared without reservation that the mobs should be put down at all hazards —if this speech had been his only utterance, then the bitter denunciations against him would have been deserved.   It would have been pusillanimous, cowardly, and unworthy the Governor of the State.   But he spoke in his official capacity, not only firmly, emphatically, and in no ambiguous terms, but he had hurried up the military, and used every means in his power to accumulate and concentrate the forces under his control to put down the riot.   No faint-heartedness or sentimental qualmishness marked any of his official acts. Prompt, energetic, and determined, he placed no conditions on his subordinates in the manner of putting down the mob, and restoring the supremacy of the law. But here in this address he was speaking to men who, as a body at least, had as yet committed no overt act ; and many doubtless were assembled expecting some public declaration from the City Hall.   He was not addressing the plunderers and rioters that were firing houses and killing negroes, but a mixed assembly, the excitement of which he thought best to allay, if possible.   Some said he began his address with " My friends ; " others, " Fellow-citizens."   Whether he did one, or the other, or neither, is of no consequence and meant nothing.   To have commenced, " Ye villains and cut-throats, disperse at once, or I'll mow you down with grape-shot !" might have sounded very brave, but if that was all he was going to say, he had better kept his room.

A *proclamation* like this address would have been infamous. Here is where the mistake was made in the criticisms heaped upon it. His official acts were all such as became the Chief Magistrate of New York. The speech, therefore, must be judged rather by the rules of taste and propriety, than by those which apply to him officially. If a man's official acts are all right, it is unjust to let them go for nothing, and bring into prominence a short address made without premeditation in the front of an excited, promiscuous assembly, moved by different motives. That it was open to criticism in some respects, is true. It should have been imbued more with the spirit of determination to maintain order and suppress violence, and less been said of the measures that had or would be taken to test the constitutionality of the draft, and of his purpose, if it were decided in the courts to be wrong, to oppose it. Such talk had better be deferred till after order is restored. When men begin to burn and plunder dwellings, attack station-houses, hang negroes, and shoot down policemen, it is too late to attempt to restore peace by talking about the constitutionality of laws. The upholding of laws about the constitutionality of which there is no doubt, is the only thing deserving of consideration. The Common Council of the city exhibited in this respect a most pusillanimous spirit, by offering resolutions to have the constitutionality of the law tested, when the entire constitution and laws of the State were being subverted! Unquestionably, some charity should be extended to men who are pleading for those whose votes elevated them to office. Brutuses are rare nowadays ; and politicians do not like to shoot down their own voters—they would much rather make more voters out of men no more fit to exercise the right of suffrage than horses and mules.

Governed by a similar spirit, Archbishop Hughes, although he had yielded to the pressure made on him and issued an address to the Irish, calling on them to abstain from violence, yet accompanied it with a letter to Horace Greeley, directly calculated to awaken or intensify, rather than allay their passions. He more than intimated that they had been abused and oppressed, and thought it high time the war was ended. The proclamation was short, but the letter was a long one, full of a vindictive spirit, and showing unmistakably with whom his sympathies were.

Towards evening a mob assembled over in Ninth Avenue, and went to work with some system and forethought. Instead of wandering round, firing and plundering as the whim seized them, they began to throw up barricades, behind which they could rally when the military and police came to attack them. Indeed, the same thing had been done on the east side of the city ; while railroads had been torn up, and stages stopped, to keep them from carrying policemen rapidly from one quarter to another. During the day, Colonel Frothingham had stood in Third Avenue, and stopped and emptied every car as it approached, and filled it with soldiers, to be carried to the upper part of the city. Acton, too, had sent round to collect all the stages still running in Broadway and the Bowery, and in a short time they came rumbling into Mulberry Street, forming a long line in front of head-quarters. A telegram from Second Avenue demanded immediate help, and the police were bundled into them and hurried off. One driver refused to stir, saying, roughly, he was not hired to carry policemen. Acton had no time to argue the case, and quickly turning to a policeman, he said: "Put that man in cell Number 92." In a twinkling he was jerked from his seat and hurried away. Turning to another policeman, he said: "Mount that box and drive." The next moment the stage, with a long string of others, loaded inside and out with the bluecoats, was whirling through the streets. He had done the same with the Sixth Avenue cars. The son-in-law of George Law remonstrated, saying that it would provoke the mob to tear down the railroad buildings. There was no time to stand on ceremony; the cars were seized, and the company, to save their property, paid a large sum to the ringleaders of the rioters. In fact, a great many factories and buildings were bought off in the same way; so that the leaders drove quite a thriving business.

But, as before remarked, the commencement of barricades to obstruct the movements of the police and military, after the Parisian fashion, was a serious thing, and must be nipped in the bud; and Captain Walling, of the Twentieth Precinct, who had been busy in this part of the city all the afternoon in dispersing the mob, sent to head-quarters for a military force to help remove them. He also sent to General Sandford, at the arsenal, for a company of soldiers, which was promised, but never sent. At six o'clock a force of regulars arrived from General Brown, and repaired to the Precinct station-house. Captain Slott, of the Twentieth Precinct, took command of the police force detailed to coöperate with the troops, but delayed action till the

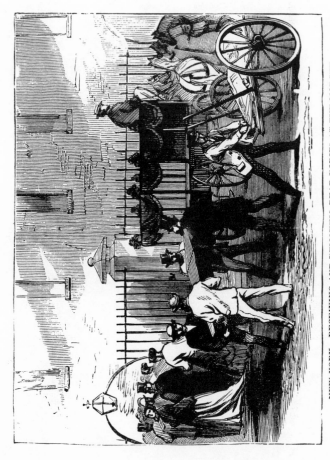

NEW YORK—RECEIVING AND REMOVING DEAD BODIES AT THE MORGUE.

arrival of the company promised from the arsenal. Meanwhile, the rioters kept strengthening the barricades between Thirty-seventh and Forty-third Streets, in Eighth Avenue, by lashing carts, wagons, and telegraph poles together with wire·stripped from the latter. The cross streets were also barricaded. Time passed on, and yet the bayonets of the expected reinforcement from the arsenal did not appear. The two commanding officers now began to grow anxious ; it would not do to defer the attack till after dark, for such work as was before them required daylight. At length, as the sun stooped to the western horizon, it was resolved to wait no longer, and the order to move forward was given. As they approached the first barricade, by Thirty-seventh Street, a volley was poured into them from behind it, followed by stones and brick-bats.

The police now fell back to the left, and the regulars advancing, returned the fire. The rioters, however, stood their ground, and for a time nothing was heard but the rapid roll of musketry. But the steady, well-directed fire of the troops, at length began to tell on the mob, and they at last broke, and fled to the next barricade. The police then advanced, and tore down the barricade, when the whole force moved on to the next. Here the fight was renewed, but the close and rapid volley of the troops soon scattered the wretches, when this also was removed. They kept on in this way, till the last barricade was abandoned, when the uncovered crowd broke and fled in wild disorder. The soldiers pressed after, breaking up into squads, and chasing and firing into the disjointed fragments as they drifted down the various streets.

10*

There was more or less disturbance in this section, however, till midnight. At nine o'clock, an attack was made on a gun and hardware store, in Thirty-seventh Street, between Eighth and Ninth Avenues, but Sergeant Petty was sent thither with a small force, and scattered them at the first charge. At midnight, an attempt was made to destroy the colored church in Thirtieth Street, between Seventh and Eighth Avenues; but before the rioters had accomplished their work, Captain Walling, with his entire force and the regulars, came up, and though met with a volley, fell on them in such a headlong charge, that they scattered down the street.

All this time the arsenal presented the appearance of a regular camp; videttes were kept out, sentries established, howitzers commanded the streets, and everything wore the look of a besieged fortress.

Sandford, whom Wool wished to take command of all the troops, evidently thought that he had as much as he could do to hold that building, without doing anything to quell the riot in the city.

One of the first companies that came up from the forts the day before, and hence belonged to General Brown's force, got, no one could hardly tell how, into the arsenal, and were there cooped up as useless as though in garrison—for if seven hundred men with cannon sweeping every approach could not hold it, seven thousand could not. General Brown and Acton needed this company badly, but how to get it was the question. Governor Seymour held no direct communication with the Police Commissioners; for they were not on friendly terms, as they were holding their places in defiance of him, he having removed them some time before. Mr. Hawley, the chief clerk, who knew the Governor personally, acted, therefore, as the channel of communication between them. He now went to him, and asked him how things were at the arsenal. He replied, he did not know—no report had been sent him. Hawley then asked him to send an officer and ascertain, and get back the company belonging to General Brown's command. He replied he had no one to send. Hawley then offered to go himself, if he would give an order to this company of United States troops to report at once to General Brown at police head-quarters. He did so, and Hawley, reaching the arsenal in safety, gave the order to the adjutant-general, before calling on Sandford, so as to be sure it was obeyed.

On the northern limits of the city, serious disturbances had occurred during the day, especially in Yorkville, to which Acton was compelled to send a strong force. The mob also attempted to burn Harlem bridge, but the heavy rain of the night before had made it so wet that it would not ignite. Down town, likewise, mobs had assembled before the Western Hotel and other places, but were dispersed before they had inflicted any damage. Almost the last act in the evening was an attack on the house of Mr. Sinclair, one of the owners of the *Tribune*.

But rioters must eat and sleep like other people, and though knots of them could be seen in various parts of the city, the main portion seemed to have retired soon after midnight.

In the police head-quarters, men were lying around on the floor in the warm July night, snatching, as best they could, a little repose. General Brown and staff, in their chairs or stretched on a settee, nodded in this lull of the storm, though ready at a moment's notice to do their duty. But there was no rest for Acton. He had not closed his eyes for nearly forty hours, and he was not to close them for more than forty to come.

With his nerves strung to their utmost tension, and resolved to put down that mob though the streets ran blood, he gave his whole soul to the work before him. He infused his determined, fearless spirit into every one who approached him. Anonymous letters, telling him he had not another day to live, he flung aside with a scornful smile, to attend to the telegraph dispatches from the different precincts.

Troops and men were stationed at various points, and gunboats were patrolling the rivers, and he must be on the alert every moment. The fate of a great city lay on his heart, and he could not sleep.

# CHAPTER XVII.

## DRAFT RIOT—THIRD DAY.

Scenes in the City and at Head-quarters.—Fight in Eighth Avenue.—Cannon sweep the Streets.—Narrow Escape of Captain Howell and Colonel Mott.—Battle for Jackson's Foundry.—Howitzers clear the Street.—State of Things shown by Telegraph Despatches.—General Sandford sends out a Force against a Mob, at Corner of Twenty-ninth Street and Seventh Avenue.—Colonel Gardin's Fight with the Mob.—Is Wounded.—Mob Victorious.—Dead and Wounded Soldiers left in the Street.—Captain Putnam sent to bring them away.—Disperses the Mob.—Terrific Night.

TUESDAY had been a day of constant success to the police and military, and many thought that the rioters were thoroughly disheartened, and but little more hard fighting would be done. There had been two days of exhausting work, and both parties were well tired out. The commissioners, certainly, could not stand this terrible strain much longer. Forty-eight hours without sleep or rest, and all the time under the intensest mental strain, was telling on even the wiry Acton, though he would confess to no fatigue.

To one who could take in all that was passing in New York on this morning, the city would have presented a strange appearance.

The magnitude and demonstrations of the mob had aroused great fear for the Navy Yard and the naval property of the Government, and the marine company that had been on duty with the police was recalled by

Admiral Paulding for their protection; and this morning six war-vessels, carrying in all over ninety guns, shotted and trained, could be seen drawn up, so as to command every avenue to the yard, while the iron-clad battery *Passaic* and a gun-boat lay off the Battery to protect Fort Columbus during the absence of its garrison. Marines armed to the teeth, and howitzers, guarded all the entrances to the Navy Yard. Broadway was almost deserted—no stages were running, street-cars had disappeared—only here and there shutters were taken down from the stores, and it looked like Sabbath day in the city. But at police headquarters all was activity. The African church nearly opposite was filled with soldiers stretched on the seats and floor of the building. Another house, a few doors from the police building, was also crowded with soldiers. The owner of this empty house, having sent a flat refusal to Acton's request for the use of it, the latter quietly told the policemen to stave in the door. It took but a few minutes to send it from its hinges; and now the troops were quartered in it also; for all those in the service of the United States, under General Brown, had their head-quarters here.

In the basement of the police building was the telegraph, with the wires running like nerves to every part of the city, over which inquiries and answers were continually passing. Rooms all around were filled with rations obtained from a neighboring grocery and meat-market, taken with or without leave. On the main floor, on one side, in their office sat the weary commissioners; on the other, were Inspectors Carpenter, Dilks, and Leonard, fit, each one to be a general, while scattered around were police captains, detectives, and

patrolmen. On the second story were the clerks, copy-
ists, etc.; while the top floor was crowded with colored
refugees, who had fled thither for protection. Some
were standing and conversing, others sitting in groups
on boxes, or walking from room to room; many of
these sad and serious, as they thought of missing relatives and friends, while the colored man placed over
them, with his shirt sleeves rolled up, was, with his
assistants, dealing out provisions.

But soon it was announced that a vast crowd, numbering some five thousand, was assembled near Eighth
Avenue and Thirty-second Street, sacking houses and
hanging negroes. General Dodge and Colonel Mott,
with Captain Howell, commanding Eighth Regiment
Artillery, were at once despatched thither. As they
marched up the avenue, they saw three negroes hanging dead, while the crowd around filled the air with
fiendish shouts. As the firm, compact head of the
column moved forward, the mob fell back, but did
not scatter. Colonel Mott dashed forward on horseback and cut down one of the negroes with his sword.
This seemed to be the signal for the mob to commence
the attack, and the next moment they rushed forward
on the soldiers with stones, brick-bats, and slung-shots.
Colonel Mott then told Captain Howell to bring two
pieces into battery on the corner of Thirty-second
Street and Seventh Avenue, so as to sweep the streets;
but he could not get through the dense crowd to do so.
The infantry and cavalry were then ordered up and
told to clear the way. The former, with level bayonets,
and the latter with drawn sabres, charged on the mass,
which parted and fell back some distance, and then
halted. Captain Howell then advanced alone, and

ordered the rioters to disperse, or he should fire on them. To this they replied in sullen silence. The apparent unwillingness of the captain to fire emboldened them to believe that he would not fire at all. Although they refused to disperse, the officers, as long as they made no assault, declined to give the word to fire. This delay encouraged the rioters still more; and either believing the guns, whose muzzles pointed so threateningly on them, were loaded with blank cartridges, or grown desperate and reckless with rage, they suddenly, as though moved by a common impulse, rushed forward and rained stones and missiles of every kind on the soldiers. Seeing that their object was to seize the guns and turn them on the troops, the word to fire was given. The next moment a puff of smoke rolled out, followed with a report that shook the buildings. As the murderous shot tore through the crowded mass, they stopped, and swayed heavily back for a moment, when the pieces were quickly reloaded, and again sent their deadly contents into their midst, strewing the pavements with the dead and dying. Those, however, in the rear, being protected by the mass in front, refused to give way, and it was not till five or six rounds had been fired that they finally broke and fled down the side streets. The military then broke into columns and marched up and down the streets, scattering everything before them, and arresting many of the rioters.

Having finished their work, they returned to headquarters. As they left the district, the mob, or a portion of it, gathered together again, and strung up afresh the lifeless bodies of the negroes.

A few hours later, Captain Brower, with a police

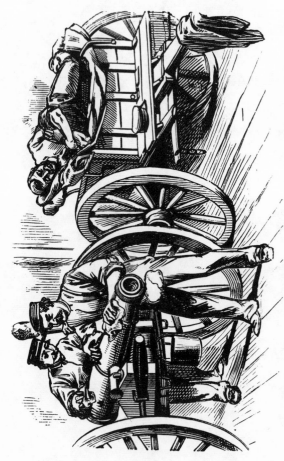

NEW YORK CITY—BATTERY B, N. G. S N. Y., EQUIPPING FOR A MOVE.

force, was sent thither, to take down and remove the bodies of any negroes that might be still hanging. He did so without molestation.

Captain Howell's murderous fire on the mob came very near causing his death two days after. Having the curiosity to witness the scene of his struggle with the mob, he took his carriage, and drove over to it. A gang of seven or eight ruffians, seeing his uniform, cried out, " There's the man who fired on us here—let us hang him." Their shouts called others to the spot, and almost before the captain was aware of his danger, some fifty men were assembled, and at once made a dash at the driver, and ordered him to stop. Captain Howell, quickly drawing his revolver, pointed it at the driver, and ordered him to turn down Thirty-first Street, and give his horses the whip, or he would shoot him on the spot. The man obeying, lashed his horses into a run. At this moment the crowd was all around the carriage, and one man was climbing up behind, when he fell and was run over. A shower of stones and brick-bats followed, breaking in the panels of the carriage, and narrowly missing the captain's head.

One stone struck an old wound in his side, and for a moment paralyzed his arm. The crowd with yells and shouts followed after, when he turned and emptied his revolver at them through the back window, which brought them to a halt. Colonel Mott had a similar escape the day before. Passing down one of the avenues in a carriage, he was recognized by some of the rioters, who immediately assailed him with stones, and fired at him. One of the bullets passed through the cushion on which he was sitting.

Soon after this affair in Seventh Avenue, word was

telegraphed that Jackson's foundry, corner of Twenty-eighth Street, First and Second Avenues, was threatened. A military force was despatched forthwith to it, piloted by four policemen. At Twenty-first Street and First Avenue, they were fired on by the mob. The attack was continued through the street to Second Avenue, and up this to Twenty-fifth Street, without any notice being taken of it by the troops. Made reckless by this forbearance, the rioters began to close up in more dangerous proximity, when the howitzer was unlimbered and pointed down the avenue. The mob not liking the looks of this, scattered, when the column resumed its march. The mob then rallied, and followed after, with shouts and distant shots, till the foundry on Twenty-eighth Street was reached. Here another mob came up from First Avenue, and the two made a simultaneous attack. The command was then given to fire, and a volley was poured into the crowd. Rapidly loading and firing, the troops soon stretched so many on the pavement, that the rest broke and fled. The military then entered the building and held it. The mob gathered around it, threatening to storm it, but could not pluck up courage to make the attempt. They seemed especially exasperated against the policemen, and had the effrontery to send a committee to the officer in command, demanding their surrender. If their request was refused, they declared they would storm the building at all hazards; but if complied with, they would disperse. The committee had to shout out their demands from the street. In reply, the officer told them if they did not take themselves off instantly, he would fire upon them; upon which they incontinently took to their heels.

As the day wore on, things began to wear a still more threatening aspect. Despatches came in from every quarter, announcing the activity of the mob. To a question sent to the Thirteenth Precinct, a little past twelve, inquiring how things were going on in Grand Street, was returned the following reply: " Lively; store-keepers have fired into the mob; no force there yet."

" 12.20. From Twenty-first. Building corner Thirty-third Street, Second Avenue, is set on fire by the mob."

" 12.50. From Fifteenth. Send assistance to Twenty-first Precinct; they are about attacking it."

" 12.55. From Twenty-sixth. It is reported that Government stores in Greenwich, near Liberty, are on fire; fired by mob."

" 1.10. From Twenty-seventh. Send more men nere forthwith."

" 1.25. From Fourth. Fire corner of Catharine Street and East Broadway."

" 1.45. A man just in from Eleventh Precinct, reports a number of bands of robbers, numbering from fifty to one hundred each, breaking into stores in Houston, near Attorney Street."

" 1.47 P.M. From Twenty-ninth. The mob have cleared Twenty-first Precinct station-house."

" 2 P.M. From Twenty-ninth. A large mob surrounded Captain Green's house, Twenty-eighth Street, Third Avenue. He escaped out of the back window; they threatened to hang him."

" 3.10 P.M. To Eleventh. Send to foot of Fourteenth Street, East River, and if military is there, send word here forthwith."

" 3.15. From Twenty-fourth. Mob are firing the

building on Second Avenue, near Twenty-eighth Street. Immediate assistance is required. Houses occupied by negroes, who are fleeing for their lives.

3.25. From Twentieth. The mob are sacking houses at Twenty-seventh Street and Seventh Avenue. We have no force to send.

3.30. From Twenty-first. There is an attack on the colored people in Second Avenue, between Twenty-eighth and Twenty-ninth Streets.

3.40. From Eleventh. Send to 242 Stanton Street, and take possession of cavalry swords forthwith.

There were five thousand cavalry swords there, and the mob were assembling to capture them; and the telegram announcing the fact, and the one ordering a force to seize them, were received and answered the same minute.

3.55. To Twenty-first. How do things look?

*Ans.* Very bad; large crowd in Thirty-fifth Street, near Third Avenue, and no assistance from adjoining precinct.

4 o'clock. To Twenty-first. What is going on?

*Ans.* The mob have captured some five or six negroes, and are preparing to hang them; be quick with reinforcements.

4.43. From Twentieth. News have just come in that the mob are about to attack the Twenty-second Precinct station-house.

5.15. From Sixteenth. Send us one hundred special shields and clubs; the citizens are arming up well.

5.15. From Twenty-ninth. Who feeds the special men?

*Ans.* You must, far as able.

*Reply.* No money.

*Ans.* It makes no difference; they must be fed; we are responsible.

5.20. From Twenty-ninth. The rioters are now on Seventh Avenue and Twenty-eighth Street. They have just killed a negro; say they are going to cut off the Croton; they have pickaxes and crowbars; and also say they will cut off the gas; so reported by one of our men, who has been in the crowd; they were about to fire corner of Twenty-eighth Street and Seventh Avenue, when he came away.

To have cut off the water and extinguished the gas, would have been master-strokes; but the military arrived in time to prevent it.

5.25. From First. Riot at Pier 4, North River; they have killed negroes there.

Thus, at the same moment, from the two extreme ends of the city, came the news of riots and calls for help. From points five miles apart, the wires would bring simultaneously tidings that showed the mob omnipresent.

In the midst of all these incessant exhausting labors, the following telegram came from the Twentieth Precinct:

"General Sandford says he has so many negroes at the arsenal, that he must get rid of them."

Acton's answer was characteristic. He had no time for formalities or courteous exchange of views. In an instant there flashed back over the wires the curt reply:

"Tell General Sandford he must do the best he can with them there."

General Sandford had at this time about the same number of men under his command at the arsenal that General Brown had at police head-quarters; yet the former, up to this morning, had not sent out a single company to assist the police to arrest the devastations of the mob. He apparently did not know what was going on, had hardly kept up any communication with the Police Commissioners or Governor Seymour, but now begs the former to relieve him of some colored refugees, as if the overworked commissioners had not enough on their hands already. This request is especially noteworthy, when taken in connection with his after report, in which he states that on this morning the riot was substantially over; so much so, at least, that the police could do all that was necessary without the aid of the military. It would seem that if he really thought that the rest of the work should be left to them, he might have sent off some of his troops, and made room for the negroes in the arsenal.

At about two o'clock in the afternoon word was received that a large number of muskets were secreted in a store on Broadway, near Thirty-third Street; and Colonel Meyer was ordered to proceed thither, with thirty-three soldiers belonging to Hawkins' Zouaves, and take possession of them. Reaching the place, he found a large mob gathered, which was momentarily increasing. He, however, succeeded in entering the building, and brought out the arms. An Irishman happening to pass by in his cart, the colonel seized it, and pitching in the guns, closed around it, and moved off.

Citizens offering their services were coming in all day, and a company was formed and placed under the command of Charles A. Lamont, and did good service. Others also were enrolled and placed on duty.

Colonel Sherwood's battery of rifled cannon arrived

in the afternoon, and was put in position in front of
the arsenal, where the firing of pickets all day would
indicate that an attack was momentarily expected.
This did not look as if General Sandford thought the
riot substantially over.

At about five o'clock, it was ordered by Sandford, with
an infantry force of one hundred and fifty, to corner of
Twenty-seventh Street and Seventh Avenue, to quell a
mob assembled in large numbers at that point, and
which were gutting, and plundering, and firing houses.
As they approached, they saw flames bursting from windows, while, to complete the terror of the scene, the
body of a negro hung suspended from a lamp-post, his
last struggle just ended. At the same time that the
military arrived, firemen, who had come to put out the
fire, reached the spot in another direction. One portion
of the mob immediately took shelter behind the latter,
so that the troops dared not fire and clear the streets,
while another ran up to the house-tops, armed with guns
and pistols, for the purpose of firing into the ranks
below. The colonel told his men to keep a sharp look-
out, and at the first shot fire. Scores of guns were immediately pointed towards the roofs of the houses. In
the meantime, from some cause not fully explained,
the imposing force, after this demonstration, marched
away, leaving the mob in full possession of the field.
It had hardly reached the protection of the arsenal
again, when the plundering and violence recommenced;
and in a short time two more negroes were amusing
the spectators with their death throes, as they hung by
the neck from lamp-posts. This was the second expedition sent out by Sandford, the commander-in-chief of
the military, during the riot.

Towards evening word was brought to the Seventh Regiment armory that the mob had gathered in great force in First Avenue, between Eighteenth and Nineteenth Streets.

Colonel Winston, in command, immediately ordered out a force, composed in part of the military, and in part of enrolled citizens, and with a battery of two howitzers, under command of Colonel Jardine, of Hawkins' Zouaves, marched rapidly to the scene of disturbance. Passing down Nineteenth Street to the avenue, it halted, and unlimbering the pieces, trained them so as to command the avenue, while the infantry formed in line to support them. As soon as the rioters saw the guns bearing on them, they dodged into basements, and mounted to the windows and roofs of the tenement buildings that abounded in that vicinity. A number of them armed with muskets and pistols, and the rest with stones and brick-bats, began a fierce and determined attack on the troops. The howitzers, loaded with grape and canister, at once swept the street. After the first discharge, but few ventured to show themselves in the avenue, until after they heard the report, when they would dodge from behind corners and fire back. But from the tops of the houses an incessant fusillade was kept up. The soldiers endeavored to pick them off, but the rioters presented a small mark compared to that which the troops, massed in the open streets, furnished; and it was soon apparent that the fight was unequal. If they had only had a police force to enter the buildings, and hunt the men from the roofs, the fight would soon have been over. But the commander, thinking he could not spare a sufficient number to do this work, or

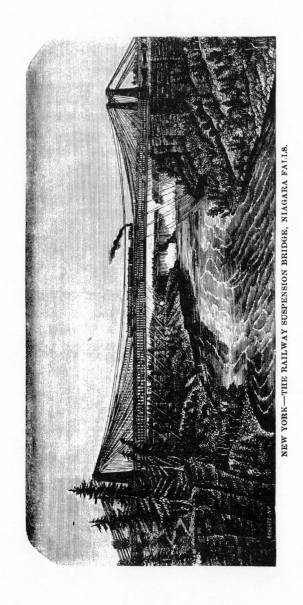

NEW YORK—THE RAILWAY SUSPENSION BRIDGE, NIAGARA FALLS.

that the soldiers, cumbered with their muskets, which, after the first discharge, would have to be clubbed, could make no headway in such a hand-to-hand fight, made no effort to dislodge the wretches, who loaded and fired with the most imperturbable coolness. One man was seen to step round the corner, after the discharge of the battery, and resting his gun on the shoulder of a fellow-rioter, take as deliberate aim at Colonel Jardine as he would at a squirrel on the limb of a tree, and fire. The ball struck the colonel in the thigh, and brought him to the pavement. Other officers shared his fate, while at every discharge, men would drop in the ranks. The howitzers rattled their shot on the deserted pavements and walls of the houses, but did no damage to the only portion of the enemy they had to fear, while the fight between the infantry and the rioters was like that between soldiers in the open field and Indians in ambush. Colonel Winston soon saw that it was madness to keep his men there, to be picked off in detail, and ordered a retreat. At the first sign of a retrograde movement, a cry rang along the avenue; and from the side streets, and basements, and houses, the mob swarmed forth so furiously, that it assumed huge proportions at once, and chased the retiring soldiers with yells and taunts, and pressed them so hotly that they could not bring off all their killed and wounded. Among those left behind was Colonel Jardine. He took refuge in a basement, where the mob found him, and would have killed him on the spot, had not one of them recognized him as an old acquaintance, and for some reason or other protected him from further violence; and he was eventually carried to the house of a surgeon near by.

11

The mob were left masters of the field, and soon began their depredations. The state of things was at length reported to police head-quarters, and General Brown sent off Captain Putman, with Captain Shelby and a hundred and fifty regulars and two field-pieces, to disperse the mob and bring away the dead and wounded of Winston's force that might remain. They reached the spot between ten and eleven o'clock at night. The dimly lighted streets were black with men, while many, apprised of the approach of the military, mounted again to the roofs as before. Putnam immediately charged on the crowd in the street, scattering them like a whirlwind. He then turned his guns on the buildings, and opened such a deadly fire on them that they were soon cleared. Having restored order, he halted his command, and remained on the ground till half-past twelve.

At the same time a mob was pulling down the negro houses in York Street, which they soon left a heap of ruins. Houses plundered or set on fire in various parts of the city, combined with the ringing of fire-bells, thunder of cannon, and marching of troops, made this night like its predecessor—one of horror.

There was also a disturbance in Brooklyn. Shaw's and Fancher's elevators, and Wheeler's store on the docks, were set on fire, and a force ordered to put them out.

The illumination of the windows from the *Times* building this evening shed a brilliant glow over Printing-house Square, and flooded the Park to the City Hall with light, while an armed force within was ready to fire on any mob that should dare expose itself in the circle of its influence.

At 12.15 the following telegram was sent:

"To all stations.   How are things in your precinct?"

*Answer.*   "All quiet."

Thus the third night of this terrible riot passed away still unsubdued, and still Acton sat at his post, awake, while others slept, and kept feeling through the telegraph wires the pulse of the huge, fevered city.   The regiments coming back from Pennsylvania might arrive at any time, and he was anxious to know the moment they reached the New York docks.   The Seventh Regiment, especially, he knew was expected to reach the city that night by special train.   Policemen were therefore kept on the watch; but the regiment did not arrive till after daylight.   About half-past four in the morning, the steady ranks were seen marching along Canal Street towards Broadway, and soon drew up in front of St. Nicholas Hotel.

# CHAPTER XVIII.

## FOURTH DAY.

ONLY the principal disturbances of the third day were given, and of these the accounts were very succinct. The movements of the mobs and the conflicts with them were so similar in character, that a detailed description of them would be a mere repetition of what had gone before. After the police force, and the troops under General Brown had become organized so as to move and act together, each fight with the rioters was almost a repetition of its predecessor. Having adopted a plan of procedure, they seldom deviated from it, and the story of one fight became the story of all—a short struggle and a quick victory.

It was hoped this morning that the rioters would conclude that they could not carry out their mad de-

signs; for the enrolment of large bodies of citizens,
and the announcement of the speedy return of several
regiments, showed that all the force necessary to subdue them was, or soon would be, on hand. The day
before, the Governor had issued a proclamation, declaring the city to be in a state of insurrection; but this
morning appeared a proclamation from Mayor Opdyke,
announcing that the insurrection was practically ended.
It is true he called on the citizens to form voluntary
associations, with competent leaders, to patrol their
separate districts, to protect themselves from roaming gangs of plunderers, and so spare the exhausted
police and military. Yet he called on the citizens to
resume their usual avocations, and directed the railroad
and stage lines to resume their routes. This opinion of
the Mayor was strengthened by the positive announcement that the draft had been suspended, and the passage of an ordinance by the City Council, appropriating
$2,500,000 towards paying $300 exemption money to
the poor who might be drafted. It was plain, if the
draft was the cause of the continued riot, it would now
cease. But in spite of all this, bad news came from
Harlem, and Yorkville, and other sections. In fact, it
was evident that the Police Commissioners did not
share fully in the pleasant anticipations of the Mayor.
Having ascertained that the leaders of the mob, learn-
ing from experience, had organized more intelligently,
and designed to act in several distinct and separate
bodies in different sections, they, with General Brown,
divided the city into four districts, in each one of which
were to be stationed strong bodies of the police and
military, so that they could act with more expedition
and efficiency than if they were sent out from the com-

mon head-quarters in Mulberry Street. It would, beside, save the fatigue of long marches. Those separate
stations were in Harlem, Eighteenth, Twenty-ninth,
and Twenty-sixth Precincts. A good deal was also
expected by an invitation given by Archbishop Hughes,
that appeared in the morning papers, to the Irish to
meet him next day in front of his house, where, though
crippled from rheumatism, he would address them
from the balcony. The Eighth Avenue cars had been
started, as well as those of the Third; and many stores
were opened. Still, on the east side of the city, in the
neighborhood of First Avenue, most of the shops were
closed.

It should be here remarked to the credit of the German population, which were very numerous in certain
localities on this side of the city, that they had no sympathy with the rioters; on the contrary, sent word to
the Police Commissioners not to be concerned about
their locality; they had organized, and would see that
order was maintained there. No better title to American citizenship than this could be shown.

Though early in the morning, it was comparatively
quiet on the east side of the city; yet near First Avenue knots of men could be seen here and there, engaged in loud and angry conversation. They looked
exhausted and haggard, but talked defiant as ever,
swearing terrible vengeance against the military; for,
though hidden from sight, in the miserable tenement-
houses near by, lay their dead, dying, and wounded
friends by scores. Near Nineteenth Street, the scene
of the conflict the evening previous, there were stones,
brick-bats, shivered awning-posts, and other wrecks of
the fight. The grog-shops were open, in which men with

bloody noses, and bruised and battered faces, obtained
the necessary stimulus to continue the desperate struggle.
Dirty, slovenly-dressed women stood in the door-ways
or on the steps, swearing and denouncing both police
and military in the coarsest language. Though the
immense gatherings of the preceding days were not
witnessed, yet there was a ground-swell of passion
that showed the lawless spirit was not subdued, though
overawed. But the Police Commissioners were now
prepared for whatever might occur. The Seventh
Regiment had been stationed on the west side of the
city, with a wide district to keep in order, thus enabling them to concentrate larger forces in other directions. But, although everything wore this favorable
aspect to the authorities, it was evident towards noon,
from the steadily increasing size of the groups observed
in the morning, that they had resolved to try again
their strength with the military. The state of things
was telegraphed to police head-quarters, but the report making the mob not formidable, only a company
of about twenty-five men were sent out. Finding the
rioters numbered about two hundred or more, and not
daring to fire their howitzer, lest, before it could be reloaded, the former would rush forward and seize it, they
concluded to retire. The mob at once set furiously on
them, and forced them to take refuge in Jackson's
foundry. The following telegram to head-quarters
announced the fact:

"1.25. From Twenty-first. The mob has charged
our military, about twenty-five in number, and driven
them into Jackson's foundry, First Avenue and Twenty-eighth Street. The mob are armed, and every time
a regular shows himself they fire. A few good skir-

mishers would pick off these riflemen and relieve the military."

This was soon succeeded by the following:

" 1.54.   From Twenty-first.   Send military assistance immediately to First Avenue and Twenty-eighth Street.   The mob increases, and will murder the military force."

*Ans.*   " They are on their way up."

They soon arrived, and were at once furiously attacked by the mob.   The soldiers fired into them, but they boldly held their ground, and were evidently bent on a desperate fight.

The former now took up their stations at the junction of the streets, and were about to sweep them with canister, when from some cause a delay was ordered. This increased the boldness of the mob, and they taunted and derided the soldiers.   But in a few minutes a reinforcement of regulars arrived on the ground and charged bayonets.   The rioters fell back, but rallying, forced the soldiers to retire in turn.   The latter, however, returned to the charge, when the mob again gave way, but still stubbornly refused to disperse.

News of the magnitude of the struggle reached the Seventh Regiment, and they rapidly marched to the spot.   Their steady tramp along the pavement, and well-set ranks, discouraged the crowd, and they marched and counter-marched through the streets without molestation.

The mob, however, dispersed only to reassemble again in Twenty-ninth Street, and began to plunder the stores in the vicinity, and spread devastation on every side.

This being reported to head-quarters, a military force

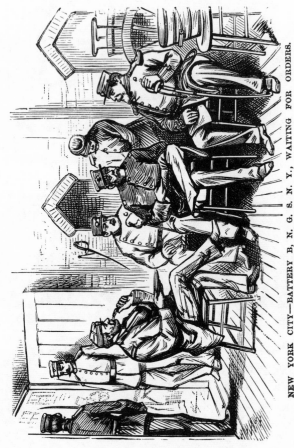

NEW YORK CITY—BATTERY B, N. G. S. N. Y., WAITING FOR ORDERS.

was despatched to disperse them. The rioters, however, instead of retreating, attacked them with the greatest fury. Almost every house was filled with them, and they lined the roofs with muskets and pistols, from which they poured down a deadly fire. For nearly a half an hour the fire was kept up without cessation, and many were killed. A sergeant was knocked down by a brick-bat, and then seized and beaten to death. The troops finding themselves unable to dislodge the assailants, retreated, leaving the body of the sergeant in the street, where it lay for three hours. General Brown not having a sufficient number of troops on hand, the mob all this time had it their own way. It was nine o'clock before he could despatch Captain Putnam with a strong force to put an end to the disgraceful scene. Arriving on the spot, the latter addressed the crowd, saying that he had come to carry away the dead body of the sergeant, and should do it at all hazards. But he had hardly placed it in a wagon, when the crowd began to assail his troops. He immediately unlimbered his pieces, when it scattered in every direction. But the rioters came together again at the corner of Thirty-first Street and Second Avenue, where they were met by reinforcements, and made a stand. They filled the houses, and mounted to the roofs, armed with muskets and revolvers, and as Putnam appeared, commenced a rapid fire. Placing his pieces in position, this gallant officer swept the street with canister, which soon cleared it. Eleven of the ringleaders were shot down, and bodies lay thick on the pavement. But this did not intimidate those in the windows, or on the roofs, and they kept up a steady fire. Putnam, who showed by his cool

11*

courage that the fighting stock from which he came had not degenerated, now ordered his men to turn their fire on the buildings. At each discharge, the heavy volleys brought down many of the wretches, some pitching headlong from the roof, and dashing out their brains on the pavement and flagging below. But the fight was very unequal, for the assailants would expose their bodies as little as possible; Putnam saw that the houses must be stormed, and gave the order to do it. The fight was now transferred to the inside, and became close and murderous. In the narrow halls and on the stairways, numbers were of no avail, and the rioters fought with a desperation they had not before exhibited. There was no way of escape, and they seemed to prefer death to being taken prisoners, and for a half an hour maintained the conflict in the darkened rooms and passages with a ferocity that was appalling. At last, however, with their numbers sadly thinned, they were forced to yield, and took refuge in flight. Many, unable to get away, hid under beds and in closets, but the soldiers ferreted them out, and carried them to police head-quarters.

The arsenal had not been attacked, as Sandford seemed every day to think it would be. Many colored people, as before stated, took refuge in it; and about noon on this day, a body of police arrived before it, with the children of the Colored Orphan Asylum that had been burned on Monday, in charge. They had since that time been scattered round in station-houses, but were now to be escorted to Blackwell's Island, for better security. It was an impressive spectacle this army of children presented, as they drew up in line in front of the arsenal to wait for those within to join them. The block was filled with them. The frightened little fugitives, fleeing from they scarce knew what, looked bewildered at their novel position. It seemed impossible that they ever could have been the objects of any one's vengeance. With a strong body of police in front and rear, and a detachment of soldiers on either side, they toddled slowly down to the foot of Thirty-fifth Street, from whence they were taken by boats to the Island.

The Sixty-fifth New York Regiment arrived from Harrisburg in the afternoon, and just before midnight the One Hundred and Fifty-second also reached the city, and marched up Broadway to police headquarters, where they were stowed away to get some rest.

A heavy storm that set in during the evening, helped to scatter the crowd that would otherwise have gathered on this warm July night, but it at the same time gave a sombre aspect to the city. The crescent moon was veiled in black, and thunderous clouds that swept heavily over the city, deepened the gloom, and seemed portentous of greater evil. The closing of all the stores and shop-windows at nightfall, through fear, left the streets lighted only by the scattering lamps. This unusual stretch of blank dead walls, emitting no ray of light, rendered the darkness made by the overhanging storm still more impenetrable. Flashes of lightning would reveal small groups of men bent on plunder, in sections where the military and police were not stationed, but no open violence was attempted. In other directions, the bayonets of the soldiers would gleam out of the dense shadows, as they silently held the posts assigned them, ready to march at a moment's notice. This was the fourth night, and the cannon planted in the streets, and the increased military force, showed that peace was not yet fully restored. The Seventh Regiment was quartered in Thirty-fourth Street, part of the soldiers within a building, and crowding every window to catch the first sign of disturbance, and part stationed below, or marching back and forth in the street. Other troops and policemen were massed at head-quarters, ready to move, at the word of command, to any point threatened by the mob.

The fourth night was passing away, and still Acton clung to his post, and refused to take even a moment's rest. His whole nature had been keyed up to meet the grave responsibilities that lay upon him, and through the wires he still watched every threatened point in the city, with sleepless vigilance. In the meantime, over a thousand special policemen had been sworn in, and five hundred or more citizens had volunteered their services, while the steady arrival of returning regiments swelled the military force into formidable proportions.

During the day, Senators Connolly and O'Brien had waited on General Brown, and asked him to remove the military from their ward, as their presence excited the people. The General very bluntly refused, saying he should not permit his troops to retire from before an armed mob. He was asked also to order the troops to leave Jackson's foundry for the same reason, and gave an equally emphatic refusal. There was now to be no compromise with the rioters, no agreement entered into. They had got beyond the character of citizens with rights to be respected—they were assassins and murderers, to whom was submitted the simple question of subjection to law and authority, or death.

The fighting through the day had been severe, but the disturbance had not been so wide-spread and general. Outside of the city, there had been threatening rumors. It was reported that there was danger of an uprising in Westchester, where some leading Democrats had taken open opposition to the draft, and a gun-boat had gone up as far as Tarrytown; but nothing serious occurred.

The rioters being almost exclusively Irish, it was thought that an address from Archbishop Hughes would go far to quiet the ringleaders, and he had therefore issued the following call, already referred to:

To the men of New York, who are now called in many of the papers rioters.

## MEN!

I am not able, owing to rheumatism in my limbs, to visit you, but that is not a reason why you should not pay me a visit in your whole strength. Come, then, to-morrow (Friday) at two o'clock, to my residence, north-west corner of Madison Avenue and Thirty-sixth street. There is abundant space for the meeting, around my house. I can address you from the corner of the balcony. If I should not be able to stand during its delivery, you will permit me to address you sitting; my voice is much stronger than my limbs. I take upon myself the responsibility of assuring you, that in paying me this visit or in retiring from it, you shall not be disturbed by any exhibition of municipal or military presence.  You who are Catholics, or as many of you as are, have a right to visit your bishop without molestation.

† JOHN HUGHES,

Archbishop of New York.

NEW YORK, *July* 16, 1863.

A curious incident was related subsequently in one of the New York papers, respecting the manner in which an interview was brought about between him and Governor Seymour, and which resulted in the resolution of the Archbishop to address the rioters.  The substance of the account was, that a young widow of high culture, formerly the wife of a well-known lawyer of this city—a woman living in an atmosphere of art, and refinement, and spending her time in study, became so excited over the violence and bloodshed that the authorities seemed unable to suppress, and finding that the Irish were at the bottom of the trouble, determined to appeal to Archbishop Hughes personally, to use his high authority and influence to bring these terrible scenes to a close.

Acting on this determination, she set out this morning for the Archbishop's residence, but on arriving was told that he was at the residence of Vicar-general Starrs, in Mulberry Street.  Hastening thither, she asked for an interview.  Her request was denied, when she repeated it; and though again refused, would not be repelled, and sent word that her business was urgent, and that she would not detain him ten minutes.  The Archbishop finally consented to see her.  As she entered the library, her manner and bearing—both said to

be remarkably impressive—arrested the attention of the
prelate. Without any explanation or apology, she told
him at once her errand—that it was one of mercy and
charity. She had been educated in a Roman Catholic
convent herself, in which her father was a professor,
and she urged him, in the name of God, to get on horseback, and go forth into the streets and quell the excitement of his flock. She told him he must, like Mark
Antony, address the people; and in rescuing this
great metropolis from vandalism, would become a second Constantine, an immortal hero. It was his duty, she
boldly declared; and though she did not profess to be a
Jeanne d'Arc or Madame Roland, but a plain woman
of the present day, she would ride fearlessly by his side,
and if he were threatened, would place her body between
him and danger, and take the blow aimed at him. The
cautious and crafty prelate was almost carried away by
the impassioned and dramatic force of this woman, but
he told her it would be presumption in him to do so; in
fact, impossible, as he was so crippled with rheumatism
and gout, that he could not walk. She then asked him
to call the crowd, and address them from the balcony
of his house. He replied that he was just then busy
in writing an answer to an attack on him in the *Tribune*. She assured him that such a controversy was
worse than useless—that another and higher duty rested
on him. She pressed him with such importunity and en-
thusiasm, that he finally consented; but as a last effort
to get rid of her, said he feared the military would
interfere and attack the mob. She assured him they
would not, and hurried off to the St. Nicholas to see
Governor Seymour about it. She found the ante-room
filled with officials and other personages on important

business, waiting their turn to be admitted.  But her determined, earnest manner so impressed every one with the importance of her mission, that precedence was granted her, and she found herself at once beside the astonished Governor.  Without any preliminaries, she told him she had just come from the head of the church, and wanted his excellency to visit him immediately.  No business was of such vital importance as this.  The self-possessed Governor coolly replied that he should be glad to see the Archbishop, but business was too pressing to allow him to be absent even a half an hour from his duties.  She hastened back to Archbishop Hughes, and prevailed on him to write a note to Governor Seymour, asking him to call and see him, as he was unable to get out.  Fortified with this, she now took a priest with her, and providing herself with a carriage, returned to head-quarters, and absolutely forced, by her energy and determination and persuasive manner, the Governor to leave his business, and go to the Archbishop's.  The invitation to the Irish to meet him was the result of this interview.

Why Archbishop Hughes took no more active part than he did in quelling this insurrection, when there was scarcely a man in it except members of his own flock, seems strange.  It is true he had published an address to them, urging them to keep the peace; but it was prefaced by a long, undignified, and angry attack on Mr. Greeley, of the *Tribune*, and showed that he was in sympathy with the rioters, at least in their condemnation of the draft.  The pretence that it would be unsafe for him to pass through the streets, is absurd; for on three different occasions common priests had mingled with the mob, not only with impunity, but

BALTIMORE—ATTACKING THE SOLDIERS AT THE ARMORY.

with good effect. He could not, therefore, have thought himself to be in any great danger. One thing, at any rate, is evident: had an Irish mob threatened to burn down a Roman Catholic church, or a Roman Catholic orphan asylum, or threatened any of the institutions or property of the Roman Church, he would have shown no such backwardness or fear. The mob would have been confronted with the most terrible anathemas of the church, and those lawless bands quailed before the maledictions of the representative of "God's vicegerent on earth." It is unjust to suppose that he wished this plunder and robbery to continue, or desired to see Irishmen shot down in the streets; it must, therefore, be left to conjecture, why he could not be moved to any interference except by outside pressure, and then show so much lukewarmness in his manner—in fact, condemning their opponents almost as much as themselves.

The excitement consequent on the draft, exhibited in outbreaks in various parts of the country, and in the vicinity of New York, was increased by the reports of violence and fighting in the latter city. In Troy there was a riot, and the mob, imitating the insane conduct of the rioters in New York, proceeded to attack an African church. But a priest, more bold or more patriotic than Archbishop Hughes, interfered and saved it. That the latter, armed with nothing but the crucifix, could have effected as much as the police and military together, there can be but little doubt. This open and decided sympathy with law and order, and bitter anathemas against the vandals who sought the destruction of the city, were the more demanded, as such a large proportion of the police force were Roman

Catholics, and in their noble devotion to duty, even to shooting down their own countrymen and men of a similar faith, deserved this encouragement from the head of the church.

# CHAPTER XIX.

## CLOSING SCENES.

Tranquil Morning.—Proclamation of the Mayor.—Mob cowed.—
Plunderers afraid of Detection.—Dirty Cellars crowded with
rich Apparel, Furniture, and Works of Art.—Archbishop Hughes'
Address.—Useless Efforts.—Acton's Forty-eight Hours without
Sleep over.—Change in Military Commanders in the City.—
General Brown relinquishes his Command.—True Words.—Noble
Character and Behavior of the Troops and Police.—General
Brown's invaluable Services.

THIS week of horrors—a week unparalleled in the
history of New York—was drawing to a close. It had
been one of terror and dismay to the inhabitants, who
thought only of the immediate effects on themselves of
the triumph of the mob. A great city laid in ashes,
given up to robbers and cut-throats, is at any time a
terrible spectacle; but New York in ruins at this time
was a republic gone—a nation uncrowned and left deso-
late; but the battle, both for the nation and city, had
been nobly fought and won; and Friday, the fifth day
of this protracted struggle, dawned bright and tranquil.
The storm of the night before had passed away, and
the streets, thoroughly washed by the drenching rain,
stretched clean and quiet between the long rows of
buildings, emblematic of the tranquillity that had returned to the city.

The cars were seen once more speeding down to the
business centres, loaded with passengers. Broadway

shook to the rumbling of the heavy omnibuses; shutters were taken down, and the windows again shone with their rich adornments. The anxious look had departed from the pedestrians, for the heavy cloud, so full of present woe and future forebodings, had lifted and passed away.

The following proclamation of Mayor Opdyke will show the true state of things on this morning, and what the people had most to fear:

"The riotous assemblages have been dispersed. Business is running in its usual channels. The various lines of omnibuses, railway, and telegraph have resumed their ordinary operations. Few symptoms of disorder remain, except in a small district in the eastern part of the city, comprising a part of the Eighteenth and Twenty-first Wards. The police is everywhere alert. A sufficient military force is now here to suppress any illegal movement, however formidable.

"Let me exhort you, therefore, to pursue your ordinary business. Avoid especially all crowds. Remain quietly at your homes, except when engaged in business, or assisting the authorities in some organized force. When the military appear in the street, do not gather about it, being sure that it is doing its duty in obedience to orders from superior authority. Your homes at your places of business you have a right to defend, and it is your duty to defend them, at all hazards. Yield to no intimidation, and to no demand for money as the price of your safety. If any person warns you to desist from your accustomed business, give no heed to the warning, but arrest him and bring him to the nearest station-house as a conspirator.

"Be assured that the public authorities have the ability and the will to protect you from those who have conspired alike against your peace, against the government of your choice, and against the laws which your representatives have enacted.

"GEORGE OPDYKE, Mayor."

Down-town there was scarcely anything to show that New York had for nearly a week been swept by one of the most frightful storms that ever desolated a city. Even in the disaffected districts, no crowds were assembled. In the corner groggèries, small groups of men might be seen, discussing the past, and uttering curses and threats; and ruined houses and battered walls and hanging blinds here and there arrested the eye, showing what wild work had been wrought; but it was evident that the struggle was over. The mob was thoroughly subdued, and the law-breakers now thought more of escaping future punishment than of further acts of violence. Bruised heads and battered forms were scattered through the low tenement-houses in every direction, which friends were anxious to keep concealed from the notice of the authorities. In dirty cellars and squalid apartments were piled away the richest stuffs—brocaded silks, cashmere shawls, elegant chairs, vases, bronzes, and articles of virtu, huddled promiscuously together, damning evidences of guilt, which were sure not to escape, in the end, the searching eye of the police, who had already begun to gather up the plunder. Thus the objects mostly coveted but a few hours ago now awakened the greatest solicitude and fear.

Even if the military under Generai Brown and the police had not shown the mob that they were its masters, the arrival of so many regiments, occupying all the infected districts, was overwhelming evidence that the day of lawless triumph was over, and that of retribution had come. Some acts of individual hostility were witnessed, but nothing more.

Archbishop Hughes had his meeting, and some five thousand assembled to hear him. They were on the whole a peaceable-looking crowd, and it was evidently composed chiefly, if not wholly, of those who had taken no part in the riot. None of the bloody heads and gashed faces, of which there were so many at that moment in the city, appeared. The address was well enough, but it came too late to be of any service. It might have saved many lives and much destruction, had it been delivered two days before, but now it was like the bombardment of a fortress after it had surrendered—a mere waste of ammunition. The fight was over, and to use his own not very refined illustration, he "spak' too late." The reports that came in to Acton from all the precincts convinced him of this, and he began to think of rest.

The strain was off, and overtasked nature made her demand, and he was compelled to yield to it. The tremendo  work that had been laid upon him had been right nobly accomplished. Had he been a weak and vacillating man, the rioters would have acquired a headway that could not have been stopped, without a more terrible sacrifice of life and property—perhaps even of half the city. Comprehending intuitively the gravity of the situation, and the danger of procrastination or temporizing, he sprang at once for the enemy's throat, and never ceased his hold until he had strangled him to death. If he had waited to consult authorities about the legality of his action, or listened to the voice of pity, or yielded to the clamors of leading politicians or threats of enemies, both he and the city, in all human probability, would have been swept away in the hurricane of popular fury.

On this day a most remarkable announcement was published: that a sudden change had been made in the military command of the troops of the city and harbor. General Dix superseded General Wool, and Canby, General Brown. That Wool should have been removed at any time, might have been expected; not from incapacity, but on account of his age, and because any one could perform the mere nominal duties that devolved on him. But why General Brown should have been removed at this critical moment, when he and the Police Commissioners were performing their herculean task so faithfully and well, is not so plain; unless it was the result of one of those freaks of passion or despotic impulse, for which the Secretary of War was so ignobly distinguished. But unlike many other blunders which the War Department committed at this time, it did not result in any evil consequences, for the fight was over. But of this fact the Secretary of War was ignorant when he made out th rder.

General Brown, in relinquishing his command, spoke warmly of the noble behavior of the troops during the riots, saying: "Engaged night and day in constant conflict with the mob, they have in some fifteen or twenty severe contests—in most of them outnumbered more than ten to one, many of the mob being armed—whipped and effectually dispersed them, and have been uniformly successful.   In not a single instance has assistance been required by the police, when it has not been promptly rendered; and all property, public and private, which has been under their protection, has been perfectly and efficiently protected; and with pride he desires to record, that in this city, surrounded by grog-shops, but one single instance of drunkenness has fallen under his observation.

" To Lieutenant-colonel Frothingham, his able and efficient adjutant-general, he tenders his thanks for his untiring assistance.

" Having during the present insurrection been in immediate and constant co-operation with police department of this city, he desires the privilege of expressing his unbounded admiration of it.   Never in civil or military life has he seen such untiring devotion and such efficient service.

" To President Acton and Commissioner Bergen he offers his thanks for their courtesy to him and their kindness to his command.

" HARVEY BROWN, *Brigadier-general.*"

The praise he bestows both on the police and soldiers was richly deserved; and he may well say that " with pride he desires to record that in this city, surrounded with grog-shops, but one single instance of drunkenness has fallen under his observation."   With all a soldier's tendency to indulge in spirituous liquor, to be thrown right amid drinking-places, which by harboring rioters had lost all claim to protection—part of the time suffering from want of food, and often drenched

BALTIMORE—U. S. ARTILLERY GUARDING THE CAMDEN ST. DEPOT

to the skin, and weary from hard fighting and want of sleep—not to step away occasionally in the confusion and darkness of night, and solace himself with stimulating drinks, was something marvellous. After hard fighting, and long marching, and short rations, a soldier feels he has a right to indulge in liquor, if he can get it; and their abstinence from it in such lawless times, not only speaks well for their discipline, but their character. A single instance shows under what perfect control the troops were. One day Colonel Ladue, seeing that his men were exhausted and hungry, desired to let them have a little beer to refresh them, and the following telegram was sent from the precinct where they were on duty:

"5.45 P.M. From 9th. Colonel Ladue wishes his men allowed to have beer in station-house."

*Answer.* "Mr. Acton says he is opposed to beer, but the colonel can give his men as much as he pleases."

"Acton is opposed to beer," but the troops are not under his command, and he has no heart to deny the poor fellows the station-house in which to refresh themselves after their hard day's work. This incident also shows the strict discipline maintained in the police department.

General Brown had done a noble work. Taking his place beside the Police Commissioners, he bent all his energies to the single task of carrying out their plans, and save the city from the hands of the rioters. He never thought what deference might be due him on the score of etiquette, or on account of his military rank; he thought only of putting down the mob at all hazards. His refusal, at first, to serve under General Sandford was not merely that it was an improper

12

thing to place a general of the regular army under the orders of a mere militia general,* having no rank whatever in the United States army, but he knew it would paralyze his influence, and in all human probability result in the useless sacrifice of his troops. The absurdity of not moving until he received orders from his superior officer, cooped up in the arsenal, where he remained practically in a state of siege, was so apparent that he refused to countenance it. He was willing that President Acton should be his superior officer, and give his orders, and he would carry them out; for thus he could act efficiently and make his disciplined battalion tell in the struggle; but for the sake of his own reputation and that of his troops, he would not consent to hold a position that would only bring disgrace on both. His views are clearly expressed in his reply to a highly complimentary letter addressed to him by the mayor and a large number of prominent citizens, for the signal services he had rendered. He says: " I never for a moment forgot that to the police was confided the conservation of the peace of the city; and that only in conjunction with the city authorities, and on their requisition, could the United States forces be lawfully and properly employed in suppressing the riot, and in restoring that peace and good order which had been so lawlessly broken. Acting in accordance with this principle, and as aids to the gallant city police, the officers and soldiers of my command performed the most unpleasant and arduous duty, with that prompt energy and fearless patriotism which may ever be expected from the soldiers of the Republic."

* Because he was especially assigned to the command of the city by the Secretary of War.

# CHAPTER XX.

On Saturday morning it was announced that the
authorities at Washington had resolved to enforce the
draft. It had been repeatedly asserted during the
riot that it was abandoned, and the report received
very general credence. Still, the official denial of it
produced no disturbance. The spirit of insurrection
was effectually laid.

It is a little singular, that, in all these tremendous
gatherings and movements, no prominent recognized
leaders could be found. A man by the name of An-
drews had been arrested and imprisoned as one, but
the charge rested wholly on some exciting harangues
he had made, not from any *active* leadership he had
assumed.

There were, perhaps, in the city this morning not far
from ten thousand troops—quite enough to preserve
the peace, if the riot should break out afresh; and
orders therefore were given to arrest the march of regiments hastening from various sections to the city,
under the requisition of the Governor. Still, the ter-

ror that had taken possession of men could not be allayed in an hour, and although the police had resumed their patrols, and dared to be seen alone in the streets, there was constant dread of personal violence among the citizens.   Especially was this true of the negro population.   Although many sought their ruined homes, yet aware of the intense hatred entertained toward them by the mob, they felt unsafe, and began to organize in self-defence.   But the day wore away without disturbance, and the Sabbath dawned peaceably, and order reigned from the Battery to Harlem. The military did not show themselves in the street, and thousands thronged without fear the avenues in which the fighting had taken place, to look at the ruins it had left behind.   On Monday there was more or less rebellious feeling exhibited by the rioters, on account of the general search of the police for stolen goods, and the arrest of suspected persons.   It exhibited itself, however, only in threats and curses—not a policemen was assaulted.   It was amusing, sometimes, to see what strange articles the poor wretches had stowed away in their dirty cellars.   There was everything from barrels of sugar and starch to tobacco and bird-seed.   Said a morning paper: " Mahogany and rosewood chairs with brocade upholstering, marble-top tables and stands, costly paintings, and hundreds of delicate and valuable mantel ornaments, are daily found in low hovels up-town.   Every person in whose possession these articles are discovered disclaims all knowledge of the same, except that they found them in the street, and took them in to prevent them being burned.   The entire city will be searched, and it is expected that the greatest portion of the property taken from the buildings sacked by the mob will be recovered." The rivers and outlets to the city were closely watched, to prevent its being carried off. In the meantime, arrests were constantly made.

It would be invidious to single out any portion of the police for special commendation, where all did their duty so nobly; but it is not improper to speak of the sanitary police, whose specific duties do not lead them to take part in quelling mobs.

They have to report all nuisances, examine tenement-houses and unsafe buildings, look after the public schools, but more especially examine steam-boilers, and license persons qualified to run steam-engines. Hence, it is composed of men of considerable scientific knowledge. But all such business being suspended during the riot, they at once, with their Captain, B. G. Lord, assumed the duties of the common policemen, and from Monday night till order was restored, were on constant duty, participating in the fights, and enduring the fatigues with unflinching firmness, and did not return to their regular duties till Monday morning.

The drill-officer also, Sergeant T. S. Copeland, became, instead of a drill-officer, a gallant, active leader of his men in some of the most desperate fights that occurred. His military knowledge enabled him to form commands ordered hastily off, with great despatch. But not content with this, he led them, when formed, to the charge, and gave such lessons in drill, in the midst of the fight, as the police will never forget.

With the details of what followed we have nothing to do. The Grand Jury indicted many of the prisoners, and in the term of the court that met the 3d of August, twenty were tried and nineteen convicted, and sentenced to a longer or shorter term of imprisonment. Of course a large number on preliminary examinations got off, sometimes from want of sufficient evidence, and sometimes from the venality of the judges before whom they were brought. Claims for damages were brought in, the examination of which was long and tedious. The details are published in two large volumes, and the entire cost to the city was probably three millions of dollars. Some of the claims went before the courts, where they lingered along indefinitely. The number of rioters killed, or died from the effects of their wounds, was put down by the Police Commissioners at about twelve hundred. Of course this estimate is not made up from any detailed reports. The dead and wounded were hurried away, even in the midst of the fight, and hidden in obscure streets, or taken out of the city for fear of future arrests or complications. Hence there was no direct way of getting at the exact number of those who fell victims to the riot. The loss of life, therefore, could only be approximated by taking the regular report of the number of deaths in the city for a few weeks before the riots, and that for the same length of time after. As there was no epidemic, or any report of increased sickness from any disease, the inference naturally was, that the excess for the period after the riots was owing to the victims of them. Many of these were reported as sunstrokes, owing to men exposing themselves to the sun with pounded and battered heads. The Police Commissioners took great care to keep all the wounded policemen indoors until perfectly cured. Only one ventured to neglect their orders, and he died of a sunstroke.

The difference of mortality in the city for the month

previous to the riots, and the month during and subsequent, was about twelve hundred, which excess
Mr. Acton thought should be put down to the deaths
caused directly and indirectly by the riots. Although
many policemen were wounded, only three were killed
or died from the injuries they received.

Immediately after the riot, Mr. Leonard W. Jerome
and others interested themselves in raising a fund for
the relief of members of the Police, Militia, and Fire
Departments who had sustained injuries in the discharge of their duty in suppressing the riots. Sub-
scriptions to the amount of $54,980 were paid in, and
$22,721.53 distributed by the Trustees of the Riot Re-
lief Fund, in sums from $50 to $1,000, each, through
Isaac Bell, Treasurer, to 101 policemen, 16 militiamen,
and 7 firemen.

The balance was securely invested, to meet future
emergencies, a portion of which was paid to sufferers
by the Orange Riot of 1871.

The following is the list of colored people known to
be killed by the mob, together with the circumstances
attending their murder, as given by David Barnes, in
his Metropolitan record, to which reference has heretofore been made.

### COLORED VICTIMS OF THE RIOT.

WILLIAM HENRY NICHOLS (colored). Nichols resided at No. 147 East Twenty-eighth Street. Mrs.
Staat, his mother, was visiting him. On Wednesday,
July 15th, at 3 o'clock, the house was attacked by
a mob with showers of bricks and stones. In one
of the rooms was a woman with a child but three days

old.  The rioters broke open the door with axes and
rushed in.  Nichols and his mother fled to the basement ; in a few moments the babe referred to was
dashed by the rioters from the upper window to the
yard, and instantly killed.  The mob cut the water-
pipes above, and the basement was being deluged ; ten
persons, mostly women and children, were there, and
they fled to the yard ; in attempting to climb the fence,
Mrs. Staats fell back from exhaustion ; the rioters were
instantly upon her ; her son sprang to her rescue, ex-
claiming, " Save my mother, if you kill me."  Two ruffians instantly seized him, each taking hold of an arm,
while a third, armed with a crowbar, calling upon
them to hold his arms apart, deliberately struck him a
savage blow on the head, felling him like a bullock.
He died in the N. Y. Hospital two days after.

JAMES COSTELLO (colored).—James Costello, No. 97
West Thirty-third Street, killed on Tuesday morning,
July 14th.  Costello was a shoemaker, an active man
in his business, industrious and sober.  He went out
early in the morning upon an errand, was accosted, and
finally was pursued by a powerful man.  He ran down
the street ; endeavored to make his escape ; was nearly
overtaken by his pursuer ; in self-defence he turned
and shot the rioter with a revolver.  The shot proved
to be mortal ; he died two days after.  Costello was
immediately set upon by the mob.  They first mangled
his body, then hanged it.  They then cut down his
body and dragged it through the gutters, smashing it
with stones, and finally burnt it.  The mob then attempted to kill Mrs. Costello and her children, but she
escaped by climbing fences and taking refuge in a
police station-house.

BALTIMORE—SCENE AFTER THE FIRST VOLLEY BY THE SIXTH REGIMENT.

ABRAHAM FRANKLIN (colored).—This young man, who was murdered by the mob on the corner of Twenty-seventh Street and Seventh Avenue, was a quiet, inoffensive man, of unexceptionable character. He was a cripple, but supported himself and his mother, being employed as a coachman. A short time previous to the assault, he called upon his mother to see if anything could be done by him for her safety. The old lady said she considered herself perfectly safe; but if her time to die had come, she was ready to die. Her son then knelt down by her side, and implored the protection of Heaven in behalf of his mother. The old lady said that it seemed to her that good angels were present in the room. Scarcely had the supplicant risen from his knees, when the mob broke down the door, seized him, beat him over the head and face with fists and clubs, and then hanged him in the presence of his parent. While they were thus engaged, the military came and drove them away, cutting down the body of Franklin, who raised his arm once slightly and gave a few signs of life. The military then moved on to quell other riots, when the mob returned and again suspended the now probably lifeless body of Franklin, cutting out pieces of flesh, and otherwise shockingly mutilating it.

AUGUSTUS STUART (colored).—Died at Hospital, Blackwell's Island, July 22, from the effects of a blow received at the hands of the mob, on Wednesday evening of the Riot Week. He had been badly beaten previously by a band of rioters, and was frightened and insane from the effects of the blows which he had received. He was running toward the arsenal (State), Seventh Avenue and Thirty-seventh Street, for safety,

12*

when he was overtaken by the mob, from whom he received his death-blow.

PETER HEUSTON.—Peter Heuston, sixty-three years of age, a Mohawk Indian, dark complexion, but straight hair, and for several years a resident of New York, proved a victim to the riots. Heuston served with the New York Volunteers in the Mexican war. He was brutally attacked and shockingly beaten, on the 13th of July, by a gang of ruffians, who thought him to be of the African race because of his dark complexion. He died within four days, at Bellevue Hospital, from his injuries.

JEREMIAH ROBINSON (colored).—He was killed in Madison near Catharine Street. His widow stated that her husband, in order to escape, dressed himself in some of her clothes, and, in company with herself and one other woman, left their residence and went toward one of the Brooklyn ferries. Robinson wore a hood, which failed to hide his beard. Some boys, seeing his beard, lifted up the skirts of his dress, which exposed his heavy boots. Immediately the mob set upon him, and the atrocities they perpetrated are so revolting that they are unfit for publication. They finally killed him and threw his body into the river. His wife and her companion ran up Madison Street, and escaped across the Grand Street Ferry to Brooklyn.

WILLIAM JONES (colored).—A crowd of rioters in Clarkson Street, in pursuit of a negro, who in self-defence had fired on some rowdies, met an inoffensive colored man returning from a bakery with a loaf of bread under his arm. They instantly set upon and beat him and, after nearly killing him, hung him to a lamp-post. His body was left suspended for several hours.

A fire was made underneath him, and he was literally roasted as he hung, the mob revelling in their demoniac act. Recognition of the remains, on their being recovered, was impossible; and two women mourned for upwards of two weeks, in the case of this man, for the loss of their husbands. At the end of that time, the husband of one of the mourners, to her great joy, returned like one recovered from the grave. The principal evidence which the widow, Mary Jones, had to identify the murdered man as her husband, was the fact of his having a loaf of bread under his arm, he having left the house to get a loaf of bread a few minutes before the attack.

JOSEPH REED (colored).—This was a lad of seven years of age, residing at No. 147 East Twenty-eighth Street, with an aged grandmother and widowed mother. On Wednesday morning of the fearful week, a crowd of ruffians gathered in the neighborhood, determined on a week of plunder and death. They attacked the house, stole everything they could carry with them, and, after threatening the inmates, set fire to it. The colored people who had the sole occupancy of the building, fled in confusion into the midst of the gathering crowd. And then the child was separated from his guardians. His youth and evident illness, even from the devils around him, it would be thought, should have insured his safety. But no sooner did they see his unprotected, defenceless condition, than a gang of fiendish men seized him, beat him with sticks, and bruised him with heavy cobblestones. But one, tenfold more the servant of Satan than the rest, rushed at the child, and with the stock of a pistol struck him on the temple and felled him to the ground. A noble young fireman, by the name of John F. Govern, of No. 39 Hose Company, instantly came to the rescue, and, single-handed, held the crowd at bay. Taking the wounded and unconscious boy in his arms, he carried him to a place of safety. The terrible beating and the great fright the poor lad had undergone was too much for his feeble frame; he died on the following Tuesday.

JOSEPH JACKSON (colored), aged nineteen years, living in West Fifty-third Street, near Sixth Avenue, was in the industrious pursuit of his humble occupation of gathering provender for a herd of cattle, and when near the foot of Thirty-fourth Street, East River, July 15, was set upon by the mob, killed, and his body thrown into the river.

SAMUEL JOHNSON (colored).—On Tuesday night Johnson was attacked near Fulton Ferry by a gang who mercilessly beat and left him for dead. A proposition was made to throw him into the river, but for some reason the murderers took fright and fled. He was taken by some citizens to his home, and died the next day.

—— WILLIAMS (colored).—He was attacked on the corner of Le Roy and Washington Streets, on Tuesday morning, July 14th, knocked down, a number of men jumped upon, kicked, and stamped upon him until insensible. One of the murderers knelt on the body and drove a knife into it; the blade being too small, he threw it away and resorted to his fists. Another seized a huge stone, weighing near twenty pounds, and deliberately crushed it again and again on to the victim. A force of police, under Captain Dickson, arrived and rescued the man, who was conveyed to the New York

Hospital. He was only able to articulate "Williams" in response to a question as to his name, and remained insensible thereafter, dying in a few days.

ANN DERRICKSON.—This was a white woman, the wife of a colored man, and lived at No. 11 York Street. On Wednesday, July 15th, the rioters seized a son of deceased, a lad of about twelve years, saturated his clothes and hair with camphene, and then procuring a rope, fastened one end to a lamp-post, the other around his neck, and were about to set him on fire, and hang him; they were interfered with by some citizens and by the police of the First Ward, and their diabolical attempt at murder frustrated. While Mrs. Derrickson was attempting to save the life of her son she was horribly bruised and beaten with a cart-rung. The victim, after lingering three or four weeks, died from the effects of her injuries.

Reports from the captains of the several precincts, with all the details of their operations, were made out —also from the subordinate military officers to their immediate superiors. The final reports of General Wool, commanding the Eastern Department, and Major-general Sandford, commanding the city troops, caused much remark in the city papers, and called forth a reply from General Brown, who considered himself unjustly assailed in them. Explanation of the disagreement between him and General Wool having been fully given, it is not necessary to repeat it here. The same may be said of the statement of General Wool, regarding his orders on Monday the 13th, respecting the troops in the harbor. But in this report of General Wool to Governor Seymour, there are other statements which General Brown felt it his duty

to correct.   General Wool says, that finding there was
a want of harmony between Generals Sandford and
Brown in the disposition of troops, he issued the following order:

MAJOR-GENERAL   SANDFORD,   BREVET   BRIGADIER-GENERAL
    BROWN.

GENTLEMEN :—It is indispensable to collect your
troops not stationed, and have them divided into
suitable parties, with a due proportion of police to
each, and to patrol in such parts of the city as may be
in the greatest danger from the rioters.   This ought to
be done as soon as practicable.

JOHN E. WOOL, *Major-general.*

After this had been issued, General Sandford reporting to me that his orders were not obeyed by General Brown, I issued the following order:
"All the troops called out for the protection of
the city are placed under the command of General
Sandford."
General Brown in his reply says, that he "*never saw
or heard of this first order.*"   The only explanation of
this, consistent with the character of both, is that General Wool sent this order to General Sandford alone—
either forgetting to transmit it to General Brown, or
expecting General Sandford to do it.
At all events, sent or not, it was a foolish order.
One would infer from it that the whole task of putting
down the riots belonged to the military, the commanders of which were to order out what co-operating force
of police they deemed necessary and march up and

down the disaffected districts, trampling out the law-lessness according to rule. This might be all well enough, but the question was, how were these troops, strangers to the city, to find out where " *such parts of the city* " were in which was " *the greatest danger from the rioters?* " It showed a lamentable ignorance of mobs ; they don't stay in one spot and fight it out, nor keep in one mass, nor give notice beforehand where they will strike next. Such knowledge could only be obtained from police head-quarters, the focus of the telegraph system, and *there* the troops should have been ordered to concentrate at once, and put themselves under the direction of the Police Commissioners. Again, General Wool says he issued the following order to General Brown, on Tuesday :

" Sir :—It is reported that the rioters have already recommenced their work of destruction. To-day there must be no child's play. Some of the troops under your command should be sent immediately to attack and stop those who have commenced their infernal ras-cality in Yorkville and Harlem."

This order, too, General Brown says he never received. Thinking it strange, he addressed a note to General Wool's assistant adjutant-general, respecting both these orders, which had thus strangely wandered out of the way. The latter, Major Christensen, replied as follows :

" The orders of General Wool published in his re-port to Governor Seymour, viz. : 'That patrols of mili-tary and police should be sent through the disaffected districts ; ' and the one July 14th, 'To-day there must be no child's play,' etc., were not issued by me, and I cannot therefore say whether copies were sent to you or not. They were certainly *not* sent by me.

"C. F. CHRISTENSEN,

"Major, Assistant Adjutant-general."

We have explained how the error may have occurred with regard to the first order. But there is no explanation of this, except on the ground that General Wool perhaps sketched out this order, without sending it, and afterwards seeing it amid his papers, thought it was a copy of one he had sent. He was well advanced in years, and might easily fall into some such error.

It is not necessary to go into detailed account of all the statements contained in General Wool's letter which General Brown emphatically denies; but the following is worthy of notice. He says that General Brown issued orders that General Sandford countermanded, and that General Brown acted through the riots under his (Wool's) orders; whereas the latter says, he never received but three orders from Wool during the whole time, and only *one* of those referred to any action towards the rioters, and that was to bring off some killed and wounded men left by a military force sent out either by Sandford or Wool, and which had been chased from the field by the mob.

But the statements of General Wool are entirely thrown into the shade by the following assertion of General Sandford, in his report. He says: "With the remnant of the [his] division (left in the city), and the first reinforcements from General Wool, detachments were sent to all parts of the city, and the rioters everywhere beaten and dispersed on Monday afternoon, Monday night, and Tuesday morning. In a few hours, but

BALTIMORE—THE MOB ASSAULTING A MEMBER OF THE SIXTH

BALTIMORE—THE MOB FIRING THE CAMDEN STREET STATION.

for the interference of Brigadier-general Brown, who, in disobedience of orders," etc.

The perfect gravity with which this assertion is made is something marvellous. One would infer that the police was of no account, except to maintain order after it was fully restored by the military on Tuesday morning. General Sandford might well be ignorant of the state of things in the city, for he was cooped up in the arsenal, intent only on holding his fortress. So far as he was concerned, the whole city might have been burned up before Tuesday noon, and he would scarcely have known it, except as he saw the smoke and flames from the roof of the arsenal. He never sent out a detachment until after the Tuesday afternoon, when, as he says, but for General Brown's action, the riot would have been virtually over. The simple truth is, these reports of Generals Wool and Sandford are both mere after-thoughts, growing out of the annoyance they felt on knowing that their *martinetism* was a total failure, and the whole work had been done by General Brown and the Police Commissioners from their head-quarters in Mulberry Street. Acton and Brown had no time to grumble or dispute about etiquette. They had something more serious on hand, and they bent their entire energies to their accomplishment. General Sandford held the arsenal, an important point, indeed a vital one, and let him claim and receive all the credit due that achievement; but to assume any special merit in quelling the riots in the streets is simply ridiculous. That was the work of the police and the military under the commissioners and General Brown.

The statement of the Police Commissioners, Acton and Bergen, on this point is conclusive. They say that General Sandford's error consisted in "not choosing to be in close communication with this department, when alone through the police telegraph, and other certain means, trustworthy information of the movements of the mob could be promptly had."

That single statement is enough to overthrow all of General Sandford's assertions about the riot. It was hardly necessary for them to declare further in their letter to General Brown:

"So far from your action having had the effect supposed by General Sandford, we are of the opinion, already expressed in our address to the police force, that through your prompt, vigorous, and intelligent action, the intrepidity and steady valor of the small military force under you, acting with the police force, the riotous proceedings were arrested on Thursday night, and that without such aid mob violence would have continued much longer."

### WELL-EARNED PRAISE.

On the week after the riot the Board of Police Commissioners issued the following address to the force, in which a well-earned tribute is paid to the military:

*To the Metropolitan Police Force.*

On the morning of Monday, the 13th inst., the peace and good order of the city were broken by a mob collected in several quarters of the city, for the avowed purpose of resisting the process of drafting names to recruit the armies of the Union.

Vast crowds of men collected and fired the offices

where drafting was in progress, beating and driving the officers from duty.

From the beginning, these violent proceedings were accompanied by arson, robbery, and murder.

Private property, unofficial persons of all ages, sexes, and conditions, were indiscriminately assailed—none were spared, except those who were supposed by the mob to sympathize with their proceedings.

Early in the day the Superintendent was assaulted, cruelly beaten, robbed, and disabled by the mob which was engaged in burning the provost marshal's office in Third Avenue, thus in a manner disarranging the organization at the Central Department, throwing new, unwonted, and responsible duties upon the Board.

At this juncture the telegraph wires of the department were cut, and the movement of the railroads and stages violently interrupted, interfering seriously with our accustomed means of transmitting orders and concentrating forces.

The militia of the city were absent at the seat of war, fighting the battles of the nation against treason and secession, and there was no adequate force in the city for the first twelve hours to resist at all points the vast and infuriated mob. The police force was not strong enough in any precinct to make head, unaided, against the overwhelming force. No course was left but to concentrate the whole force at the Central Department, and thence send detachments able to encounter and conquer the rioters. This course was promptly adopted on Monday morning. The military were called upon to act in aid of the civil force to subdue the treasonable mob, protect life and property, and restore public order.

Under such adverse circumstances you were called upon to encounter a mob of such strength as have never before been seen in this country. The force of militia under General Sandford, who were called into service by the authority of this Board, were concentrated by him at and held the arsenal in Seventh Avenue, throughout the contest. The military forces in command of Brevet Brigadier-general Harvey Brown reported at the Central Department, and there General Brown established his head-quarters, and from there expeditions, combined of police and military force, were sent out that in all cases conquered, defeated, or dispersed the mob force, and subjected them to severe chastisement. In no instance did these detachments from the Central Department, whether of police alone or police and military combined, meet with defeat or serious check.

In all cases they achieved prompt and decisive victories. The contest continued through Monday, Tuesday, Wednesday, Thursday, and till 11 o'clock on Thursday night, like a continuous battle, when it ended by a total and sanguinary rout of the insurgents.

During the whole of those anxious days and nights, Brigadier-general Brown remained at the Central Department, ordering the movements of the military in carefully considered combinations with the police force, and throughout the struggle, and until its close, commanded the admiration and gratitude of the Police Department and all who witnessed his firm intelligence and soldierly conduct.

It is understood that he had at no time under his immediate command more than three hundred troops, but they were of the highest order, and were commanded by officers of courage and ability. They cordially acted with, supported, and were supported by, the police, and victory in every contest against fearful odds, was the result of brave fighting and intelligent command.

In the judgment of this Board, the escape of the city from the power of an infuriated mob is due to the aid furnished the police by Brigadier-general Brown and the small military force under his command. No one can doubt, who saw him, as we did, that during those anxious and eventful days and nights Brigadier-general Harvey Brown was equal to the situation, and was the right man in the right place.

We avail ourselves of this occasion to tender to him, in the most earnest and public manner, the thanks of the department and our own.

To the soldiers under his command we are grateful as to brave men who perilled all to save the city from a reign of terror. To Captains Putnam, Franklin, and Shelley, Lieutenant Ryer, and Lieutenant-colonel Berens, officers of corps under the command of Brigadier-general Brown, we are especially indebted, and we only discharge a duty when we commend them to their superiors in rank and to the War Department for their courageous and effective service.

Of the Inspectors, Captains, and Sergeants of police who led parties in the fearful contest, we are proud to say that none faltered or failed. Each was equal to the hour and the emergency. Not one failed to overcome the danger, however imminent, or to defeat the enemy, however numerous. Especial commendation is due to Drill-sergeant Copeland for his most valuable aid in commanding the movements of larger detachments of the police.

The patrolmen who were on duty fought through the numerous and fierce conflicts with the steady courage of veteran soldiers, and have won, as they deserve, the highest commendations from the public and from this Board. In their ranks there was neither faltering nor straggling. Devotion to duty and courage in the performance of it were universal.

The public and the department owe a debt of gratitude to the citizens who voluntarily became special patrolmen, some three thousand of whom, for several days and nights, did regular patrolmen's duty with great effect.

In the name of the public, and of the department in which they were volunteers, we thank them.

Mr. Crowley, the superintendent of the police telegraph, and the attachés of his department, by untiring and sleepless vigilance in transmitting information by telegraph unceasingly through more than ten days and nights, have more than sustained the high reputation they have always possessed.

Through all these bloody contests, through all the wearing fatigue and wasting labor, you have demeaned yourselves like worthy members of the Metropolitan Police.

The public judgment will commend and reward you. A kind Providence has permitted you to escape with less casualties than could have been expected. You have lost one comrade, whom you have buried with honor. Your wounded will, it is hoped, all recover, to join you and share honor. It is hoped that the severe but just chastisement which has been inflicted upon those guilty of riot, pillage, arson, and murder, will deter further attempts of that character.   But if, arising out of political or other causes, there should be another attempt to interrupt public order, we shall call on you again to crush its authors, confident that you will respond like brave men, as you ever have, to the calls of duty; and in future, whenever the attempt may be made, you will have to aid you large forces of military, ably commanded, and thus be enabled to crush in the bud any attempted riot or revolution.

To General Canby, who, on the morning of Friday, the 17th inst., took command of the military, relieving Brigadier-general Brown, and to Gen. Dix, who succeeded General Wool, the public are indebted for prompt, vigorous, and willing aid to the police force in all the expeditions which have been called for since they assumed their commands.   Charged particularly with the protection of the immense amount of Federal property and interests in the Metropolitan district, and the police force charged with the maintenance of public order, the duties of the two forces are always coincident.

Whatever menaces or disturbs one equally menaces and disturbs the other.

We are happy to know that at all times the several authorities have co-operated with that concert and harmony which is necessary to secure vigor and efficiency in action.

Sergeant Young, of the detective force, aided by Mr. Newcomb and other special patrolmen, rendered most effective service in arranging the commissary supplies for the large number of police, military, special patrolmen, and destitute colored refugees, whose subsistence was thrown unexpectedly on the department. The duty was arduous and responsible, and was performed with vigor and fidelity. All the clerks of the department, each in his sphere, performed a manly share of the heavy duties growing out of these extraordinary circumstances. The Central Department became a home of refuge for large numbers of poor, persecuted colored men, women, and children, many of whom were wounded and sick, and all of whom were helpless, exposed, and poor. Mr. John H. Keyser, with his accustomed philanthropy, volunteered, and was appointed to superintend these wretched victims of violence and prejudice, and has devoted unwearied days to the duty. The pitiable condition of these poor people appeals in the strongest terms to the Christian charity of the benevolent and humane. The members of the force will do an acceptable service by calling the attention to their condition of those who are able and willing to contribute in charity to their relief.

BALTIMORE—CARRYING OFF THE DEAD RIOTERS

# CHAPTER XXI.

## ORANGE RIOTS OF 1870 AND 1871.

IN a free country like ours, where toleration of all
religions alike is one of the fundamental principles of
the Government, one would naturally think that open
persecution of any sect or body of religionists was
impossible. But the Irish, unfortunately, have brought
with them to this country not merely many of their
old customs and national fêtes, but their old religious
feuds.

Nearly two hundred years ago, William of Nassau,
Prince of Orange, or William the Third, a Protestant,
met the Catholic King, James the Second, of England,
in deadly battle, in the vales of Meath, through which
the Boyne River flows, and utterly routed him, and com-

13

pelled him to flee to the Continent for safety. According to old style, this was on the first day of July, as the old ballad says:

"'Twas bright July's first morning clear,
    Of unforgotten glory,
That made this stream, through ages dear,
    Renowned in song and story."

According to new style, however, this has become the twelfth of the month. The Ulster Protestant Society, known as Orangemen, was founded in 1795. It was a secret political organization, founded, it is said, to counteract the Ribbonmen, or Protectors, as they were called. Its object in this country, it is asserted, is entirely different, and more in harmony with other societies that have their annual celebration in New York City and other places.

It is not necessary to go over the bitter feuds between these and the Catholic Irish in the old country. The hates they engendered were brought here, but kept from any great outward manifestation, because the Orangemen indulged in no public displays. We believe that there had been only one procession previous to this. In this year, however, an imposing display was resolved upon, but no trouble was anticipated, and no precautions taken by the police. It was not proposed to parade the streets, but to form, and march in procession up Eighth Avenue, to Elm Park, corner of Ninetieth Street and Eighth Avenue, and have a picnic, and wind up with a dance. As the procession passed Fourth Street, in full Orange regalia, and about twenty-five hundred strong (men, women, and children), playing "Boyne Water," "Derry," and other tunes obnoxious to the Catholics, some two hundred Irishmen followed it with curses and threats.

Violence was, however, not feared, and the procession continued on, and at length reached the new Boulevard road, where a large body of Irishmen were at work. Beyond, however, the interchange of some words, nothing transpired, and it entered the park, and began the festivities of the day.

In the meanwhile, however, the rabble that had followed them came upon the Ribbonmen at work on the Boulevard road, and persuaded them to throw up work and join them, and the whole crowd, numbering probably about five hundred, started for the park. The foreman of the gang of three hundred workmen saw at once the danger, and hurried to the Thirty-first Precinct station, corner of One Hundredth Street and Ninth Avenue, and told Captain Helme of the state of things.

The latter immediately thought of the picnic, and, anticipating trouble, telegraphed to Jourdan for reinforcements. In the meanwhile, the mob, loaded with stones, advanced tumultuously towards the park, within which the unsuspecting Orangemen were giving themselves up to enjoyment. Suddenly a shower of stones fell among them, knocking over women and children, and sending consternation through the crowd. Shouts and curses followed, and the Orangemen, rallying, rushed out and fell furiously on their assailants. Shovels, clubs, and stones were freely used, and a scene of terrific confusion followed. The fight was close and bloody, and continued for nearly half an hour, when Sergeant John Kelly, with a force of sixteen men, arrived, and rushing in between the combatants, separated them, and drove the Orangemen back into the park. The mob then divided into two portions, of between two and three hundred each. One party went by way of Ninth Avenue, and, breaking down the fence on that side, entered the park, and fell with brutal fury on men, women, and children alike. A terrible fight followed, and amid the shouts and oaths of the men and screams of the women and children, occasional pistol-shots were heard, showing that murder was being done. The enraged, unarmed Orangemen, wrenched hand rails from the fence, tore up small trees, and seized anything and everything that would serve for a weapon, and maintained the fight for a half an hour, before the police arrived. The second portion went by Eighth Avenue, and intercepted a large body of Orangemen that had retreated from the woods, and a desperate battle followed. There were only two policemen here, and of course could do nothing but stand and look on the murderous conflict. In the meantime, the force telegraphed for by Captain Helme arrived. It consisted of twenty men, to which Captain Helme added the reserve force, with a sergeant from the Eighth, Ninth, Fifteenth, Sixteenth, and Nineteenth Precincts, making in all some fifty men. These he divided into two portions, one of which he sent over to Eighth Avenue to protect the cars, into which the fugitives were crowding, while the other dashed furiously into the park, and fell on the combatants with their clubs. They soon cleared a lane between them, when turning on the Ribbonmen, they drove them out of the park. They then formed the Orangemen into a procession, and escorted them down the city. A portion, however, had fled for the

Eighth Avenue cars; but a party of Ribbonmen were lying in wait here, and another fight followed. Huge stones were thrown through the windows of the cars, the sides broken in, over the wreck of which the mob rushed, knocking down men, women, and children alike, whose shouts, and oaths, and screams could be heard blocks off. The scene was terrific, until the arrival of the police put an end to it, and bore the dead and wounded away.

About seven o'clock, Superintendent Jourdan arrived in the precinct, accompanied by Inspectors Dilks and Walling, and Detectives Farley and Avery. In the basement of the Thirty-first Precinct station, on a low trestle bed, three bloody corpses were stretched, while the neighboring precincts were filled with the wounded. Two more died before morning. The street near each station was crowded with Orangemen inquiring after friends.

Although no more outbreaks occurred, the most intense excitement prevailed among the Irish population of the city, and it was evident that it needed only a suitable occasion to bring on another conflict.

### THE RIOT OF 1871.

When the next anniversary of the Orangemen came round, it was discovered that a conspiracy had been formed by a large body of the Catholic population to prevent its public celebration. The air was full of rumors, while the city authorities were in possession of the fullest evidence that if the Orangemen paraded, they would be attacked, and probably many lives be lost. They were in great dilemma as to what course to pur sue. If they allowed the procession to take place, they would be compelled to protect it, and shoot down the men whose votes helped largely to place them in power. If they forbade it, they feared the public indignation that would be aroused against such a truckling, unjust course. As the day drew near, however, and the extensive preparations of the Irish Catholics became more apparent, they finally determined to risk the latter course, and it was decided that Superintendent Kelso should issue an order forbidding the Orangemen to parade. This ludicrous attempt on the part of the Mayor to shift the responsibility from his own shoulders, awakened only scorn, and the appearance of the order was followed by a storm of indignation that was appalling The leading papers, without regard to politics, opened on him and his advisers, with such a torrent of denunciations that they quailed before it. Processions of all kinds and nationalities were allowed on the streets, and to forbid only one, and that because it was *Protestant*, was an insult to every American citizen. Even Wall Street forgot its usual excitement, and leading men were heard violently denouncing this cowardly surrender of Mayor Hall to the threats of a mob. An impromptu meeting was called in the Produce Exchange, and a petition drawn up, asking the president to call a formal meeting, and excited men stood in line two hours, waiting their turn to sign it. The building was thronged, and the vice-president called the meeting to order, and informed it that the rules required twenty-four hours' notice for such a meeting. The members, however, would listen to no delay, and with an unanimous and thundering vote, declared the rules suspended. The action of the city authorities

was denounced in withering terms, and a committee of
leading men appointed to wait on them, and remon-
strate with the Mayor.  One could scarcely have
dreamed that this order would stir New York so profoundly.  But the people, peculiarly sensitive to any
attack on religious freedom, were the more fiercely
aroused, that in this case it was a Catholic mob using
the city authority to strike down Protestantism.  The
Mayor and his subordinates were appalled at the tempest they had raised, and calling a council, resolved to
revoke the order.  In the meantime, Governor Hoffman was telegraphed to from Albany.  Hastening to
the city, he, after a consultation with Mayor Hall, decided to issue the following proclamation :

"Having been only this day apprised, while at the
capital, of the actual condition of things here, with
reference to proposed processions to-morrow, and
having, in the belief that my presence was needed,
repaired hither immediately, I do make this proclamation :

" The order heretofore issued by the police authorities, in reference to said processions, being duly re-
voked, I hereby give notice that any and all bodies of
men desiring to assemble in peaceable procession to-
morrow, the 12th inst., will be permitted to do so.
They will be protected to the fullest extent possible by
the military and police authorities.  A police and
military escort will be furnished to any body of men
desiring it, on application to me at my head-quarters
(which will be at police head-quarters in this city) at
any time during the day.  I warn all persons to abstain
from interference with any such assembly or procession,

except by authority from me ; and I give notice that all the powers of my command, civil and military, will be used to preserve the public peace, and put down at all hazards, every attempt at disturbances ; and I call upon all citizens, of every race and religion, to unite with me and the local authorities in this determination to preserve the peace and honor of the city and State.

Dated at New York, this eleventh day of July, A. D. 1871.                          JOHN T. HOFFMAN.

It was thought by many that this would counteract the effects of the cowardly order of the police super-intendent.  But whatever its effect might have been, had it been issued earlier, it now came too late to do any good.  The preparations of the Roman Catholics were all made.  A secret circular had fallen into the hands of the police, showing that the organization of the rioters was complete—the watchwords and signals all arranged, and even the points designated where the attacks on the procession were to be made.  Arms had been collected and transported to certain localities, and everything betokened a stormy morrow.  Consequently, General Shaler issued orders to the commanders of the several regiments of militia, directing them to have their men in readiness at their respective armories at 7 o'clock next morning, prepared to march at a moment's warning.  His head-quarters, like those of General Brown in the draft riots, were at the police head-quarters, so as to have the use of the police tele-graph, in conveying orders to different sections of the city.  Meanwhile, detachments were placed on guard at the different armories, to frustrate any attempt on the part of the mob to seize arms.

BALTIMORE—A NIGHT SKIRMISH AT EUTAW STREET.

The night, however, wore quietly away, and in the morning the Governor's proclamation appeared in the morning papers, showing the rioters the nature of the work before them, if they undertook to carry out their infamous plans. It seemed to have no effect, however. Early in the morning sullen groups of Irishmen gathered on the corners of the streets, where the Irish resided in greatest numbers, among which were women, gesticulating and talking violently, apparently wholly unaware that the authorities had any power, or, at least, thought they dared not use it. Other groups traversed the streets, while at the several rendezvous of the Hibernians, many carried muskets or rifles without any attempt at concealment. In the upper part of the city, a body of rioters began to move southward, compelling all the workmen on their way to leave work and join them. One or two armories were attacked, but the rioters were easily repulsed. The demonstrations at length became so threatening, that by ten o'clock the police seized Hibernia Hall.

About the same time, the Orangemen—who on the issue of Kelso's order had determined not to parade but on the appearance of the Governor's proclamation changed their mind—began to assemble at Lamartine Hall, on the corner of Eighth Avenue and Twenty-ninth Street. Their room was in the fourth story, and the delegates from the various lodges brought with them their badges and banners, which they displayed from the windows. This brought a crowd in front of the building, curious to know what was going on in the lodge room. Soon five hundred policemen, ten or fifteen of them on horseback, appeared under the command of Inspectors Walling and Jamieson, and occu-

13*

pied both sides of Twenty-ninth Street, between Eighth
and Ninth Avenues. Several policemen also stood on
Eighth Avenue, while the door of the hall was guarded
by others. Inside the hall there were probably some
seventy-five or a hundred Orangemen, discussing the
parade. Some stated that a great many, concluding
there would be none, had gone to their usual work,
while others, alarmed at the threats of the Hibernians,
would not join it. But after some discussion, it was
resolved, that although the number would be small,
they would parade at all hazards; and at eleven o'clock
the door was thrown open, and the Orangemen, wearing orange colors, were admitted, amid the wildest
cheering. An invitation was sent to the lodges of
Jersey City to join them, but they declined, preferring
to celebrate the day at home.

Two o'clock was the hour fixed upon for the parade
to begin, and the authorities at police head-quarters
were so advised. In the meantime a banner had been
prepared on which was inscribed in large letters,

"AMERICANS! FREEMEN!! FALL IN!!!"

in order to get accessions from outsiders, but without
success.

The line of march finally resolved upon was down
Eighth Avenue to Twenty-third Street, and up it to
Fifth Avenue, down Fifth Avenue to Fourteenth
Street, along it to Union Square, saluting the Lincoln
and Washington statues as they passed, and then down
Fourth Avenue to Cooper Institute, where the pro-
cession would break up.

About one o'clock, a party of men came rushing

down Eighth Avenue, opposite Lamartine Hall, cheering and shouting, led by a man waving a sword cane. As he swung it above his head it parted, disclosing a long dirk. The police immediately advanced and swept the street. Eighth Avenue was cleared from Thirtieth Street to Twenty-eighth Street, and the police formed several deep, leaving only room enough for the cars to pass.

In the meantime, around police head-quarters, in Mott Street, things wore a serious aspect. From six o'clock in the morning, the various detachments of police kept arriving until Bleecker, Houston, Mulberry, and Mott Streets were dark with the massed battalions, ready to move at a moment's notice. Rations were served out to them standing. Early in the day, Governor Hoffman and staff arrived, and were quartered in the Superintendent's room, while General Shaler and staff were quartered in the fire marshal's office. Commissioners Manierre, Smith, and Barr were in their own rooms, receiving reports from the various precincts over the wires. A little after nine a dispatch came, stating that the quarrymen near Central Park had quitted work, and were gathering in excited groups, swearing that the Orangemen should not parade. Immediately Inspector Jamieson, with two hundred and fifty policemen, was despatched in stages to Forty-seventh Street and Eighth Avenue, to watch the course of events. Another dispatch stated that an attack was threatened on Harper's building, in Franklin Square, and Captain Allaire, of the Seventh Precinct, was hurried off with fifty men to protect it. A little later came the news that the Orangemen had determined to parade at two o'clock, and a police force of five hundred, as we have already stated, were massed in Eighth Avenue, opposite Lamartine Hall. About noon, a body of rioters made an attack on the armory, No. 19 Avenue A, in which were a hundred and thirty-eight stands of arms. Fortunately, the janitor of the building saw them in time to fasten the doors before they reached it, and then ran to the nearest police-station for help, from which a dispatch was sent to head-quarters. Captain Mount, with a hundred policemen, was hurried off to the threatened point. He arrived before the doors were broken in, and falling on the rioters with clubs, drove them in all directions. During the forenoon, Drill-captain Copeland was given five companies, and told to seize Hibernia Hall, where arms were being distributed. As he approached, he ordered the mob to disperse, but was answered with taunts and curses, while the women hurled stones at his face. He then gave the order to charge, when the men fell on the crowd with such fury, that they broke and fled in wild confusion. Meanwhile, the detectives had been busy, and secured eighteen of the ring-leaders, whom they marched to police head-quarters.

As the hour for the procession to form drew near, the most intense excitement prevailed at police head-quarters, and the telegraph was watched with anxious solicitude. The terrible punishment inflicted on the rioters in 1863 seemed to have been forgotten by the mob, and it had evidently resolved to try once more its strength with the city authorities. Around the Orange head-quarters a still deeper excitement prevailed. The hum of the vast multitude seemed like the first murmurings of the coming storm, and many a face turned pale as the Orangemen, with their banners and badges, only ninety in all, passed out of the door into the street. John Johnston, their marshal, mounted on a spirited horse, placed himself at their head. In a few minutes, the bayonets of the military force designed to act as an escort could be seen flashing in the sun, as the troops with measured tread moved steadily forward. Crowds followed them on the sidewalks, or hung from windows and house-tops, while low curses could be heard on every side, especially when the Twenty-second Regiment deliberately loaded their pieces with ball and cartridge. The little band of Orangemen looked serious but firm, while the military officers showed by their preparations and order that they expected bloody work. The Orangemen formed line in Twenty-ninth Street, close to the Eighth Avenue, and flung their banners to the breeze. A half an hour later, they were ready to march, and at the order wheeled into Eighth Avenue. At that instant a single shot rang out but a few rods distant. Heads were turned anxiously to see who was hit. More was expected as the procession moved on. A strong body of police marched in advance. Next came the Ninth Regiment, followed at a short interval by the Sixth. Then came more police, followed by the little band of Orangemen, flanked on either side, so as fully to protect them, by the Twenty-second and Eighty-fourth Regiments. To these succeeded more police. The imposing column was closed up by the Seventh Regiment, arresting all eyes by its even tread and martial bearing. The sidewalks, doorsteps, windows, and roofs were black with people. The band struck up a martial air, and the procession moved on towards Twenty-eighth Street. Just before they reached it, another shot rang clear and sharp above the music.

No one was seen to fall, and the march continued. At the corner of Twenty-seventh Street, a group of desperate-looking fellows were assembled on a wooden shed that projected over the sidewalk. Warned to get down and go away, they hesitated, when a company of soldiers levelled their pieces at them. Uttering defiant threats, they hurried down and disappeared. As the next corner was reached, another shot was fired, followed by a shower of stones. A scene of confusion now ensued. The police fell on the bystanders occupying the sidewalks, and clubbed them right and left without distinction, and the order rolled down the line to the inmates of the houses to shut their windows. Terror now took the place of curiosity; heads disappeared, and the quick, fierce slamming of blinds was heard above the uproar blocks away. The procession kept on till it reached Twenty-fourth Street, when a halt was ordered. The next moment a shot was fired from the second-story windows of a house on the northeast corner. It struck the Eighty-fourth Regiment, and in an instant a line of muskets was pointed at the spot, as though the order to fire was expected. One gun went off, when, without orders, a sudden, unexpected volley rolled down the line of the Sixth, Ninth, and Eighty-fourth Regiments. The officers were wholly taken by surprise at this unprecedented conduct; but, recovering themselves, rushed among the ranks and shouted out their orders to cease firing. But the work was done; and as the smoke slowly lifted in the hot atmosphere, a scene of indescribable confusion presented itself. Men, women, and children, screaming in wild terror, were fleeing in every direction; the strong trampling down the weak, while eleven corpses lay stretched on the sidewalk, some piled across each other. A pause of a few minutes now followed, while the troops reloaded their guns. A new attack was momentarily expected, and no one moved from the ranks to succor the wounded or lift up the dead. Here a dead woman lay across a dead man ; there a man streaming with blood was creeping painfully up a doorstep, while crouching, bleeding forms appeared in every direction. Women from the windows looked down on the ghastly spectacle, gesticulating wildly. The police now cleared the avenue and side streets, when the dead and wounded were attended to, and the order to move on was given. General Varian, indignant at the conduct of the Eighty-fourth in firing first without orders, sent it to the rear, and replaced it on the flank of the Orangemen with a portion of the Ninth. The procession, as it now resumed its march and moved through Twenty-fourth Street, was a sad and mournful one. The windows were filled with spectators, and crowds lined the sidewalks, but all were silent and serious. Not till it reached Fifth Avenue Hotel were there any greetings of welcome. Here some three thousand people were assembled, who rent the air with cheers. No more attacks were made, and it reached Cooper Institute and disbanded without any further incident.

In the meantime, the scene at the Bellevue Hospital was a sad and painful one. The ambulances kept discharging their bloody loads at the door, and groans of distress and shrieks of pain filled the air. Long rows of cots, filled with mangled forms, were stretched on every side, while the tables were covered with bodies, held down, as the surgeons dressed their wounds. The dead were carried to the Morgue, around which, as night came on, a clamorous crowd was gathered, seeking admission, to look after their dead friends. A similar crowd gathered at the door of the Mount Sinai Hospital, filling the air with cries and lamentations. As darkness settled over the city, wild, rough-looking men from the lowest ranks of society gathered in the street where the slaughter took place, among whom were seen bare-headed women roaming about, making night hideous with their curses.

A pile of dead men's hats stood on the corner of Eighth Avenue and Twenty-fifth Street untouched, and pale faces stooped over pools of blood on the pavement. The stores were all shut, and everything wore a gloomy aspect. The police stood near, revealed in the lamplight, but made no effort to clear the street. It seemed at one time that a serious outbreak would take place, but the night passed off quietly, and the riot was ended, and the mob once more taught the terrible lesson it is so apt to forget.

Two of the police and military were killed, and twenty-four wounded; while of the rioters thirty-one were killed, and sixty-seven wounded—making in all one hundred and twenty-eight victims.

There was much indignation expressed at the troops for firing without orders, and firing so wildly as to shoot some of their own men. It was, of course, deserving the deepest condemnation, yet it may have saved greater bloodshed. The fight evidently did not occur at the expected point, and doubtless the result here, prevented one where the mob was better organized, and would have made a more stubborn resistance.

BALTIMORE—ARRIVAL OF GATLING GUNS AT CAMDEN ST. DEPOT.

That innocent persons were killed is true; but if they will mingle in with a mob, they must expect to share its fate, and alone must bear the blame.   Troops are called out to fire on the people if they persist in violation of the peace and rights of the community.   Of this all are fully aware, and hence take the risk of being shot.   Soldiers cannot be expected to discriminate in a mob.   If the military are not to fire on a crowd of rioters until no women and children can be seen in it, they had better stay at home.

To a casual observer, this calling out of seven hundred policemen and several regiments of soldiers, in order to let ninety men take a foolish promenade through a few streets, would seem a very absurd and useless display of the power of the city; and the killing of sixty or seventy men a heavy price to pay for such an amusement.   But it was not ninety Orangemen only that those policemen and soldiers enclosed and shielded.   They had in their keeping the laws and authority of the city, set at defiance by a mob, and also the principle of religious toleration and of equal rights, which were of more consequence than the lives of ten thousand men.   The day when New York City allows itself to be dictated to by a mob, and Protestants not be permitted to march as such quietly through the streets, her prosperity and greatness will come to an end.   The taking of life is a serious thing, but it is not to weigh a moment against the preservation of authority and the supremacy of the law.

One thing should not be overlooked—the almost universal faithfulness of the Roman Catholic Irish police to their duty.   In this, as well as in the draft riots, they have left a record of which any city might be proud. To defend Protestant Irishmen against Roman Catholic friends and perhaps relatives, is a severe test of fidelity ; but the Irish police have stood it nobly, and won the regard of all good citizens.*

# OFFICIAL REPORTS ON THE DRAFT RIOTS.

## REPORT OF CAPTAIN PUTNAM.

FORT HAMILTON, July 21, 1863.

SIR:—I have the honor herewith to make the following report of the operations of my command, during the late riots in New York City.

At the commencement of the riot I was in command of the fort at Sandy Hook, New York Harbor. On the night of the 13th of July, I received orders from General Brown, to proceed with my company to New York City. In thirty minutes my command was ready, with twenty rounds of ammunition. On my arrival in the city, I proceeded to the St. Nicholas Hotel, and remained in that vicinity about two hours. I was then ordered to report to the Mayor, at the City Hall. I marched my company down Broadway to the City Hall, as directed, and was immediately ordered back to the St. Nicholas by General Wool, and from there General Wool ordered me to proceed to General Brown's headquarters, No. 300 Mulberry Street. On my reporting to General Brown, I was ordered to proceed with my company to Forty-sixth Street, where the mob was burning buildings.

We were accompanied by a force of sixty policemen, under Captain Walling. On our arrival there, we found the mob in strong force, burning and destroying property. We immediately charged on the rioters with our whole force, both military and police. The mob fought desperately for about five minutes, when they broke in all directions, leaving a number of dead and wounded in the street. Their loss in killed and wounded would not fall short of forty. One of my company was badly wounded, and was sent to the Jewish hospital. Several others were more or less injured by stones thrown by the mob. My company numbered eighty-two enlisted men. Lieutenant Stacey, Twelfth Infantry, was the only company officer beside myself with the company.

After dispersing the mob, we returned about 5 P.M. to head-quarters—the men having marched during the day not less than twelve miles.

### Operations on Tuesday night.

10.30 P.M. My company, together with a police force of one hundred men, were ordered out and marched through a large portion of the city. Found everything quiet. Distance marched about seven miles. Returned to head-quarters at 1.30 A.M.

### Operations on Wednesday, July 15.

About one o'clock P.M., received orders to march up the Bowery and Third Avenue, and disperse the mob wherever found. After getting into Third Avenue a short distance, we met a regiment or part of a regiment of militia, commanded by a major. I think he had four companies. The rioters were collected in great force, and were firing on the militia with both muskets and revolvers. The troops were retiring before the mob, who had completely filled the avenue for some distance, also the cross streets in the vicinity.

We immediately marched by the militia, when the mob commenced firing on us. I ordered my skirmishers to fire on them, which they did with effect. We advanced steadily, the fight being between the skirmishers and the mob, which soon gave way, and ran in all di-rections.

We then marched up to Fourth Avenue, but found no disturbance there.

At this time I was informed by a special policeman,

that the mob had again collected in greater numbers than ever, on Third Avenue, and were determined not to let me march back on that street. I immediately marched down the nearest cross street to Third Avenue again; when the mob saw us, they scattered without firing a shot.

I then returned to head-quarters with my command, which consisted of my own company and one field piece of artillery, under command of Captain Rawolle, of General Brown's staff. The men of my command behaved like veterans.

### Operations on Wednesday night.

About nine o'clock I was informed by General Brown, that a force of militia, under Colonel Jardine, had been driven from Nineteenth Street by the mob, leaving a number killed and wounded, including their commanding officer, in the hands of the mob.

The general ordered me to take my own company (the permanent guard from Fort Hamilton being for the time under the command of Captain Shelley, aide-de-camp,) and Captain Rawolle, with one gun from his battery, and proceed to Nineteenth Street, disperse the mob, and bring Colonel Jardine and the wounded officers and men of his command to head-quarters. We marched down Nineteenth Street, and met the mob near First Avenue. I immediately ordered Sergeant Roche, with the skirmishers, to attack them, which he did, Lieutenant Stacey, Twelfth Infantry, supporting him with the first platoon of company F (my own). The mob were driven back, but continued to fire on us. At this time I left Lieutenant Stacey to take care of the mob, and commenced a search for Colonel Jardine and others of his command. We found the colonel in a house, the family having hid him. He was very badly wounded in the thigh. We also found another wounded officer, whose name I did not learn. They were placed in a carriage. In the meantime, the mob had gathered on Second Avenue, and commenced firing on Captain Shelley's company, which I had posted near there; a few shots from the skirmishers drove them away, and the mob being entirely dispersed, and everything quiet, we returned to head-quarters, bringing the wounded officers with us, also a number of ladies, to a place of safety. I forgot to mention a detachment of the Thirtieth Militia, which was ordered by Colonel Winston to accompany my command; they behaved well. Colonel Winston was with me during this affair, and although having no command, conducted himself as only a soldier can. I did not lose a man killed, and only a few slightly injured, during the evening.

### Operations on Thursday.

At nine o'clock A.M., went up Third Avenue. Inspector Carpenter, deputy superintendent of police, accompanied me. Marched through several streets for a distance of about five miles, found everything quiet, and returned to head-quarters.

### Operations on Thursday evening.

About six o'clock P.M., General Dodge and Colonel Mott informed General Brown, that the troops at Grammercy Park had marched down Twenty-second Street, and been attacked by an armed mob; that they had been driven back, leaving their dead in the street. The general ordered me to take my company, and portion of the Twentieth and Twenty-eighth New York volunteer batteries, about eighty men, armed as infantry, commanded by Lieutenant B. F. Ryer. Lieutenant Ryer had with him Lieutenant Robert F. Joyce and Lieutenant F. M. Chase, Twenty-eighth New York battery. My whole command amounted to one hundred and sixty men.

With this force I marched to the Grammercy Hotel. At a short distance from the hotel, I saw some of the rioters fire from a house on some of Colonel Mott's command. I immediately sent Lieutenant Joyce with a few men to search the house. The search was fruitless, the men having escaped to the rear. I then told the women in the house that the artillery would open on the house, if any more shots were fired from it. We then marched down Twenty-second Street, between Second and Third Avenues, found the body of a sergeant of Davis' Cavalry, who had been killed two hours before. I ordered a livery-stable keeper to put his horses to a carriage, and accompany me, for the purpose of carrying the dead and wounded. He replied that the mob would kill him if he did, and that he dare not do it. He was informed that he would be protected if he went, but if he refused he would be instantly shot. The horses were speedily harnessed, and the body put into the carriage. The mob at this time commenced firing on us from the houses. We at once commenced searching the houses, while my skirmishers drove the rioters back from every window and from the roofs. The houses were searched from cellar to the roof. The mob, made a desperate fight, and evidently seemed to think they could whip us. Every house that was used to conceal these rioters was cleared. A large number was killed, and several prisoners taken. We then marched to Second Avenue, where we found the mob in great force and concealed in houses. They fired on us from house-tops, and from windows, and also from cross streets. We soon cleared the streets, and then commenced searching the houses. We searched thirteen houses, killed those within that resisted, and took the remainder prisoners. Some of them fought like incarnate fiends, and would not surrender. All such were shot on the spot. The soldiers captured a large number of revolvers of large size, which I allowed them to keep. The mob at this place were well armed; nearly every one had some kind of fire-arms, and had one blunderbuss which they fired on us.

If they had been cool and steady, they might have

done us great harm. As it was, they fired wildly, running to a window and firing, and then retreating back out of danger.

When my soldiers once got into a house they made short work of it. The fight lasted about forty minutes and was more severe than all the rest in which my command was engaged. There were none of my men killed. Sergeant Cadro, of company F, Twelfth Infantry (my own), was slightly wounded in the hand; private Krouse was also slightly wounded.

The mob being entirely dispersed, we returned to head-quarters.

I remained at head-quarters till Saturday, when I was ordered by General Canby to Fort Hamilton. I have since been informed by Mr. Acton, President of the Board of Police Commissioners, that our fight (that of Thursday night) had the effect of crushing the rioters in the city, and that there has been no trouble since.

I would respectfully call the attention of the general to the noble conduct of the officers who served with me on different occasions, during the riot, and beg leave to mention their names, together with some of the non-commissioned officers.

First Lieutenant M. H. Stacey, Twelfth Infantry.

Captain Rawolle, aide-de-camp, commanding Artillery.

Captain Shelley, aide-de-camp, commanding Fort Hamilton permanent guard.

Lieutenant B. F. Ryer, Twentieth New York Artillery.

Lieutenant R. F. Joyce, Twenty-eighth New York battery.

Lieutenant F. M. Chase, Twenty-eighth New York battery.

First Sergeant J. E. Putnam, company F, Twelfth Infantry.

Sergeant R. W. Tompson, company F, Twelfth Infantry.

PITTSBURGH—RIOTERS DISTRIBUTING STOLEN WHISKY.

Sergeant Frank Westcott, company F, Twelfth Infantry.

Sergeant Patrick Roach, company F, Twelfth Infantry, had charge of the skirmishers, and behaved nobly.

Sergeant Peter Cadro, company F, Twelfth Infantry, who was slightly wounded on Thursday night.

Sergeant Kimball, of the permanent guard. I do not know the names of the sergeants of the other companies, but all, as well as privates, without exception, acted like veterans.

I am, sir, very respectfully your obedient servant,

H. R. PUTNAM,
*Capt. Twelfth U. S. Infantry Com. company F,*
*Second Battery.*

First Lieutenant J. P. McELRATH,
*Fifth U. S. Art. A. A. A. G.*

---

### REPORT OF CAPTAIN FRANKLIN.

FORT RICHMOND, NEW YORK HARBOR, July 23, 1863.

SIR:—I have the honor to make the following report in regard to the part taken by " H " company, second battalion, Twelfth United States Infantry, and the troops attached to it, in quelling the late disturbances in New York City.

Monday, July 14, about three o'clock P.M., I received an order for one platoon to report to Lieutenant Wood. Fifteen minutes after the order was received, thirty-five men were on the boat, with thirty rounds of ammunition in their boxes. I accompanied the men over to Fort Lafayette, and there received an order from General Brown, to take charge of Lieutenant Wood's men, numbering fifty-four, and proceed to Leonard Street, New York, and report to Colonel Nugent, assistant provost marshal general. On my arrival at the corner of Leonard Street and Broadway, I received an order from Colonel Nugent, to report to him at the arsenal, corner of Thirty-fifth Street and Seventh Avenue.

The command proceeded up Eighth Avenue to Thirty-fifth Street to the arsenal, and reported to Colonel Nugent as ordered. The company remained at the arsenal till eleven o'clock that night, when it was ordered to report to General Brown, at the police head-quarters, No. 300 Mulberry Street.

Finding that General Brown had been relieved of his command, I reported in person to General Wool, who directed me to remain at the police head-quarters, at the same time detaching Lieutenant Wood, and ordering him to command the Fort Hamilton permanent guard. Tuesday morning, about nine o'clock, I received an order from General Brown, to proceed to Thirty-fourth Street and Second Avenue, to quell a disturbance which was raging there. I immediately took possession of the Fourth Avenue cars, and proceeded as directed at a rapid rate. On approaching near the scene of the riot, I heard firing, and forming my company by platoons, marched up Fourth Avenue to Thirty-fourth Street, down Thirty-fourth Street to a point where two field-pieces were in position. I was followed and surrounded by a threatening mob from the time I left the cars. The crowd soon commenced throwing stones and brick-bats, at the same time brandishing clubs, and beckoning to their comrades to come on; but on facing the rear platoon about, and coming to a "ready," they suddenly disappeared, and gave me no further trouble till I reported to Colonel O'Brien.

The colonel seemed to have the mob pretty well scattered before we reached them, but there was firing still going on by his men, who were deployed as skirmishers. I held my company as a reserve, near the field-pieces, and continued to do so till we returned to police head-quarters. I was joined before going on this expedition, by 36 men of company " H," so that the total number I had, leaving behind the number of sick, was about 115. After being at the police headquarters about thirty minutes, my company was ordered to go with a party of police to Grand Street. Lieutenant Penny, the only commissioned officer I had with me, was taken sick at this time, and was not able to join me till Wednesday. We marched down Grand Street to East River, and back, but did not find any mob.

About two o'clock, my company, with about 150 policemen, was ordered to proceed to Twenty-second Street and First and Second Avenues. On reaching Second Avenue, we found a large crowd collected, which soon retreated to First Avenue, firing with stones and muskets continually. The police making way for me, the company was marched in three sections down Twenty-second Street to First Avenue, and down First Avenue to Twenty-first Street. The crowd grew more insolent, and increased the firing as we advanced. In Twenty-second Street the police took possession of between 200 and 300 carbines, which the mob was in the act of taking when we arrived; they were all brought safely to the station-house. At the corner of Twenty-first Street and First Avenue I halted the company, and fired by sections, allowing each section to fall to the rear to load as fast as it had fired. The crowd soon retired to the houses and roofs, from which they kept up a fire for some minutes, but soon ceased altogether, as a number of them had been killed, and it became rather dangerous for them to show a head anywhere. I then withdrew my company by the same routes and in the same manner I had advanced. Going down Second Avenue, the crowd seemed to increase very rapidly, and became more and more threatening. They were allowed to get quite close to us, when I faced the rear section about, and fired one or two volleys, which must have been very effective, as they dispersed, and did not give us any further trouble, till we reached police head-quarters. Some of my men received blows from stones, but none were seri-ously hurt.

After resting an hour or two, my men were put in stages, and ordered to go to Twenty-first Street and Eighth Avenue. I marched the company up and down the avenues, and through several of the streets, but did not find a crowd that offered any resistance.

We took the stages again, and proceeded to Twenty-ninth Street and Eighth avenue, and found there that a house had been just sacked, and some of the plunder-ers being found in it, were instantly killed. My com-pany charged wherever there was a crowd, and it was instantly scattered.

Marching up to Fifth Avenue, and not finding any mob, we took the stages to police head-quarters. The company was not called on again during the night.

Wednesday morning, about twelve o'clock, it was ordered with 50 policemen to proceed to Harlem. On arriving there, we found that the mob had disappeared as soon as they heard of our coming. They had burned one or two buildings, but did not give us or the citizens of Harlem any trouble during our stay there. I was relieved by a company of the N. G. Seventy-first, and ordered to proceed to Fort Rich-mond on Monday morning, July 21st. In compliance with your request, that I should mention any officers, non-commissioned officers, or privates who had partic-ularly distinguished themselves, I have to make the following statement. Lieutenant Penny, the only com-missioned officer I had with me, was taken sick on Monday evening, and was only able to march with me to Thirty-fourth Street; he joined me again when we moved to Harlem.

Among non-commissioned officers and privates, all of whom acted so exceedingly well, it is very hard to make any distinction. First Sergeant Eggemeyer, who at the battle of Gaines' Mill, in Virginia, had sole charge of a company, and fought it all through that day till wounded and taken prisoner, did equally well on this occasion. Sergeants Livingstone, Corsa, Ruby, Burke, and Jackson, and Corporals Williams, Bothwell, Yonkers, Brandon, and Raymond were very cool, and did excellent service. The men, amid the numerous temptations they had to drink, and the fatigue they endured in marching over stone pavements, kept perfectly sober, and bore the threats and insults of the mob with perfect coolness.

Corporal Raymond and eight of my men were detailed to guard the house of Mayor Opdyke, which duty they performed till they were relieved on Monday.

My company at no time numbered more than 120 men, and generally about 105.

I am, sir, very respectfully,
Your obedient servant,

WALTER S. FRANKLIN,
*Captain Twelfth Infantry.*

Brev. Brig.-gen. HARVEY BROWN, Fort Hamilton, N. Y.

---

REPORT OF CAPTAIN WILKINS.

FORT COLUMBUS, NEW YORK HARBOR, July 21, 1863.

SIR:—I have the honor to report, that, in obedience to orders from Major-general Wool, I proceeded on Monday the 13th inst., at half-past one o'clock P.M., in command of 89 non-commissioned officers and privates of the permanent party, with directions "to report to Colonel Robert Nugent, A. A., provost-marshal general, 106 Leonard Street, for special service."

Arrived there, I found orders to report to Colonel Nugent, at the arsenal on Thirty-fifth Street, and marched to that point. On my arrival there I reported, and was directed to hold myself under the orders of Major-general Sandford, who was present. At about four o'clock P.M., I was ordered to take the advance of a command, consisting of my own men, the marines, and a detachment of the Invalid Corps, all under the command of General Sandford. After marching in various directions about the city—my knowledge of the streets being limited—without encountering the mob I received orders to march the entire command back to the arsenal. On the morning of the 14th, I was ordered to Mayor Opdyke's house. On my arrival, I found the mob had left, but the neighborhood threatened. Remained about two hours, and reported with command at head-quarters. Shortly after received orders to proceed to a police station, in the Twentieth Ward, situated on Thirty-fifth Street, between Eighth and Ninth Avenues. On my road to this point, I found a portion of the rioters sacking a house on a street leading into Ninth Avenue. They retired on my approach. Finding the house had been set fire to, I remained long enough to have it extinguished, and followed the rioters into Ninth Avenue. I had moved but a short distance, when an attack was made on the command from the rear. I immediately opened fire, which was kept up at intervals until we reached Thirty-fifth Street and Ninth Avenue, when I halted till the police force at that station (about 20) joined me. In front of me, on the Ninth Avenue, I observed what appeared to be a formidable barricade, guarded by a strong force of rioters. After waiting a short time, endeavoring to procure a field-piece, I concluded to storm the barricade with the small force I had, and wheeled into the avenue, advancing rapidly to the first barricade, which I found composed of empty wagons, carts, telegraph poles and wires. The rioters retreated, and under the protection of the company, the police removed the obstructions; no small task, as they had to roll the wagons away, untwist the wires, lift poles; which of course occupied time, and exposed them to the missiles of the mob. On removing the barricade, I encountered a second, and thus for four the same process was gone through. During this time, neither the mob nor my men were idle, but were constantly exchanging civilities in the shape of stones and shot.  After removing the barricades, and getting a clear street, I proceeded still farther up, when I was suddenly assailed with a terrific shower of brick-bats, thrown by unseen hands from the houses under which we were passing.  After engaging this latter party, I concluded to take post at the station-house, as it was almost too dark to operate with any success.  I returned without any molestation to the station-house, and remained there that night.  On the morning of the 15th, Lieutenant Porter, of the First Artillery, joined me, bringing orders for the company to report at headquarters.  On reporting, I was ordered to the works of the Manhattan Gas Company, on the East River, foot of Fourteenth Street.  On my arriving there, I found the works at a stand-still, on account of the workmen having been driven off by the rioters; and unless something was done, the city would soon be in darkness.  Under the protection of the company, and the exertions of the engineer in charge, labor was resumed, and continued during my stay, which was up to Saturday night, the 19th, at which time I was relieved, and ordered to report at this point.

Lieutenant Porter, during the time he was with me, was efficient and of great service.  During the time he was absent, I understand he was very active in the discharge of the various duties imposed upon him.

Being the only officer with the company in the engagement of the 14th, I relied upon and received great assistance from Sergeant McGrath (acting first sergeant), Sergeants Sutler, Foster, Finn, and Delancey; also Lance Sergeants Smith and Steward.  The entire command behaved well in the trying position in which they were placed.

I am, very respectfully, your obedient servant,
JOHN D. WILKINS,
*Captain 3d Infantry commanding P. P.*
Lieut. S. F. McELRATH, *Acting Adj. Fifth Artillery.*

List of wounded :
> Sergeant EDWARD McGRATH, contused.
> Sergeant SMITH, contused.
> Corporal LEWIS, contused.
> HUGH CAREY, contused.

REPORT OF SURGEON SMITH.

FORT WOOD, July 21, 1863.

SIR :—In obedience to your order dated July 20th, I
have the honor to make the following report :

That upon July 13th, while I was absent from this
post, an order arrived, directing me to report, with my
command, to the Mayor of New York immediately for
duty.  My first sergeant, immediately upon the arrival of the order, assembled the men, and in ten minutes was aboard the steamer, *en route* to New York.
Upon his arrival he reported to the Mayor, who gave
him an order to report to the officer commanding the
arsenal, corner of Seventh Avenue and Thirty-fifth
Street.  It was a few minutes subsequent to this that
I met my company, commanded by the Sergeant,
marching rapidly up Broadway, in obedience to the
last order.  I immediately took command, and marched
direct to the arsenal, *via* Broadway, to Twenty-eighth
Street, and Seventh Avenue, and reported to General
Sandford, who ordered me to march my men into the
arsenal, and await further orders.  Shortly after, I
received conflicting orders from various parties whose
authority was not sufficiently evident to permit their
being obeyed.  And as night was coming on, and the
crowd around the building was increasing, and there
was nothing to prevent a determined mob from carrying the first floor, and firing the building, I moved my
men down from the fourth story, and took possession
of the first floor, and put it in such a state of defence
as the means at my command permitted.  I preferred
defending the building from the inside of the first floor,
because my command was too small to permit of my

PITTSBURGH—ARREST OF A RIOTER DEFENDED BY THE MOB.

holding all of the approaches from the outside. During the night I was relieved by Captain Wilkins, Third U. S. Infantry, commanding the permanent party from Fort Columbus, and ordered to report to No. 300 Mulberry Street, which I did. Tuesday morning, July 14th, I received an order in person from General Wool, to report to Brigadier-general Brown for duty, and was by him ordered to report with my command to Captain Putnam, Twelfth U. S. Infantry, at the City Hall. Upon arriving at the City Hall, I received an order from General Wool to report to Mr. Barney, of the Custom House, to guard some stores to be transported to Fort Columbus, and to remain at Fort Columbus for the protection of the ordnance stores at that post. This order was not obeyed, because my services were not required by the Custom House officers. During the day Captain Putnam was ordered elsewhere, and I was left with a section of artillery belonging to the Fifteenth New York. In compliance with your instructions, the command was so disposed as to protect the immediate vicinity as completely as possible. The artillery was posted, supported by my own men, so as to sweep all the points to be defended. In this position I remained till July 18th, when, by order of General Canby, I was relieved and ordered to return with my company to this post.

The behavior of my men during the time we were on duty was soldierly and prompt to the highest degree. Upon Saturday, after five days and nights of unremitting service, constantly exposed, my whole original detachment was on duty, without exception, and all doing their duty cheerfully and willingly, although some of them were suffering severely from old wounds, which had become irritable from the severe duty they had been performing. The strength of this command during the period we were on duty in New York was fifty-three men. JOSEPH L. SMITH,
*Assistant Surgeon U. S. A.*

Brigadier-general BROWN, U. S. A.

REPORT OF LIEUTENANT WOOD.

FORT LAFAYETTE, N. Y. H., July 20, 1863.

SIR :—I have the honor to report that my command, as ordered by you, came in contact with the rioters for the first time about ten o'clock on the morning of the 14th inst., in Pitt Street. My command consisted of detachments from Forts Lafayette, Hamilton, and Richmond, and numbered one hundred and thirty men.

Previous to my order to fire, I commanded the rioters, which were about five thousand strong, to disperse, which they refused to do, and commenced an assault with clubs, stones, and other missiles. I then gave the order to fire, with the following result : fourteen killed and seventeen wounded. After reloading, I charged bayonets, and the rioters fled in every direction. I then proceeded to the corner of Division and Grand Streets, where another large body of rioters were assembled. I halted my command about thirty paces from them, and ordered them to disperse, telling them if they did not, I would fire upon them. They wavered. I charged upon them, and dispersed them at the point of the bayonet. I then cleared the neighboring streets of all rioters ; and when everything was quiet, returned to the head-quarters in Mulberry Street, before reaching which place, I unfortunately fell, and sprained my leg so badly as to incapacitate me from any further active service during the riot.

I cannot speak too praiseworthily of my men. They all acted bravely ; but particular mention should be made of Lance Sergeant Louis Bluff, general service, acting first sergeant of the detachment, for his coolness and bravery ; there being no commissioned officer with me, his position being one of great responsibility ; also Private James McCarthy, of the permanent guard of Fort Hamilton. The latter, after the volley was fired into the rioters in Pitt Street, rushed from the ranks into their midst, bayoneted one of them who carried a flag, captured the flag, and returned with it to the command. The number of men from this command on duty in New York during the riot was eighty.

Very respectfully, your obedient servant,

THOMAS O. WOOD,
*First Lieutenant Ninth U. S. Infantry.*

---

REPORT OF LIEUTENANT RYER.

OFFICE OF THE SUPERINTENDENT OF POLICE,
300 MULBERRY STREET, NEW YORK, July 20th, 1863.

SIR:—I have the honor to transmit herewith, a report of the operations of my command during the period of the late riots in New York City.

Pursuant to orders from General Brown, I reported to him with my command, which comprised parts of the Twenty-sixth and Twenty-eighth batteries (numbering one hundred men, well armed and equipped, with rifles), on Tuesday, the 14th inst., at about 6 P.M. Immediately on reporting, I received orders to march to Thirty-sixth Street and Second and Third Avenues, to recover the body of Colonel O'Brien, who had been killed in that neighborhood. On arriving there we found that the body had been removed, and no sign of the mob remaining. I immediately marched back to head-quarters in Mulberry Street, and reported the fact about twelve o'clock. I then marched my men through Grand Street, nearly to the ferry, and then backward and forward, through the various narrow streets in that part of the city, without being able to discover any disorderly persons. In this way I marched for four hours, and returned again to head-quarters, at four o'clock A.M., the 15th inst.

About seven o'clock, I again received orders to proceed to Thirty-second Street and Seventh Avenue, and quell the disturbance there at all hazards. I marched there through a heavy rain, and found a crowd of some two hundred or three hundred rioters, who had been engaged in hanging a negro. They immediately dispersed, without my having to fire a shot; I then repaired to the arsenal, Seventh Avenue, to obtain information where I could next meet the mob. I was ordered by General Sandford to march my command inside the lines of his " videttes " and outer pickets. I was then ordered to march to Thirty-second Street and Seventh Avenue, and quell the disturbance, which had broken out anew—the mob trying to break into a house in which a number of negro families had taken refuge. I dispersed the mob, and brought the negroes, some fourteen in number, into the arsenal. I then placed one half of my command across Seventh Avenue and Thirty-second Street, and while in this position, the mob made a rush up the avenue, but were promptly met by two volleys of musketry from my command, when they retired with considerable loss. Soon after one of the rioters endeavored to wrest the musket from the hands of one of my sentries, but received the contents instead. During the time I was engaged with the rioters in Seventh Avenue, Lieutenant Robert F. Joyce, in command of the second platoon, received information that a large number of muskets were concealed in a house on Thirty-second Street, near Broadway, and taking fifteen men from his command, proceeded to the house, and overcoming all the obstacles that were thrown in his way, succeeded in taking seventy-three Enfield rifles with accoutrements; and placing them on a cart brought them to the arsenal, although he was threatened by 500 men in the streets. About four o'clock, information reached me that a large mob had collected in Forty-second Street, between Tenth and Eleventh Avenues, and were endeavoring to burn buildings in that neighborhood. I immediately marched my command, numbering about fifty men (the remainder being on guard near the arsenal), to the scene of the disturbance; on arriving in Forty-second Street, between Ninth and Tenth Avenues, we were saluted with groans, hisses, etc., and when at the corner of Tenth Avenue, received a storm of bricks, and missiles of every description, and shots from the roofs and windows of the buildings.

Wheeling the platoons right and left, I formed them so as to sweep the streets and avenue in all directions. I advised the mob to disperse in one minute, or I would fire, there being 2,000 men at least. A few of them moved away, but the greater part remained, when I ordered my troops to fire, and had to fire at least five volleys before I could disperse the mob; when they again commenced firing on us from the windows, and house-tops; one shot fired on us from the windows came near depriving us of a man, as the ball grazed his head, but terminated in nothing serious. I then ordered Lieutenant F. M. Chase to take ten men, and search the houses from top to bottom, which he immediately did, and captured two prisoners. I succeeded finally in clearing the streets and closing the houses, and I remained on the ground as long as there was any necessity for a force there. I then started for the arsenal, but had not progressed more than half a block, when the mob, who had been joined by another crowd of rioters, made a rush up the street, as if to overpower my force. I allowed them to approach very close, with the impression that I was falling back, when I suddenly halted my command, and faced the second platoon to the rear, and fired two more volleys into them. They immediately dispersed, and I was informed it was their last gathering in that locality. There were at least fifty killed, and a large number wounded, and I marched off with my command, without hardly a scratch. Having delivered our prisoners over to the authorities at the Twentieth Precinct station-house, I again returned to the arsenal, and after a slight disturbance there, in which I arrested two of the rioters, I had the privilege of a few minutes rest, when we were placed on guard, and kept there without a relief, until ordered back to these head-quarters by General Brown. I was then ordered to proceed with Captain Putnam, Twelfth U. S. Infantry, to the Second Avenue and Twenty-eighth Street. This report will inform you of the nature of our duties at that point.

I now most respectfully beg leave to call your attention to the officers of my command, Lieutenant R. F. Joyce and Lieutenant F. M. Chase, who have nobly seconded every movement that was contemplated and executed. My sincere thanks are due commissioners and members of the police force, for the prompt and efficient service they have rendered us, as well as their excellent management in providing rations for my men, when so many others called their attentions away.

I am very respectfully your obedient servant,

B. FRANKLIN RYER,
*First Lieut. Comd'g Twentieth Battery, N. Y. V. A.*

Lieut.-col. B. FROTHINGHAM, *A. A. General.*

---

### REPORT OF CAPTAIN FRANKLIN.

FORT RICHMOND, NEW YORK HARBOR, July 20, 1863.

SIR:—In reply to your request of the 26th instant, I have the honor to make the following statement:

On the afternoon of the 13th, I received an order from General Brown for one platoon of my company, to report to Lieutenant Wood, at Fort Lafayette. I accompanied it, and finding General Brown at the wharf, reported to him, with the request that I might go with my own men. He granted my request, and ordered Lieutenant Wood to report to me, and at the same time gave me an order to report with my whole command to Colonel Nugent, in Leonard Street. Arriving at that point, I was met by General Brown, who ordered me to report to Colonel Nugent, at the arsenal, corner of Thirty-fifth Street and Seventh Avenue. On arriving at the arsenal, I found everything in a great state of confusion. No one seemed to know who was in command ; some said Colonel Nugent, and others, some colonel whose name I do not recollect. There was no officer of the day on guard, and no guard stationed, except one at the arsenal door.

The street, during the evening, became filled with a noisy crowd, and I suggested to Colonel Nugent that the streets be cleared, and that a guard be posted at all the four streets approaching the arsenal. This was soon done by the marines, and the guard posted as I suggested. My company relieved the marines, and remained on guard till it was ordered to report to General Brown, at 300 Mulberry Street. I marched the company down, about 11.30 P.M., through the rain, accompanied by the marines. I found on my arrival that General Brown had been relieved. I then went to the hotel and reported to General Wool. A section of battery had just arrived from Fort Hamilton, with no one but a volunteer quartermaster in charge. The general did not seem to know what to do with it. I suggested to a member of his staff, that Lieutenant Wood be ordered to relieve Lieutenant McElrath, then commanding an infantry company, and that Lieutenant McElrath be ordered to take command of the section.

The room at this time was filled with gentlemen, and the general seemed to be very much confused : it was a long time before the attempts made by several of his staff to make him understand this were successful.

Finally he issued the order, and Lieutenant Wood started up with the section to relieve Lieutenant McElrath. General Wool seemed, during all the time I was there, very much confused and worn out, and I should judge unable to perform any duty. Soon after that, he gave orders to Colonel Nugent to take command of the regular troops, who ordered me to remain at police head-quarters, all night.  About 12 o'clock, I think it was, all the gentlemen and the general's staff left him for the night.  I think only one orderly remained with him, and he on the outside of the door.

The next morning General Brown was in command again, and I received orders from him, up to the time he was relieved by General Canby.  From this time, everything seemed to work well.  Every time there was any notice of any disturbance, in any part of the city, east or west, troops were sent with great promptness, and up to the time I left, with success.  The statement of General Sandford, that General Brown confined his labors to the east side of the city, is a mistake.  My company was ordered to Twentieth Street, Eighth and Ninth Avenues, on Tuesday evening, and dispersed the mob that had just finished sacking the house on Twenty-ninth Street, between Seventh and Eighth Avenues, on the same evening.

I obeyed no orders during the riot except those received from General Brown, General Canby, and Colonel Nugent.  Everything seemed to be working with perfect harmony and success, up to the time I left (Wednesday noon, July 15th) for Harlem.

Respectfully your obedient servant,

WALTER S. FRANKLIN,
*Capt. Comd'g Company H, Twelfth Infantry.*

First Lieut. McELRATH, *Acting Adjt. 5th Artillery.*

---

REPORT OF LIEUTENANT MCELRATH.

FORT HAMILTON, N. Y. H., July 28, 1863.

GENERAL :—In response to your letter of the 26th inst., requesting a statement of all facts in my possession connected with the service of the troops of your command, during the riot in New York, on and after the 13th inst., I respectfully state: On the 13th of

PENNSYLVANIA RAILROAD BRIDGE, FAIRMOUNT PARK.

July I was acting assistant adjutant-general of the city and harbor of New York. On the afternoon of the 13th inst., I received an order from, General Wool, to send immediately to New York a portion of the troops from Fort Lafayette, and half the company then garrisoning Fort Richmond. The whole force thus detached did not exceed eighty men. Upon reporting to you the terms of the order, you expressed your surprise at the small number of men ordered to the city, and directed me to immediately have all the troops at Fort Hamilton, Fort Lafayette, Fort Richmond, got in readiness to move at a moment's notice.

In the meanwhile, you hastened to New York to endeavor to have them ordered to the city. While waiting your orders, I occupied myself, by your direction, in organizing a section of artillery, using for the purpose the guns used for the instruction of the men of the Fifth Artillery, and the. horses of the quartermaster department of this post. I filled the limbers with canister, and giving the command of one of the pieces to Drum-major George S. Browning, Fifth Artillery, and that of the other to Com. Sergeant H. S. Hetherington, I directed the officers in charge to proceed to New York, and report to you at St. Nicholas Hotel.

About 8 P.M., two boats arrived. I sent one to Sandy Hook by your order, to carry Captain Putman's company to your city, replacing it with a company of volunteer artillery, and in the other I proceeded myself, with the remainder of the troops above-mentioned. These consisted of the permanent guard of Fort Hamilton and the balance of the garrisons of Forts Lafayette and Richmond, in all about 140 effective soldiers, excellently disciplined and trained to fight. Arriving at the St. Nicholas, I found that you had been relieved of command, and I reported to 'General Wool, who sent me to the arsenal in Seventh Avenue. I reported there to General Sandford for orders. He gave my men quarters in an upper room. About 11.30

P.M., or 12, threats having been made of an early attack on the arsenal by the mob, General Sandford,
who for some reason did not wear his uniform at any
time during the riot, put on his hat, and bidding us
good-evening, took his departure for his private residence, leaving two of his staff to act during his absence.
There appeared to be constant uncertainty throughout
the night, as to which of these officers was really in
command.

About 2 A.M., Lieutenant C. O. Wood, Ninth United States Infantry, reported at the arsenal, having
brought with him the section of artillery organized by
me.  With the consent of Major Hamilton, of General
Sandford's staff, who had just at that moment appeared
to be in charge, Lieutenant Wood and I made a transfer of our commands—he taking my company of infantry and I assuming command of the artillery.  Major
Hamilton directed me to bring my two guns immediately inside.  I proceeded to the street and examined
the building, and discovered there were no embrasures
in the work.  I returned and requested permission to
place my guns in position in the street, where they
could be put to some use.  I believe I remarked to
Major Hamilton, that he had already too much ordnance hidden in the building.  My application was
granted, and I put my guns in battery in the Seventh
Avenue, at the corners of Thirty-fifth and Thirty-
sixth Streets, pointing up and down the avenue.  One
hundred infantry and those two guns could have defended the arsenal against any mob that was concentrated in the city during the riot.  In the morning the
battery was ordered, by a Colonel Moore, claiming to
be in command, to Yorkville, in company with the Eleventh New York Volunteers, under a volunteer officer
whom I had detailed to accompany the battery from
Fort Hamilton.  I hastened to report to General Wool
the fact of my command being taken away from me,
but met you at the St. Nicholas, and was ordered to
serve on your personal staff.  It was during this inter-

val that, I think in Second Avenue, three rounds were fired from the Battery *over the heads* of the mob. Who is responsible for this injudicious proceeding I do not know ; but had another course been adopted at the time, the terrible murder of Colonel O'Brien would, I think, have been avoided. On Tuesday afternoon, the battery having been reported to you for duty, I was sent in command of it, supported by the permanent guard, under Lieutenant Porter, First United States Artillery, to disperse a mob in the neighborhood of the arsenal, corner of Thirty-fifth Street and Seventh Avenue. I went into battery on the corner of Thirty-sixth Street and Seventh Avenue, but the crowd scattering with haste, as the guns approached, it was unnecessary to fire. By the order of General Sandford, I remained where I was until Wednesday morning. On the morning of the 15th, my feet giving me great pain, I was obliged to apply to be temporarily relieved of the command, and returned that day to Fort Hamilton, whence on Thursday I was about to return to New York with a small detachment, unavoidably left behind on Monday, when I received orders from you to remain at the fort. The battery returned to this post the next day, having been in the meantime under the command of Captain Rawolle, of General Wool's staff.

I am, General, very respectfully your obedient servant,

T. P. McELRATH,
*First Lieut. and Adj. Fifth U. S. Art.*

Brevet-general BROWN,
*Colonel Fifth United States Artillery.*

---

REPORT OF CAPTAIN SHELLEY.

FORT HAMILTON, N. Y. H., Wednesday, July 29, 1863.

BREVET BRIGADIER-GENERAL HARVEY BROWN.

GENERAL:—I have the honor to submit the following

report of the part taken by the " permanent guard " of
Fort Hamilton, N. Y. H., in quelling the recent riots in
the city of New York.  On Tuesday night, July 14th,
at 11 o'clock P.M., I received your order to proceed to
the state arsenal, Thirty-fifth Street and Seventh Avenue, and assume the command of the " permanent
guard " of Fort Hamilton, then temporarily commanded
by Captain Dole, Lieutenant McElrath having charge
of the artillery.

In obedience to your orders, I marched my command
to the head-quarters, Mulberry Street, to act as a reserve ; all the troops then stationed there being act-
ively engaged in different parts of the city in putting
down the riot.

## Operations on Wednesday, July 15th.

At 7 o'clock A.M. received orders to proceed to
Thirty-second Street and Seventh Avenue, and disperse
the mob wherever found.  On arriving at Thirty-
second Street, I found a force of about 300 militia
drawn up in column of platoon, with two pieces of
artillery from the arsenal at Thirty-fifth Street, under
the command of a brigadier-general, whose name I do
not know.  I also learned that the mob had, in this
vicinity, hung and brutally mutilated a colored citizen.

The militia force was resting on Thirty-second Street,
near Seventh Avenue, with their artillery unlimbered
and placed in battery to sweep Seventh Avenue, where
the rioters were then in force, concealed in the houses.
About this time the rain fell in torrents, and injured
the ammunition of the artillery, so that it could not be
used with effect.  After consulting with the commanding officer of the militia force, I determined to pass
my command by their flank to the front, and march
down Seventh Avenue, which I accordingly did, dispersing the mob wherever found, and then returning
to head-quarters to await further orders.

## *Operations on Wednesday night.*

About 9 o'clock P.M. I was ordered to proceed to Nineteenth Street, with a detachment of the Twelfth United States Infantry, with one piece of artillery commanded by Captain Rawolle, the whole to be commanded by Captain H. R. Putnam, Twelfth United States Infantry, who displayed the command so that my company on the march to Nineteenth Street protected the rear. On arriving at Nineteenth Street and First Avenue, the head of the column became engaged with the rioters, and shortly afterwards they collected in force on our rear in Second Avenue, and commenced firing at us. By direction of Captain Putnam, I ordered my skirmishers, who were posted about fifty yards in rear of my column of platoons, to attack them, which they did effectually, and after a few shots they were driven off. Having recovered two wounded officers, left to the mercy of the mob by some of the militia force engaged during the day, and having dispersed the mob, we returned to head-quarters, about 12 o'clock A.M.

## *Operations on Thursday morning.*

About one o'clock in the morning, I was ordered to proceed with my command to Grammercy Park, for the purpose of protecting the property in that vicinity, as the mob were then collecting there in force, and had made threats to burn and rob the houses of certain parties residing in the immediate vicinity.

The scouts employed by the mob warned them of my approach, so that when I arrived there I found everything quiet. I immediately posted pickets on the corners of the different streets, and made the necessary disposition of my command for the protection of the place. About four o'clock in the morning my pickets gave the alarm, the mob had collected in Fourth Ave-

nue and commenced plundering a store. I immediately marched to the place indicated and attacked
them, when they scattered and fled in all directions.
I returned to Grammercy Park, and remained till 3
o'clock A.M., when I received your orders to return to
head-quarters, which I accordingly did.

*Thursday noon.*

Was informed that the mob was in force near Fifty-
second Street and Eleventh Avenue, with artillery. I
received your orders to move my command to that
place and disperse the mob and capture their artillery.
On arriving at Forty-seventh Street, I learned that the
mob had broken into a bullet factory on Fifty-second
Street, and had taken a large quantity of bullets. I
immediately marched through Eighth Avenue to Fifty-
second Street, and dispersed the mob and took possession of the piece of artillery, returning to the station-
house on Forty-second Street, where I remained that
night to protect the depot and stables of the Eighth
and Ninth Avenue railroads, which the mob had
threatened to burn.

On Friday morning I received an official notification,
that General Canby had assumed command of the
United States troops in the city and harbor of New
York, together with an order to remove my command
to the station-house on Thirty-fifth Street, between
Eighth and Ninth Avenues, where I remained till
Monday morning, when I was relieved by two companies of militia, and ordered to report to Fort Hamilton with my command.

Before closing this report, I would respectfully call
attention to the gallant conduct of Sergeants G. A.
Kimball and S. E. Tiffany and other non-commissioned
officers of the company. Being the only officers with
the command I relied on, received very efficient aid
and assistance from them. The men of the command
acted like veterans, and are entitled to the highest

praise. Although worn out with fatigue from incessant marching night and day, they performed the arduous duties with alacrity and willingness.

During the different engagements, I had three men badly wounded, and five or six slightly injured from various missiles thrown at us by the mob.

Very respectfully your obedient servant,

RICHARD L. SHELLEY,
*Capt. Com. Permanent Guard, Fort Hamilton.*

PENN. R. R.—VIEW OF HARRISBURGH.

# CHAPTER XXII.

## THE RAILROAD RIOTS OF 1877.

TRADES Unions, "Co-operative" Societies, and all those various societies and organizations among the laboring classes for their own protection or benefit, are a part of the spirit of the age. The great material results which are constantly being accomplished are secured by the concentration and organization of capital. It is simply carrying out the old proverb, "In union there is strength." That labor, as it becomes intelligent, should take advantage of this well-established principle, is natural and right. Although there have been some failures, there have been successes enough to prove that those organizations which have reference to supplying the necessaries of life can cheapen very much the cost of living. Those organizations or unions which are designed solely to affect the price of wages, whether among manufacturers or railroad men, or any class of laborers, look for success only in their ability at any given moment to "strike," or in other words, suddenly

15

refuse to labor. At first these met with more or less
success, for the losses entailed on large companies by
the sudden suspension of work would compel them to
accede to the terms of their employés, as the lesser
evil of the two.

The history of strikes proves this. The formation
of workingmen's societies for their own protection
began with the present century. Wool-carders, cotton-
spinners, scissors-grinders, tailors, men of all trades in
England, formed organizations at first to keep out ex-
ceptional men from their own peculiar occupations,
afterwards to control wages. Severe laws were passed
against them. These were at length abolished, and a
system adopted allowing these combinations to exist,
and men to leave work when they chose, but denouncing
all attempts to prevent other men from taking their
places. Believing that simply striking would bring
the employers to terms, it was at once started and
great trouble occurred in the manufacturing districts
of Great Britain. The following is a list of the principal strikes that have taken place in England since
the repeal of the laws referred to :

Manchester cotton-spinners in 1829 ; number of idle
10,000 ; duration six months.

Ashton and Staleybridge cotton-spinners in 1830 ;
number of idle, 30,000 ; duration ten weeks.

Liverpoo building trades in 1833 ; duration six
months.

Preston cotton-spinners in 1854 ; number of idle,
17,000 ; duration nine months.

London building trades in 1859 ; number of idle,
8,000.

General lockout in the iron trade in 1865 ; number
of idle, 200,000 ; duration sixteen weeks.

Clyde ship-building trade in 1867; number of idle, 18,000; duration nine weeks.

North of England iron trade in 1866; number of idle, 12,000; duration five months.

In 1871, there was a general strike about harvest time among the laborers, because the farmers cut down their wages, but the former were the chief sufferers. The last great strike occurred in Wales in 1875, and embraced 120,000 persons, whose aggregate loss during its continuance amounted to $15,000,000.

In America, no attempt has been made to prevent the organization of societies among laboring men for the protection of their own interests. The following is a list of them, with branches in different States:

|  | Established. | Branches. | Membership. |
|---|---|---|---|
| International Typographical Union........ | 1852 | 175 | 10,950 |
| Machinists and blacksmiths.............. | 1859 | 164 | 8,000 |
| Iron Moulders' Association.............. | 1859 | 152 | 7,500 |
| Brotherhood of Locomotive Engineers..... | 1863 | 192 | 14,000 |
| Journeymen Tailors' National Trade Union. | 1865 | 40 | 2,800 |
| Coopers' International Union............. | 1870 | 68 | 5,000 |
| Cigar-Makers' Union.................... | 1871 | 103 | 5,000 |
| Miners' National Union.... ............ | 1873 | 347 | 35,315 |
| United Sons of Vulcan.................. | 1874 | —— | 4,000 |

The Miners' Union comprises organizations which existed for years in different States—Pennsylvania, Ohio, Illinois, Indiana, Iowa, Maryland, Missouri, Kansas, Tennessee, and West Virginia. The Society of the United Sons of Vulcan comprises iron puddlers and other workers in metals. The local unions are called "forges." In addition to the above there are the Bricklayers' National Union, the United Order of American Plasterers, the House Painters' Union, the Hat Finishers' Association, the Knights of St. Crispin (shoemakers), the Order of Morocco Dressers, the Journeyman Horseshoers' Union, the Society of Locomotive Firemen, and the Mule-Spinners of Cotton Factories.

Now all these organizations proposed to secure the results they desired by stopping work, thus compelling the great industries of the country to accede to their demands or lie idle. This course was to some extent successful, as it was in England, and compromises were made. They may still succeed in those branches of industry where skilled labor is employed, but in the vast majority of cases, companies of nearly all kinds soon learned to be prepared for such emergencies, and replaced the "*strikers*" with new men. This at once rendered those vast organizations harmless. That laborers had a right thus to organize and act in unison, when they thought they were not sufficiently compensated for their work, no one will question, how muchsoever men may differ as to the wisdom of such a course. Strikes, therefore, as meaning simply to refuse to labor because the pay is not satisfactory, are, except in isolated cases, things of the past. These organizations saw that to be of any avail they must take another step forward, and not only refuse to work themselves, but prevent any one else from working in their places. They thus passed from legitimate organizations into riotous proceedings, and at once lost the sympathy and countenance of the great mass of the people, and laid themselves open to the penalties of law, which guarantees, first of all, the right of every man to labor for any wages he may agree to receive. They lost sympathy, because, instead of waging war against monopolists, they themselves at once became the most tyrannical, outrageous monopolists in the country—indeed, the worst that can exist—the monopo-

lists of labor. Large capitalists may, with some show
of justice, claim the right to keep and control for their
own benefit the wealth they have accumulated by labor,
intelligence, or successful ventures, but no man can
take from another the right to work. It is God-given,
and the man or the men who seek to deprive their fellows of it are guilty of one of the greatest wrongs that
he can commit. Here, for instance, are 10,000 men employed as laborers on a single line of railroad. They
band together, and simultaneously refuse to labor without an advance of wages. Ten thousand other men,
with needy families, who are anxious to work, step
forward, thankful for the opportunity to do this work
for the wages given. The first 10,000 men say, " No!
No matter how needy your families may be, you shall
not do this work. Nobody shall do it but ourselves,
and we will not do it except on our own terms." This
is a monopoly and despotism of the most oppressive
kind. It is the merest sophistry to say that they are
acting for the general good of the laboring class, to
protect their rights, and elevate the standard of labor.
These 10,000 men are scattered workingmen, and if
they are allowed no place on this railroad must pick
up work where they can find it, and get such remuneration for it as they can.

So that we see that strikes have necessarily run into
riots. Violence must be used and willing laborers must
be clubbed from the places they are eager to occupy,
and which their straitened circumstances urgently
demand, and their employers, if they attempt to defend
them, must be shot down and their buildings and property destroyed. This is not striking for just wages—it
is striking at the very foundation of society, and abro-

gating law itself. Hence the question of strikes has passed from the domain of argument into one of force —a fight between lawless despotism and guaranteed rights—between self-interest and law—between anarchy and good government. There can be but one end to this struggle—the putting down of such lawless, violent conduct at whatever cost of life, or the utter abandonment of government. What the result will be admits of no doubt. How long we shall be in reaching it, depends on the promptness, energy, and fearlessness of those in power.

But there is another class of men, who at once join hands with strikers, of a still more dangerous type— communists and plunderers. The first believes there is an irreconcilable war between labor and capital, and that the latter must be put down at all hazards, and hence are glad of any opportunity to destroy property which has been accumulated by capital.

### COMMUNISM.

Communism assumes different phases in different countries, as well as among different classes of men; but the principles that lie at the bottom are the same. The fundamental principles are :—First, that the earth was made for men to enjoy equally ; that it produces enough to satisfy the wants of all, and hence its products belong to all alike. Accumulation, therefore, in one place causes distress in another. In short, from accumulation, whether in individuals or corporations, springs all the pauperism of the earth, and consequently most of its misery and crimes. In the second place, Communists believe that all class distinctions are wrong ; that men were made to be equal, and no one should have any special rights and privileges, such as nobles or aristocrats, of whatever kind.

Under this head come also all churches, clergymen, and religious institutions, etc. Now while these are in brief their principles, the manner in which they attempt to give them success varies. Quakers, Fourierites, and various kindred communities repudiate violence of all kinds, and believe in the law of example, the advocacy of truth, and the spread of light. The Communists of France and Germany, on the other hand, believe that all accumulation of wealth in palaces, monopolies, structures, and institutions of extravagance, to be wrong, and should be destroyed forthwith —indeed, that it ought to be the first move in the work of reform.

There is a difference also in their religious and social belief. Those like the Oneida Community believe that all marriage exclusiveness should be done away with, and woman, like property, be held in common, and hence are often called socialists.

Others require a strict morality, whether they practice it or not. Some have a form of religious belief peculiar to themselves; others, like the French and German, for the main part have none at all, but are open infidels.

These are some of the various forms in which Communism develops itself; but the underlying principle remains the same, and is what its name implies, " commune," " common," all things in common.

The Communism that prevailed after the overthrow of the late Napoleon had some features that do not naturally belong to it. The Communists hoped to control France—in fact, make it one great Communist

society, but they could not ignore their external rela-
tions to other nations. Obligations were to be met,
debts to be paid, etc., etc., which they must recognize,
and hence certain political articles had to be inserted
into their creed which had nothing to do with their
principles, and hence need not be noticed here.

It is sad, but true, that this antagonism between the
poor and rich increases with the advance of republican
principles. The masses can.read the declaration that
" all men are born free and equal " in only one way—
if their equality is a fact and not a delusion, then they
have an equal right to the good things of this world.
It is a worthless doctrine to them if it means simply
equal rights to *vote* with the rich or to walk about, free
to consult their own pleasure where they can find it.
They must have the food, clothing, nay, a share of the
luxuries of the rich, or their equality is a lie. They
all have some ground for this belief, for the doctrine
took root in the very first development of· Christianity,
when the early disciples had "all things in common."
It does seem that the wealth and good things of this
world, like snow after a heavy, disastrous storm, is
heaped up in one place where it is a curse, and swept
clean from the ground where it is needed, and moreover, what is worse, its accumulation in one place ne-
cessitates its scarcity in another. But how to right this
is one of the difficult problems connected with the
history of our race that time alone can solve. There
is *one* thing that is true, and about which there can be
but one opinion among all enlightened and good men,
and that is, the problem cannot be solved by violence, and
plunder, and murder. However much we may err in
our methods of reaching the political and social millen-

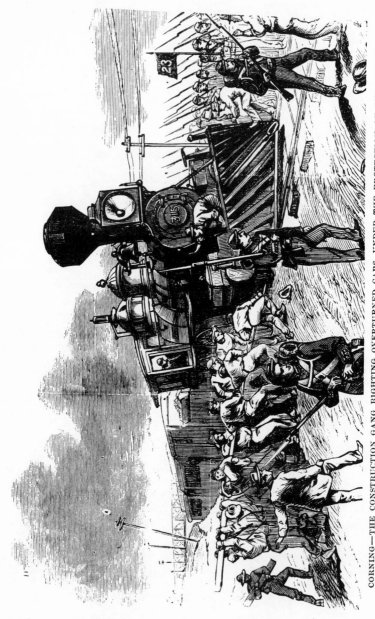

CORNING—THE CONSTRUCTION GANG RIGHTING OVERTURNED CARS, UNDER THE PROTECTION OF THE MILITIA.

nium towards which the race seems ever earnestly and longingly looking, we cannot err in putting down at any cost the violent *methods* of these communists. Here our duty is plain. To destroy property is not to distribute it equally. Robbers, and plunderers, and murderers never bring about a happy state of society. The millennium, which men are looking after, will never come in that fashion.

As these fanatical men join the regular strikers, so that vast mass of wretched outlaws that throng our cities, and are only too thankful for any occasion in which they can safely give way to their savage and demoniacal spirit and gratify their love of blood and rapine, join them also. They thus make common cause against society and good government, and must share the same fate.

The personal character of the individuals forming these three separate classes may be very different, but the character of their actions is the same. They are all rioters, law-breakers, and must be treated exactly alike. It is idle to draw a line of distinction in favor of the strikers as a class, because their cause is just, and that their wages are inadequate for their support, and their employers are oppressive. Infraction of law must have the same penalty, no matter what the motive or character of the man may be who is guilty of it. No matter whether a man steals from a stranger or from one who has overreached him in a bargain, the penalty is the same. No matter whether he murders an innocent man or one steeped in crime, he must mount the scaffold all the same. The guilt or innocence of the party assailed has nothing to do with the crime of the assailant or his punishment in the sight of the

15*

law. The principle is fixed and unassailable that no man or set of men can be allowed to vindicate themselves or enforce their rights outside of the forms of law. If one man can be allowed to do it, then all can, and law and government become a nullity, and society disorganized. The rioters who resort to violence may be perfectly just in their demands, and yet the way they take to obtain them be the greatest crime they can commit. A large company may be oppressive and unjust, but murder is worse than oppression. They may cut down the price of wages, but that is not so criminal as to tear down houses and make wreck of human property. One crime cannot justify another and greater one. The world is full of oppression and suffering; but who is to right it? It is astonishing how the fact that because wrong is done to the laboringman, men will say he is therefore justified in taking law into his own hands. God's physical laws do not pity nor discriminate as to the character of the man who violates them. All who break them suffer alike.

The laws that uphold government and protect society are *His* laws also, given for the benefit of man, and in preventing their infraction officers and government act only as His agents. The man who is shot down while committing rapine and murder falls as really by the hand of God as though struck by lightning. The right of revolution—the right of a people to change a government from one based on injustice to one based on principles of truth and right no one denies, but all other violence leads to no government at all. Hence the miserable sentimentality that revolts at stern measures to put it down becomes a crime. The man who indulges it is more compassionate than God, who is pitiless to him who violates His physical laws. Suffering and death follow their infraction with remorseless certainty, and they must, or God would cease to govern the world, and they must equally follow the violation of the laws of good government or government will cease to exist. Men often congratulate themselves on quieting a mob by kind words, and thus they say save life. On the contrary, they have destroyed it. One life is perhaps saved to-day to render the destruction of forty lives on some future day inevitable. Blank cartridges at the outset of a riot multiplies the death-roll tenfold in the end. It is a fearful thing to shoot down fellow-citizens, but that is not the question involved—it is, will you shoot down five to-day and thus save fifty hereafter, or save one now and make the death of fifty in the future certain? Unless we wish to see mobs increase and become more dangerous and destructive, there must cease all false sympathy for them, and they be looked upon not as American citizens, but as felons and murderers. The order to lay down their arms and disperse, if disobeyed, must be followed by such decisive action that no doubt can remain of what the issue will be. If mobs knew that the first salutation after the order to disperse was given would be grape-shot and canister, we should see the end of them. The first Napoleon understood this when called before the Convention to receive the command of the troops to put down the mobs that threatened to overturn Paris. Stung by his haughty sarcasm, uttered in reply to their careful advice, Rewbell said, " But do you know that this may be a very serious affair—that the sections——" " Very well," fiercely interrupted the young Lieutenant, " I will make a serious affair of it, and the sections will be tranquil." He had seen Louis XVI. put on the red cap and show himself from the palace of the Tuilleries, to appease the mob, with disgust and indignation, and exclaimed, "What madness! He should have blown four or five hundred of them into the air, and the rest would have taken to their heels." And when on the mighty populace, backed by the National Guard, his artillery, loaded to the muzzle with grape-shot, thundered, he announced the manner in which he would treat with a mob, and as he promised, the sections became tranquil.

# CHAPTER XXIII.

## THE RAILROAD RIOTS—WEST VIRGINIA.

Commencement of the Riots.—Extent of the Strikes.—Their Cause.
—Riot in Martinsburg.—Trains Stopped.—A Man Shot.—Disgraceful Conduct of the Militia.—Never Reliable.—The Aid of
the General Government Asked.—Caution of the President.—
He Sends Aid.—His Proclamation.—End of the Strike.—Mischief of not Striking Promptly at First.

THE recent railroad strike has been unprecedented in
its extent throughout the country. Beginning at Martinsburg, on the Baltimore and Ohio Railroad, its influence reached all the great lines in the central and
western part of the Union. So rapidly did one strike
and riot follow another, that at first sight there seemed
to have been a general concert of action, but such was
evidently not the case. One followed another just as
tinder and combustible matter take fire at the first spark
that touches them, and the flames run rapidly into each
other. This is evident from the fact that, although it
was a railroad strike, the riotous element in every
place was equally on the alert and ready for action
with the railroad men. The truth is, the whole country has for some time been ready for an explosion of
some kind. Every man accustomed to watch public
feeling has been aware of this, and more or less apprehension has been felt. The hard times have pressed
heavily on everybody, and want always breeds discon-

tent and restlessness. The rich man may see his fortune crumble at his feet—there is nothing for him to
strike for. The man of moderate means may be compelled to give up one luxury after another—he cannot
strike to have them restored to him. The tradesman
may see his custom diminish, and the mechanic the demand for contracts grow less and less—he cannot strike
—he must sit still and suffer. But the laboring man has
somebody to look to when his turn comes to retrench.
As long as a man is insolvent, or a company can pay
the interest on its debt, there seems to be no reason
why his wages should be reduced. As long as money
is paid out he thinks it should be paid to him, and if it
is not he demands it with threats. The truth is, labor
has been in such demand for years, and so extrava-
gantly rewarded, that the laboring class have been able
to indulge in luxuries they never dreamed of before,
and it is the loss of these they deplore more than the
want of the necessaries of life. This is seen especially
in domestic service. There no reduction of wages will
be tolerated, simply because it would necessitate more
plainness and economy in dress. There is no doubt
that rich men and rich companies, on the other hand,
have in some cases taken advantage of the hard times
for the sole and wicked purpose of making more
money by reducing the wages of their employés beyond
what was necessary or just, and hence naturally caused
a great deal of complaint and bitter feeling. But
whatever the particular causes may have been, the dissatisfaction existed, and it needed but a spark to give
it outward expression, and this was furnished at Martinsburg when a strike took place among the railroad
men on account of a reduction in their wages. On the

night of the 16th of July the firemen there struck, and when other men offered to take their places, drove them from the engines.   The Vice-President of the road immediately telegraphed to Governor Matthews the state of things, saying that the trains both ways were in the hands of the rioters, and that the town authorities were powerless to suppress the riot, and asked for aid.   The Governor telegraphed back that he had sent word to Colonel Faulkner to aid the authorities with the two military companies of Martinsburg.   Colonel Faulkner arrived that morning with seventy-five men of the Berkeley Light Infantry Guard, and took charge of one of the west-bound freight trains that had been stopped, and endeavored to move it on its way.   As the train reached the switch one of the strikers seized the lever which moved it and endeavored to turn it off on a side-track.   A member of the militia company, named Poisal, jumped from the pilot of the engine and endeavored to prevent him.   The striker then fired at him, slightly wounding him in the head.   Poisal fired back, shooting the former through the hip.   Several shots followed, fired by the soldiers, wounding the rioter still farther.   The firing brought a crowd together, and great excitement followed, amid which the volunteer engineer and fireman that had taken charge of the train ran away.   At this Faulkner stated that he had done his duty, and if the train men deserted their posts he could do nothing more, and marching his company to the armory disbanded them, and the rioters were left in possession of the field.   The next morning the western train brought in a new company of militia, sent by Governor Matthews, and a conference was held between the officers and some of the

citizens, but nothing was done. The rioters, emboldened by their success, went at noon to the workshops
of the company and endeavored to make the men stop
work, but they refused to do so, and the former retired. The aspect of affairs in the place at this time
may be gathered from the following dispatch, dated at
12.30 P.M. :

" The rioters are still firm and determined, and the
presence of the military only seems to further exasperate them. The town is wild with excitement, and the
strikers and their friends, numbering at this time fully
1,000 men, are marching about, bidding defiance to the
military and the authorities. Some seventy-five or
eighty engines are congregated here, and none are
allowed to depart. A committee from the striking
firemen have notified the engineers that in case any engineer shall attempt to take a train out of town he will
be immediately shot. At noon a cattle train bound for
Baltimore attempted to start, whereupon the rioters
flocked on board, and with drawn revolvers, placed at the
head of the engineer and fireman, compelled them to
run the train into the stock-yards, where the cattle were
unloaded. The passenger trains are not interfered with,
as the strike is entirely confined to the transportation
men. So far the strikers have everything their own
way, and the military are passive, awaiting further
orders from the Governor, which up to this time have
not come."

The passenger trains were allowed to come and depart unmolested, but all freight trains were stopped.

It soon became very evident that no reliance could be
placed on the local militia. Indeed, there never can be
in case of a riot, embracing not rowdies or vagrants, but
ordinary laboring men. In the first place, the militia
is composed in part of these very men, while others are

NEW YORK—RIOTERS MARCHING DOWN THE NEW YORK CENTRAL
RAILROAD TRACK AT WEST ALBANY, JULY 24, 1877.

the friends, companions, and relatives of those they are
ordered to fire. into. They may be opposed to the
riot—believe it to be contrary to law, and should be
suppressed by some means—but to shoot down their
friends and companions engaged in it is quite another
thing. The rioters know this, and hence are emboldened
in their course. Regiments from distant cities or
States are better than home troops, because less likely
to be governed by local sympathy, yet still they are,
in a great measure, composed of workingmen, who do
and will sympathize with workingmen whom they hon-
estly believe to be wronged and oppressed—at least to
that extent that they will not kill them at the order
of their officers. Hence United States troops must
always, in the last resort, be looked to for protection.
It is not because they are braver or less sympathetic,
but they have been trained to do their duty regardless
of consequences. The veterans that stand unmoved in
front of a deadly battery are not more courageous
than the raw volunteers that turn and fly. But they
have been drilled and trained to do simply their duty.
This power of thorough discipline was seen a few
years ago in New York in the famous Orange riots.
Religious hatred and fanaticism yielded to this sense
of duty that had been drilled into the police, so that
Roman Catholics shot down Roman Catholics without
mercy in defence of Protestant Irishmen. Among all
the Roman Catholics that composed the police force of
the city, only one was found recreant to his duty.
For years they had been taught to regard themselves
as defenders of the city—the guardians of its peace
and citizens. This had been and was their duty, into
which they had been so thoroughly trained that they

would do it reckless of consequences to individuals. It is so with regular troops—they have nothing to do with individual wrongs—they are only to obey the orders of their government. Governor Matthews soon saw that he could not rely on his home troops, and telegraphed to the President for aid. The latter, reluctant—as the President always should be—to interfere with the internal affairs of any State, ordered the Secretary of War to telegraph for more specific information. On its reception he no longer hesitated, and the Secretary of War ordered United States troops to Martinsburg, and a dispatch was received, dated 11 o'clock P.M. :

" At ten o'clock at night a train of nine cars, drawn by engine No. 407, moved out of the Baltimore and Ohio depot in Washington, carrying the troops, comprising eight companies of artillery acting as infantry. Six of the companies have been on duty at the Arsenal, and two reached Washington from Baltimore, joining the troops there. Their strength is two hundred and fifty men, all in regular fighting trim, supplied with rations, canteens, plenty of ammunition, and in all other respects regularly equipped for whatever work may be necessary when they reach the scene of tumult. The whole detachment is under command of General French."

This news somewhat astounded the strikers. They had found such sympathy from the citizens and local troops that they flouted the authorities, and had even stoned the Governor in his hotel at Grafton ; but when the general government in its majesty began to move, matters assumed a more serious aspect. Suddenly to face the naked fact that, to succeed, they must whip the United States, startled them. That was a solemn night. The arrested trains stretched two miles away on each side of Martinsburg—enough hands were ready to start them—but no one dared to move. In the meantime, the heavy train bearing the United States troops, with artillery, was slowly approaching the place. Added to this, the rain began to fall in torrents, drenching the rioters and tending still more to dampen their courage. With the arrival of the troops came also the following proclamation of the President, which gave the rioters to understand very clearly the magnitude of the work on which they had entered.

### A PROCLAMATION.

*By the President of the United States of America :*

*Whereas*, It is provided in the Constitution of the United States that the United States shall protect every State in the Union on application of the Legislature, or of the Executive when the Legislature cannot be convened, against domestic violence ; and,

*Whereas*, The Governor of the State of West Virginia has represented that domestic violence exists in said State, at Martinsburg, and at various other points along the line of the Baltimore and Ohio Railroad, in said State, which the authorities of said State are unable to suppress ; and,

*Whereas*, The laws of the United States require that in all cases of insurrection in any State, or of obstruction to the laws thereof, whenever it may be necessary in the judgment of the President, he shall forthwith by proclamation command such insurgents to disperse and retire peaceably to their respective abodes within a limited time ;

*Now, therefore*, I, Rutherford B. Hayes, President of the United States, do hereby admonish all good citizens of the United States, and all persons within the territory and jurisdiction of the United States, against aiding, countenancing, abetting, or taking part in such unlawful proceedings; and I do hereby warn all persons engaged in or connected with said domestic violence and obstruction of laws to disperse and retire peaceably to their respective abodes on or before 12 o'clock noon of the 19th day of July inst.

In witness whereof I have hereunto set my hand and caused the seal of the United States to be affixed.

Done at the city of Washington this 18th day of July, in the year of our Lord 1877, and of the independence of the United States the 102d.

By the President,        R. B. HAYES.

F. W. SEWARD, Acting Secretary of State.

The firm attitude of the general government stopped for the time all violent demonstrations of the mob, and on the 19th two trains were started out. Seventy-three locomotives stood with their fires banked ready to start, and the civil authorities began to arrest the ringleaders of the strikers. But the mischief had been done and from every quarter came, in rapid, startling succession, the news of strikes and the sudden arrest of all transportation of freight to and from the sea-board. The sympathy of the military and the people with the strikers, and the complete control the latter had over the railroad, had been sent on telegraph wires all over the country, falling on the excited railroad men like fire on gunpowder. Had the people risen *en masse* and put down the rioters on the first day, or had the military acted with promptness and decision, and on the first attempt at violence by the mob shot down a half a dozen, dispersed the rest, and set the trains rolling on their way, the great railroad strike of 1877 would never have disgraced the country, and it would have been spared the suffering and loss that have followed. A mob is like a rolling rock that, once fairly in motion, it is difficult to stop it. One prompt, determined blow at Martinsburg would have ended the trouble. On the very day the following announcement was made from Martinsburg, Baltimore was in a tumult of excitement—the rioters parading the streets with shouts and yells, carrying dismay on every side.

July 17th.—"Information has just been received here that there is serious trouble at Keyser, and troops from this place are being sent by a special train to that place. The strikers at Keyser are collected in large force, numbering about two hundred. The small guard of ten men that arrived there this morning in charge of the first train from Martinsburg is insufficient to cope with the large body of strikers, and aid is requested. In fact, they are powerless to do much more than protect themselves from the mob.

"Trains commenced to move from here at seven o'clock this morning in charge of small detachments of United States soldiers. There were plenty of firemen and engineers at Martinsburg ready and willing to run the trains when assured that they would have protection while discharging their duties. Large numbers of strikers were to be seen along the railroad in the vicinity of the depot, but they were not permitted to get near enough to offer any obstruction to the movement of trains. Gen. French this morning issued imperative orders directing that all persons should be kept at a distance from the depot and from the vicinity of operations, no matter whether their intentions were friendly or hostile. Eight trains were dispatched from Martinsburg up to eight o'clock this morning. Up to 11 A.M. thirteen trains were started from this point, of which seven went west and six east. The last westward train took another detachment of troops, which proceeded as far as Keyser. The service of the

Wheeling militia has ended, and they will probably leave this afternoon. Officers are now out for the purpose of arresting some of those most prominently engaged in the obstruction of the trains. One man, named Davis, was arrested this morning. One of the trains which left for the West this forenoon was cut off at Sir John's Run. After a short delay it was coupled up and went on. Capt. Litchfield has gone on with two companies of troops to prevent a repetition of the act, and with orders to arrest those engaged in it. No further interference at that point is apprehended."

# CHAPTER XXIV.

## THE RAILROAD RIOTS—MARYLAND.

Governor Carroll's Proclamation.—Cause of the Outbreak in Balti-
more.—Attack on the Fifth Regiment.—Mustering of the Sixth
Regiment.—The Armory attacked by the Mob.—March of the
First Company.—It fires on the Mob.—March of the Second
Company.—Fights its Way onward.—March of the Last Com-
pany.—Attack on the Regiment.—Deadly Firing.—A Fearful
Night Scene.—Scene at the Depot.—The Fifth Regiment.—
The President asked for Troops.—Number of Killed and
Wounded.

WORD having reached Gov. Carroll that the trains
leaving Martinsburg were stopped by rioters at Cumberland, he saw at once that the trouble was extending
into Maryland, and immediately issued a proclamation
in response to the call for aid from the railroad authorities—calling on all rioters to disperse. He also called
out the Fifth Regiment of the Maryland National
Guard, to proceed, under command of General Herbert, to Cumberland, and protect the trains at that
point. This proclamation and order seemed to be the
spark that lit the flame in Baltimore, that soon spread
like a conflagration. Baltimore has long been noted
for its ferocious mobs, and the " plug uglies " have become known far and wide. There needs no railroad
strikes to excite a mob there. The mere attempt to
put one down elsewhere will bring it together. This
regiment was to march at 7 P.M. Though there had

been no outbreak in the city, the news from Martinsburg for the last three days had produced the profoundest excitement.   Angry crowds gathered around
the depot to hear the news, inquire about the non-
arrival of trains, while knots of rough-looking men
could be seen on the corners of the by-streets talking
in low and earnest tones.   It turned out that a plan
was laid to prevent the soldiers from departing to put
down the rioters and support the railroad officers.   As
the soldiers, in obedience to the order of the Governor,
hurried singly or in squads to the armory for their
muskets, they were jeered by the men and boys that
lined the streets, and occasionally a stone would be
thrown at them.   Soon after, the City Hall bell
sounded the signal 151, denoting that a riot was in
progress, and the mustering of the militia demanded.
The Fifth Regiment was soon assembled in force, and
at about seven o'clock, numbering about 250 muskets,
marched out of the armory and took its way towards
the depot, where they were to take the train to Cumberland.   An excited crowd followed them, hooting
and yelling as they advanced, and increasing in numbers at every cross-street.   When about three blocks
from the depot, at the corner of Pratt and Eutaw
Streets, it made a rush at the regiment, shouting and
cursing, and hurling stones and brick-bats.   The soldiers, with fixed bayonets, marched steadily forward
to the station, and entered it amid a shower of stones.
The mob then dashed around the lower end of the
platform and met the troops face to face.   The soldiers
immediately charged bayonets and scattered the crowd,
and entered the train.   The rioters then rushed for the
locomotive, and dragged off the engineer and fireman.

NEW YORK—THE CONSTRUCTION GANG REPAIRING THE TRACKS AT
CORNING: UNDER PROTECTION OF THE 23D REG'T, N. Y. S. N. G.

While these events were passing at the station, a more alarming state of things existed in the heart of the city. The ringing of the alarm of the City Hall bell, by whomsoever ordered, was a most unwise thing, for it instantly roused up all the bad elements of the city, and sent them hurrying to a common centre. The Sixth Regiment had been ordered to hold itself in readiness for two or three days, and, at the first sound of the alarm bell, rushed to the armory. But the streets were now thronged with angry men, whose cries and shouts sent terror to the hearts of the inhabitants. As soon as a soldier appeared a rush was made for him. The small police force stationed at the armory soon lost all control of the mob that surged in angry waves around the building. Some of the soldiers, being unarmed, turned back. One was seized and hurled over Fayette Street bridge into Jones's Falls, but he luckily caught on a timber, and, leaping the railing, fled down the street. In the meantime all was bustle and excitement inside the armory. Col. Peters, commanding the regiment, had received an order from Gen. Herbert, of the Fifth, at Camden station, to detail three companies and report to him there. The tumult was wild without, but the men appeared generally calm and cool. It was now apparent that the weak guard of four men at the door could do no good, and was, moreover, in danger of being hit by the missiles that were hurled against the armory, and Lieut. Brown was directed to go down and order them in. As they fell back a wild yell of triumph and derisive laughter greeted them, followed by a shower of brick-bats and stones. The two large glass doors were shattered into fragments, while Lieut. Brown received a severe blow on the arm. The crowd

16

thinking the soldiers were frightened, became more
clamorous and violent and swelling every moment, rent
the air with shouts, curses, and rained a perfect storm
of brick-bats and stones on the armory.

By a quarter past eight the preparations were all
completed, and the three companies prepared to start.
The police were ordered to throw open the doors, and
then stand aside.  The door opened on Front Street, and
the armory room being on the second floor, a long flight
of stairs had to be descended before the street could
be reached.  Down this the soldiers could march only two
abreast.  Company I, of only forty men, Capt. Tupper
commanding, first began to descend.  As it did so, the
very building shook with the shouts of the infuriated
multitude, and the doorway was darkened with flying missiles.  "Keep your heads down, boys, and forward march," passed down the line, and the men,
though evidently greatly excited and for a moment wa-
vering, gathered at the word of command, and marching steadily down, emerged into the street, and for a
moment faced the shouting, maddened crowd.  They
then, in solid order, commenced their desperate march
down the street, headed by Col. Peters.  Immediately
they were met by a shower of stones intermingled with
pistol shots.  The first rank of soldiers fired a volley
over the heads of the mob as they filed out and formed
into line.  But this, as it always does, only exasperated
the rioters, and they opened fire on the troops.  The
latter now levelled their pieces and fired point-blank
into the dense and yelling mass.  Men falling on the
sidewalks, or reeling backward with bullets in their
breasts, terrified the crowd, and they scattered.  The
company then marched down to Baltimore Street and

halted. The mob, not seeing the rest of the regiment
appear, thought they were afraid to leave the armory,
and began to surge back around it with derisive shouts
and cries. Company F, Capt. Fallen, was next put in
motion, but the moment they reached the street they
were met by a volley from pistols and muskets. They
returned the fire with such deadly effect that the assailants were staggered. The company then marched forward to join the first, firing volleys as they moved
along. The last company, under Lieut. Duffy, followed immediately after. This was composed of very
young men, some scarcely out of boyhood, many of
whom, as they met the fire of the mob at the door,
rushed back pell-mell upstairs. They, however, soon
rallied and marched out. The deadly fire of the last
company had intimidated the crowd, and they kept
more aloof. The firing and the shouts had called the
people far and near to the scene of disturbance, and
after the troops disappeared around the corner, the
crowd surged around the armory, beating in windows
and doors, and picking up their dead and wounded
comrades.

As the three companies marched down Baltimore
Street, the mob once more fell upon it, but was met by
such a deadly volley that it recoiled. The soldiers
were in earnest, and fired with terrible effect. It
was now about nine o'clock, and the lighted street
presented a wild and fearful aspect. In a compact
mass the some two hundred soldiers kept the middle
of the street, while behind and beside them pressed
the yelling, cursing throng. Ever now and then, as
the mob pressed too closely, a sudden volley would
light up the sea of swaying heads that would sud-

denly disappear down the side-streets as the dead fell on the pavement.

An elderly man, dressed in white, stood in front of the Carrollton House as the soldiers passed. He waved his hand and called on the crowd to come on. An enraged soldier stepped out of the ranks, and taking deliberate aim at him, shot him dead. The mob, unable to stand up against the deadly fire, soon scattered, and quiet was restored. The Fifth Regiment, down at the station, was in the meantime surrounded by a mob, and several collisions took place, and some of the soldiers were wounded. But the men not being allowed to fire on the mob, they took complete control of the engines and trains, and nothing was done. A few volleys like those of the Sixth would soon have settled the matter.

The events of the night at this point may be summed up in a few words.

Upon the entrance of the Fifth Regiment, about 7.30, an excited crowd of strikers, numbering about two hundred, began an attack upon Engine 389 with stones and pistols, and for some moments the fusillade was continued, until the wood-work of the engine was a complete wreck. The engineer and fireman escaped with a few bruises. A small force of police from the front charged on the mob, but were repulsed. At this moment Engine No. 407, Engineer Byerly, backed up to Barre Street to connect with No. 2 Chicago express, which was to leave at 8.15, when a second attack was made upon her, and soon she was also a wreck. Subsequently she was run out by the rioters, who jumped upon her, and, pulling back the throttle, let the engine go at full speed. She ran down the yard, and was **wrecked in a collision with freight trains at a point** below Lee Street. Gen. Herbert ordered Capt. Zollinger to disperse the mob. Capt. Zollinger, with Company C, Capt. Herbert, then charged the rioters with fixed bayonets, who had forced their way midway of the platform, north of Barre Street. The soldiery charged bayonets and drove them off the platform, when the rioters made a stand in the yard, near Howard Street, and assailed the troops with missiles of every description. By this fusillade Private George Wonderly, of Company C, and Lieut. Spear, of the same company, were struck in the head with stones and rendered unconscious. They were taken by their comrades back to Mr. King's private car, at the rear of the train, which had been converted into a temporary hospital. Company C again charged the mob to the intersection of Howard and Barre Streets, where they made a stand and again assaulted the militia. Numerous pistol-shots were fired by the rioters, and private Lewis, of Company K, and others were struck down. Company C had in the meantime been reinforced by Company K, but both companies were ordered back, they being unable to cope with the mob, which had increased to several thousand, and took possession of the entire vicinity. The coolness with which the two companies deported themselves was remarkable. Had extreme measures been used at the time, it would no doubt have put a stop to all further riotous acts, but Governor Carroll, who was present in consultation with Brig.-Gen. Herbert, Major Harry Gilmor, and other police authorities, counselled the use of civil power until the very latest possible moment. Notice was sent to each of the station-houses for all policemen who could be mustered, and, pending their arrival, the mob, constantly augmenting in numbers, held their position in the depot-yard and the surrounding streets. Three boys or young men, evidently crazed with liquor, boarded engine No. 407, and giving her full power, ran her down below Lee Street, where she was turned upside down. The rioters then tore up the tracks in the yard, and simultaneously demonstrations were made in front of the depot on Camden Street. Major Harry Gilmor, with a squad of men from Company C, Fifth Regiment, formed in line at the head of the platform in front of the ticket window, where the ammunition of the Fifth, in boxes, was piled. At this time a movement was made by the rioters from Barre Street, but they retreated after ascending the platform for a few yards. Anticipating the movement, the militia was ordered to load and make ready, which they did, but the retrograde movement on the part of the rioters prevented any extreme measure at this time.

Some firing was done by the policemen at Lee Street from the mob attempting to stop the firemen from doing their duty. They cut the hose of Engine No. 2, and fired on the guard. The casualties were few, while the main injury by fire was the burning of a passenger-car and the destruction of the despatcher's office. During the fire Governor Carroll sent a dispatch to President Hayes, saying that the depot had been fired by the mob, which was too strong for the force under his control, and asking for United States troops. Early in the morning the following reply was received:

WASHINGTON, July 21.
*To Gen. Barry, Commanding at Fort McHenry:*

The Secretary of War directs that you report to the Governor of Maryland with guns and all your men, to act according to his orders.

The message was sent to Fort McHenry by a mounted orderly as soon as received, returning with word that the troops were in readiness at a moment's notice. Subsequently, when quiet had been restored, these and other orders for troops were rescinded.

In the conflict with the mob between thirty and forty were killed or wounded, nine were killed outright, all of them rioters, and the removing of the bodies at eight o'clock in the morning, to their respective homes, was a sad and mournful spectacle. The crowd looked on in silence and a gloom settled down on the city.

The Police Board of Commissioners called out and organized a special force of five hundred policemen; liquor stores and saloons were closed; all trains over the road were stopped, and every precaution taken to prevent another outbreak.

In the meantime Gen. Hancock was ordered to Maryland to take command of the troops there, while the spreading disturbances alarmed the government at Washington, and measures were taken to protect its property, should an uprising occur in the city.

But while the fires were being stamped out in Martinsburg and Baltimore, the conflagration was spreading over the country, and at Pittsburg broke out with tenfold fury. If there could have been a few days' delay, till the result in the former places could have **been definitely ascertained, the strikes would not have**

extended as they did.    But the first news of the uprising seemed to run along the great railroads like an
electric spark.    The general reduction of wages had so
angered the employés everywhere that they were
ready to act on the first signal of revolt.

PENN. R. R.—VIEW OF PITTSBURGH.

# CHAPTER XXV.

## THE RAILROAD RIOTS.—PENNSYLVANIA.

The Riot in Pittsburg.—Its Origin.—The Track taken Possession of.
—Conference between the Strikers and the Superintendent of the
Road.—The Philadelphia Troops Sent for.—Their Reception.—
Attempt to Clear the Track.—The Fight.—The Troops in the
Round-house.—A Fearful Siege.—Attempt to Burn them out.—
Flight of the Soldiers.—The Work of Destruction.—A Committee
of Citizens Attempt to Quell the Rioters.—Union Depot set on
Fire.—Destruction of other Depots.—Extent of the Destruction.
—Tramps Seize a Train.—The Riot Ends.

THE very day after the riot in Baltimore, and before
the knowledge of the final result could be obtained, a
strike of the men employed on the Pennsylvania Railroad took place at Pittsburg. The ostensible cause of
this was the new order of the company, which went into
effect on that day, requiring that a double train, provided with two engines, and consisting of thirty-six cars,
be taken out with one crew of men. They claimed that
by this order two ordinary trains were taken out to Altoona, a distance of 116 miles, instead of to Derry,
which is forty-eight miles. Formerly a trip to Derry
was considered a day's work, while now the trip to Altoona is considered a day's work. This, they say, would
require one crew to do the work of two, and would en-
able the company to discharge one-half their number.

It was owing, however, doubtless to the general dis-
16*

affection growing out of the reduction of wages from former prices. The strikers ran out the freight trains on the side-track, and a man, while attempting to couple cars, was severely beaten. The strikers proceeded to East Liberty, and induced the yardmen in the stock-yard there to join them. They took possession of the main track, and stopped all freight trains going east or west. A placard was posted at the depot, signed by the President of the Tradesmen Union, calling a meeting of the train men, at Phœnix Hall, in the evening. The Engineers' Brotherhood held a secret meeting, and resolved to stand by the strikers. The latter, in the morning, after a full meeting, appointed a committee of five, composed of one from the conductors, one each from stokers, brakemen, and firemen, to wait on Mr. Pitcairn, Superintendent of the Western Division, to demand what they had resolved upon the night before, viz., that the classification of engineers be abolished, that the two per cent. reduction be restored, and the double train system abandoned. This demand was refused, and the officers of the company began to prepare for a defence of their property, and open up the road. Thus far no passenger trains had been stopped.

The local militia, consisting of three regiments and one battery, were called out at their request, but it was soon evident that no reliance could be placed on them. Aid was then sought for elsewhere, and troops were sent on from Philadelphia. This was the beginning of serious trouble. When they arrived at Pittsburg, they were received with jeers and howls by the mob. But no violence was offered, and the troops proceeded with a Gatling gun to the Union depot.

This was on Saturday, and between three and four o'clock, word being brought that the crossing at the outer depot of the Pennsylvania Railroad was blocked by the rioters, it was decided that the sheriff should proceed thither and attempt to make arrests, and on his being resisted, as no one doubted he would be, he was to call on the military for help. The troops set out, and a little before five reached the Twenty-eighth Street crossing, which they found packed with a mob that refused to leave. The Black Hussars were then ordered to clear the way, but the crowd stubbornly held its ground. Another company was then sent to their aid, and advanced with fixed bayonets. The crowd in the meantime had armed themselves with stones, sticks, and everything they could lay hands on, which they suddenly hurled full in the faces of the soldiers. Unable to make headway against this pelting storm, some say the order to fire was given, and others that the soldiers fired without order—it matters little which. Enraged at the sudden and rapid fire that followed, and which mowed down nearly twenty of their number, the rioters turned and fled in affright toward East Liberty, when the military took possession of the crossing. This unexpected slaughter caused intense excitement, some asserting that the soldiers fired before any resistance was made, so that many of those killed and wounded were mere spectators, and among these a little girl only four years old. The news, distorted and exaggerated, spread on every side, and brought together workingmen, tramps, and miners from every quarter, who filled the city with uproar. The immense throng divided, and began to roam the streets in search of arms or for plunder. Threats of the direst vengeance were uttered against the military. The city was now virtually in the hands of the mob, and the inhabitants became filled with terror. Johnson's gun factory, on Smithfield Street, was sacked, and the guns distributed among the crowd. Brown's larger establishment on Wood Street was also gutted, and the rioters, only a small portion of whom were railroad men, marched 3,000 strong down Fifth Avenue, with drums beating and flags flying, and shouting curses on the troops and General Pearson, who commanded them. In the meantime the troops had withdrawn into the round-house for better protection. This was a sad mistake, for it was a confession of weakness or timidity. With a single Gatling gun at their head, they could have cleared every street in the city in two hours. As soon as this movement was reported, the mob took courage and swarmed tumultuously around the building, bringing with them the guns belonging to the Hutchinson battery, which they had captured. These, as the papers stated, were levelled at the house, and soon the boom of cannon shook the city. A breach was made in the walls, through which some of the most desperate rioters endeavored to rush. The soldiers were then ordered to fire, and a volley was poured into the crowd, which drove them back. At this crisis some one shouted that the troops were bringing their Gatling gun to bear on them. The mere mention of this terrible arm so terrified them that they turned and fled in the wildest confusion, and did not stop till they put two or three squares between them and the dreaded danger.

In contradiction to this report it is proper to give, what is entitled to more credit and should be received perhaps as the correct account of the matter, the following statement of Captain Brett, of this same Hutchinson Battery, which of course supposes that he was in the round-house with the Philadelphia troops, or obtained his information from them.   He says:

"After the retreat into the round-house the guards were mounted, and a most vigilant watch kept on all avenues of approach.   Several times during the night attacks were made and were quickly repulsed by the sentries alone.   No general firing was permitted at any time, and not a shot was fired from the much dreaded Gatling guns either on Saturday or Saturday night.   They with two guns of my battery shotted with canister were kept ready for a grand attack our spy reported was to be made, but, it is needless to say, never was made.

"The only demonstration worth mentioning was when the mob placed one of the guns stolen from my armory in position on Liberty Street, and endeavored to fire it.   They speedily retired when opened on with sixty-five muskets, leaving several dead and wounded on the ground.   They were allowed to remove all the dead and wounded except two dead men who lay in such position that under cover of removing them they might have fired the gun.   Every man who approached that gun was warned by the sentries to keep away, and no one was shot at who heeded the warning.   At every point where attacks were made warning to keep away was given before firing.

"The stories about the round-house being bombarded are also false.   Not a shot was fired at us from a field-piece, nor would the gunnery of the mob, had they commenced firing, created the slightest excitement or produced the least confusion.   The Philadelphia men are soldiers and gentlemen, and simply obeyed the orders given them, and regret very much that obedience to those orders on Saturday caused bloodshed.

They are as steady and precise as regulars, and I or no other officer could ask or care to have a better support.

"The round-house was not evacuated till the men were suffocating from the smoke, and they retired in most excellent order."

The sudden retreat, however, is not denied, and hence shows what the effect would have been if the Gatling guns had been brought into actual requisition. It was now near midnight, and under cover of the darkness the rioters rallied again, and finding the Gatling gun was not brought into use, became emboldened, and, returning to the round-house, resolved to burn the soldiers out. The order was given, and soon " burn them! burn the wretches!" went up in one wild shout to heaven. The long blockade had filled the sidetracks with freight-cars till they extended more than two miles east from the city. Some of these were loaded with coke, and while a part of the crowd guarded the round-house, so that the troops could not escape, another part, with flaming torches, rushed for these cars, and in a moment huge volumes of black smoke rolled upwards, followed by sheets of flame that illuminated the whole surrounding region. Fire-bells were rung, increasing the terror, and soon the fire-engines came tearing down the street. But the mob kept them back and the flames had free course. The fire seemed to frenzy the mob still more, and holding torches before their pallid faces, they rushed backward and forward, setting fire to everything that would burn. They confined themselves, however, to the property of the railroad. The burning cars being too far from the round-house to set it on fire, some of the strikers took a car loaded with coke on the Alleghany Valley track and switched it off on to the Pennsylvania road. They then seized some cans of petroleum, flooded the coke with it, and then set it on fire, and shoved the car against the round-house. The troops now thought they would have to fight their way through the crowd. But the building did not easily ignite, when other flaming cars were run down against it. Morning had now dawned, and whether the mob was seized with fear lest the Gatling gun should be turned on them, or moved by some other cause, they suddenly turned and fled. The soldiers who, if they had remained much longer, would have been roasted alive, took advantage of this lull in the storm to escape. Filing out of the building, they formed into line, and marching up Thirty-third Street turned into Pennsylvania Avenue and thence into Butler Street, where stood the Arsenal, hoping to obtain shelter there. In the meantime the news of their flight had spread among the rioters, and a thousand or more of them, fully armed, started in swift pursuit. Some of the soldiers turned and fired, but this only infuriated the mob, and they pressed forward more fiercely, and soon a soldier fell on the pavement, shot through the body. Arriving at the Arsenal the troops asked to be admitted, but the commandant refused, saying he had only ten men to guard it, and they would be powerless to hold it should the mob attack it. He however, took in the wounded while the troops fled on up the street, pressed savagely by the mob, which kept up a constant fusillade upon them. The firing was kept up for a mile, when two more soldiers were killed and left on the sidewalk. The column continued on until they

got over to the north side of the Alleghany River,
which they crossed by the Sharpsburg bridge, when
they scattered, and the mob broke up and disappeared.

While one mob was thus chasing the soldiers out of
the city the other that remained behind continued the
work of destruction, and the city was in a state of anarchy.  The multitude, drunk with passion, and maddened by the sight of the roaring flames they had kindled, and which seemed to threaten the entire destruction of that part of the city, continued to swell
the conflagration by new fires.  The sun, which now
had begun to mount the summer heavens, was obliter-
ated by the huge volumes of black smoke that rolled
up the sky.  The crackling of the flames rose over the
maddened shouts of the multitude that now continued
the work of destruction without fear or hindrance.  It
was Sabbath morning, but it had dawned more like
the last day of time than the Christian's day of rest.
By seven o'clock the flames had extended from Melville
station to Twentieth Street, and long lines of cars, hundreds in number, were represented by long lines of
fire, while the extensive machine shops of the company, blacksmith shops, the depot and offices of the
United States Transfer Company, two round-houses,
and various other buildings, were set on fire and
towered in flames over the flaming cars below.  One
hundred and twenty-five first-class locomotives in the
two round-houses were totally destroyed.  The scene
on Liberty Street, along the line of which the railroad
track runs, was a strange, bewildering one.  Men with
sledges were breaking open cars loaded with merchandise, around which crowded women and children struggling to get each his share of plunder.  Goods were

CORNING, N. Y.—SECOND DETATCHMENT, 23D REGIMENT, N. G. S. N. Y., STOPPED BY RIOTERS.

pitched into the street, which was literally blocked by the plunder tossed into it. Even wagons and carts were driven up and loaded with goods. It was a scene of confusion and terror indescribable, and yet some of the exhibitions of greed were ludicrous, notwithstanding the tragedy that accompanied them. Here, a brawny woman could be seen hurrying away with pairs of white kid slippers under her arm. Another carrying an infant would be rolling a barrel of flour along the sidewalk, using her feet as the propelling power. Here a man would be seen pushing a wheelbarrow loaded with white lead. Boys hurried through the crowd with large family Bibles as their share of the plunder, while scores of women utilized aprons and dresses to carry flour, eggs, dry goods, etc. Bundles of umbrellas, fancy parasols, hams, bacon, leaf lard, calico, blankets, laces, and flour, were mixed together in the arms of robust men, or carried on hastily constructed hand-barrows.

The mayor with the police attempted to stop the pillage, but he could not stop the work of destruction that went on. It was evident that a large portion of the citizens were averse to the presence of the troops, thinking that it incensed the strikers, while they believed the men could be controlled by reason and forbearance. But now that the troops were gone, chased out of the city by a mob that shot them down as they fled, and havoc and destruction were abroad in their midst, they began to see what an incarnation of everything fiendish, a lawless, maddened mob was. About eleven o'clock a meeting of the citizens was called at the City Hall, to see what was to be done. A committee was appointed to wait on the rioters, and per-

suade them to desist from the work of destruction.
On this committee of five was Bishop Twiggs, of the
Roman Catholic Church, and Rev. Doctor Scovel,
pastor of the Presbyterian church. It was thought
that so many of the rioters being Roman Catholics the
presence of the priest would awe them into submission. But mayor and priest were alike insulted, and
narrowly escaped personal violence. It was the Sabbath day, and these peaceful servants of the Lord could
not fail, it was thought, to have a good effect. They
had yet to learn, what all history has taught, that
mobs once entered on the work of destruction are as un-
tamable as a wild beast. The only committees that
can influence them are the close and deadly volleys.
They want bullets, not sermons. The railroad authorities had fled, lest their presence should rouse the rioters
to fresh deeds of blood, and the wild work went on
unhindered, and authorities and people stood and looked on in still terror. The church-bells pealed on over
the wild chaos, but there were few worshippers in the
sanctuary. Only a small part of the rioters were railroad men. Most of the leaders in this wanton destruction of property had no complaints against the
company—they were chiefly of the class to be found
in all cities, who are always ripe for violence and
rapine—fond of them for their own sake. There
were also a great many spectators, the hillsides south
of the railroad being covered with them as they looked
on the wide-spread conflagration in silent astonish-
ment. There, too, stood the firemen, but they were not
allowed to move a finger towards putting out the fire.
Had they attempted it their engines would have shared
the general destruction. The Union depot had thus

far escaped, and it was thought the passions of the
mob would be appeased without adding this structure
to the general ruin.   But the wilder the destruction
the more insatiate seemed the mob, and about half-
past three a burning car was run down the grade
under the sheds near it, and soon the vast mass of
lumber that composed them was a sea of roaring flame.
Having started this new conflagration, the rioters
turned to the freight depot of the Pittsburg, Cincinnati, and St. Louis Railroad close by.   This they first
gutted, breaking open boxes and barrels, and carried
off their contents.   Men staggered away, loaded with
hams, flour, and plunder of all sorts.

They then applied the torch to it, and the Union
depot blazed up while the firemen looked on, afraid to
interfere.   It was a fearful spectacle.   The Union
depot was a large four-story building of brick and
stone.   It had a frontage on Liberty Street of about
seventy feet and extended back about 200 feet.   The lower floor was used as a waiting-room, ticket-offices and the
company's offices.   The upper floor was occupied by
the Keystone Hotel Company, and was one of the best
houses in the city.   The whole building was of modern style of architecture, and was considered one of the
best arranged depots in the country.   It was finished
about seven years ago.   In the rear of the depot, and
extending back 500 feet, were lines of neat pine sheds
covering different tracks to protect passengers from the
weather.   It was under these the burning car was run.
The depot is flanked by a high hill.   In front, and
across the street, stood huge grain warehouses, and
across the street on the right were numbers of small
stores and shops.   At the rear of the building platforms

and tracks were laid for the use of the several railroad lines interested in the depot. The yard was not inclosed, but long, narrow sheds covered the tracks. Connecting tracks were laid on both sides of the depot to the grain warehouse across the street and to the outer depot of the Pittsburg, Fort Wayne and Chicago road in Allegheny City.

The freight depot of the Pittsburgh and St. Louis Railroad was a large shed, built fronting on Grand Street, and extending from Washington Street to Seventh Avenue. The company's general offices were in a four-story brick building fronting on Seventh Avenue. These buildings were totally destroyed, as was also the depot of the Adams Express Company, located on Grand Street. The books and valuable papers had been removed from the Union offices, as well as from the outer buildings, before the fire reached them.

The last to follow in this wide-sweeping conflagration was the Pan Handle depot. It now seemed as if the city itself would take fire, and a panic seized the citizens. The ruin, however, was confined chiefly to the railroad property. When this last building was fired, the whole territory between Seventh Avenue and Mill Vale Station, a distance of three miles, was a mass of flames, the railway company's property being all between the south side of Liberty and the Bluff Hill, extending from Seventh Avenue to Hill Vale.

The railroad buildings destroyed here were two round-houses, one machine-shop, Superintendent's office, car repair-shop, blacksmith-shop, three or four oil houses, the Union Transfer Depot and offices, the Pullman Car Company's laundry and offices, dispatcher's office, powder-house, the Union Depot Hotel, the Pan

Handle Railroad engine-house, general offices and freight depot, and the freight depot of the Adams Express Company.

The country now became thoroughly aroused, and no one knew where the trouble would end. It was spreading like an insurrection, and reports of strikes on the following roads were received: Baltimore and Ohio, Pennsylvania Central, Erie, Lake Shore and Michigan Southern, Pittsburg, Fort Wayne and Chicago, Pittsburg, Cincinnati and St. Louis, Vandalia, Ohio and Mississippi, Cleveland, Columbus, Cincinnati and Indianapolis, Philadelphia and Reading, Philadelphia and Erie, Erie and Pittsburg, Chicago, Alton and St. Louis, Canada Southern, and some minor roads.

Governor Hartranft called on the President for aid, and the latter promised it and issued his proclamation to the people of Pennsylvania. General Hancock was put in command of the troops of the State, and General Sherman, who was in the West, was sent for. The various garrisons along the coast were heavily drawn on for regular troops, which alone could be relied on in any such crisis as had just happened in Pittsburg. The mayor of the city called on the citizens to enroll themselves for self-protection, and soon more than a thousand men were enrolled and marched, armed, through the city. The Philadelphia regiment that had been so badly handled was encamped ten miles out of the city on a hill. Fifty mounted policemen patrolled the city as also the troops, composed of the Duquesne Grays, the Nineteenth Regiment, together with some veterans, and a battery, and it was evident the riot was over. The mayor and citizens had waked up to the danger after the mischief was done.

It was confidently thought that the rioters were awed into quietness by the display of force; but the fact was they had nothing more to do. They had accomplished their work, which was the destruction of the railroad property in the place. They declared they had no intention of doing anything else, and now there was in reality no fear, except from small bands of plunderers. They could survey at leisure their work in the charred and blackened ruins around. The survey was not as satisfactory as they had anticipated in their mad frenzy, especially as they began to comprehend that they must await the slower action of the police and courts of justice.

Some strikes occurred in a few of the factories, and more or less anxiety was exhibited. People wishing to leave the place dare not, fearing their progress might be arrested at any point. On the night of the 23d the mayor received a dispatch stating that a lot of thieves and tramps from Baltimore had taken possession of a train on the Baltimore and Ohio Railroad, and were running it into the city. He immediately assembled a police force, and marching to the station, received them as they entered it, and relieving them of their arms, locked them up. But the city, on the whole, was quiet, and the inhabitants had time to reckon up the number of millions of dollars the city would have to pay for that Sabbath's wild work.

# CHAPTER XXVI.

## THE RAILROAD RIOT—PENNSYLVANIA.

### The Beginning of the Harrisburg Disturbance.—Quickly Quelled.

THE news of the riot quickly reached Harrisburg, and the next day things wore an ominous look in the streets of the city. At the depot, foot of Market Street, a vast crowd assembled and threatened the property of the railroad company.

They were not held in check through fear of the authorities, but of the 2,000 troops which, in view of the threatening aspect of affairs throughout the State, had assembled at the State Arsenal under General Siegfried, and who had put the building in a state of defence, with Gatling guns to protect it. A meeting of the strikers was held in West Harrisburg, and a resolution passed requiring the road to return to the wages of 1871, or twenty per cent. more than was now paid. All business was suspended at both the Pennsylvania and Reading depots, and everything was plainly preparing for an outbreak. A number of soldiers, on their return from Altoona, where they had been sent to protect the railroad, were put off the train about five miles from the city, and after wandering into the suburbs, were captured by the strikers, who took their guns and ammunition from them. A meeting was held in one of the round-houses, where incendiary speeches were made. Among them appeared the mayor, Patterson, who persuaded them to give up their guns, he promising they should not be used against them.

Intense excitement prevailed, and the arrival of soldiers to keep the peace exasperated them still more. At about one o'clock in the morning, a mob made an indiscriminate attack on the stores at the foot of Market Street, near the depot. Every store that was supposed to contain guns was gutted, and the mob proceeded to arm itself. A proposition from one of the leaders to burn the *Telegraph* printing-office was met with demoniac yells, and they proceeded to accomplish their purpose. In the meantime Sheriff Jennings summoned a posse of 500 citizens, armed them with revolvers and guarded the *Telegraph* building. The fire-alarm was struck, and the firemen as they responded were given places in the ranks of the sheriff's posse, and their apparatus taken back to the houses. Shortly after 12 o'clock the sheriff ordered a move on the strikers, who were massed at Fourth and Market Streets. The mob fell back, but not before two rioters with guns in their hands were captured. The posse advanced as far as the railroad track, the mob meanwhile fleeing across the canal bridge. The mayor attempted to prevent them from breaking into the gun shops, when a rioter pointed a gun at his head and snapped it. The citizens at once organized a Vigilance Committee to guard the principal buildings.

The sheriff addressed the mob, and ordered them to disperse. He was hooted and jeered, and one striker attempted to strike him. He was immediately arrested, and when his comrades advanced to rescue him, they were met by the muzzles of the revolvers of the

READING— BURNING OF THE LEBANON VALLEY BRIDGE.

police and fell back. The citizens' Vigilance Committee acted promptly, and kept so completely the upper hand that the mob was cowed, and the riot was quelled without the shedding of blood.

17

# CHAPTER XXVII.

## THE RAILROAD RIOT—PENNSYLVANIA.

The Riot in Reading.—Bloody Work.—First Outbreak.—Burning of
Lebanon Valley Bridge.—The Coal and Iron Police.—Arrival of
the Militia.—Blank Cartridges.—Point-blank Firing.—Cowardly
Troops.—Killed and Wounded.—Internal Commerce Stopped,
and Famine Threatened.

READING supplemented the wild work of the Sabbath day at Pittsburg. The terrible news that almost
momentarily kept arriving created the most intense
excitement, and groups of men in earnest conversation,
and with agitated countenances were gathered around
the depot and on street corners. At the outer depot,
the crowd which had assembled greeted the passenger
trains arriving after ten o'clock with shouts and yells.
Several hundred persons started for the Lebanon Valley Railroad tracks, west of the depot, and were quickly followed by the remainder of the crowd. The advance portion broke open a tool-house, seized the crowbars, picks, and sledges, and commenced tearing up
and blockading the tracks. Rails and sills were carried upon the tracks. Meanwhile two locomotives
were cut loose from their respective trains, having
come from Philadelphia and Allentown, and run
towards the obstruction. The engineers were motioned
back, and were greeted with volleys of stones. The

head-light of one locomotive was knocked to pieces, and the windows of the cabin were broken. The other locomotive was also damaged. Both were run back, the engineer of the hind locomotive discharging two chambers of a revolver as he pushed through the crowd.

Two cabooses were fired, and the firemen who came to the rescue were prevented from extinguishing the flames. The tracks were also blocked, and later a freight train was set on fire, and five cars burned, while the crowd increased to thousands. "At 12 o'clock, midnight, the Lebanon Valley Bridge, one of the finest in the State, was set on fire. The fire was kindled at the western end of the bridge, near the watch-tower. A portion of tin was removed from the roof, and cotton waste, saturated with oil, was dropped down among the network of timbers. The fire at first burned slowly, and it was three-quarters of an hour after the fire had been kindled before an alarm of fire was sounded. After the fire had gained headway the flames spread rapidly across the bridge until the entire structure was enveloped in flames. The sight of the burning bridge was witnessed by thousands of citizens, many of whom were on the Harrisburg bridge. The fire companies, as they reported at the scene of the fire, were prevented from throwing water upon the bridge. The police were greatly outnumbered by the sympathizers with this movement, who lined both banks of the Schuykill. The immense timbers of the bridge were licked up by the devouring element, and the entire burning mass presented a magnificent sight, one long to be remembered. Showers of sparks ascended from the fire, which swept from one end of the bridge to the other, and the work of destruction was complete. At 1.35 A.M. the spans fell into the river, the western span starting first, and taking all the others with it in quick succession. The bridge was erected in 1857, and is said to have cost $150,000. The piers were left standing."

The next morning the excited crowds thronged the streets, uttering the old Paris cry, when the mob marched on Versailles: "Bread! bread!" In the former case the cry was sincere, for the people were starving, but here it was the merest farce—there was no want of food, and many of those who uttered the cry the loudest had been spending enough for whiskey for the last two or three days to keep their families in bread a month. About noon some 500 congregated at the Philadelphia & Reading Railroad depot, and took possession of it. The passenger train from Pottsville for Philadelphia was halted, but after a short delay was allowed to proceed. A coal train, however, was stopped, and the engineer stoned from the engine. Chief of Police Cullen read the Riot Act to the crowd, and when he finished they showed their respect for it by howls of derision. As the afternoon wore away, the crowd became more excited, and it was evident it was lashing itself into fury. Their passions were excited still more when the 6 o'clock train came thundering into the depot, and a body of the Coal and Iron Police stepped out on the track. Though few in number these charged on the crowd and drove them back, till, becoming completely surrounded, they were forced to beat a retreat. An hour later another body of Coal and Iron Police arrived from Pottsville, when the two took position in one of the car-shops and awaited the course of events.  A half an hour later, the Easton Grays and two companies from Allentown arrived, and forming at once at the depot, with colors flying and drums beating, marched to the " Cut," as it was called, situated near Penn and Seventh Streets.  Here was a train which the strikers had captured, and were determined to hold against all comers.  The Cut for more than thirty rods from Penn Street was filled with rioters, while a dense crowd occupied both sides.  As the soldiers approached, the mob began to yell and throw stones and pieces of coal at them.  These falling in a shower bruised and maddened the troops, and at last they fired, but over the heads of the crowd.  But they found, for the one hundredth time, that blank cartridges are worse than useless.  The rioters greeted the harmless discharge with derisive laughter, and poured in a still heavier shower of stones and coal, and stubbornly held their ground.  The order to fire point-blank was now given, and a volley was delivered into the very midst of the crowd.  They seeing a number reeling and falling around them, immediately turned, and with wild shouts rushed from the Cut. The sight of blood seemed to craze them.  How many of their comrades lay dying or dead in that cut they could not tell, and they ran through the streets crying, " BLOOD ! BLOOD ! *Murder !* *Vengeance !* " and as one after another dead or wounded man was carried out the most frantic cries and yells rent the air.  In half an hour after, everything seemed quiet, but another half hour had scarcely elapsed before a crowd of half-drunken men and boys filled Penn Street, and breaking into the armory, seized about forty rifles, and declared they would clean out the murderers. They did not attempt, however, to carry out their threat, and by midnight comparative quiet reigned, though here and there a body of angry strikers could be met parading the streets and tearing up portions of tracks. The next day part of the Sixteenth Regiment, National Guard, and the Easton Grays of the Eighth Regiment arrived and marched down Penn Street, followed by a hooting crowd, who assailed them with the most opprobrious epithets, while they pelted the Easton Grays with stones. Enraged at this treatment, the latter wanted to fire on their assailants, but the Norristown company threatened, if they did, to fire on them. Not long after, the Norristown company basely stacked their arms and refused to act against the mob. The State militia could not be relied on, that was plain, and they were ordered away. But at evening 600 regulars—First Artillery—arrived under General Hamilton, bringing with them their camp equipage and a large amount of ammunition, showing that they meant to stay and see the matter out. Their stern appearance and measured tread told the rioters that if they attempted any more violence they would have different men to deal with than the poltroons of a few hours before, and the city at once became as quiet as on a Sunday.

It was said that ten were killed and over forty wounded in the night's engagement, besides some twenty soldiers wounded. A special police force was sworn in, and steps were taken to insure future peace. The mob still retained possession of the road. The tracks had been torn up for some distance, and mail communication was kept up by a transfer of mail matter to pony express at a point below the city. A freight-car loaded with tobacco was rifled of its contents. A large quantity of rifles and ammunition, which had been stored away by the rioters, was captured by the police.

Although the strikes kept extending, and it was plain that the local militia could not be depended upon, and no one knew what new complications might arise, or where the trouble would end, yet the prompt, decisive manner in which the rioters had been put down in their first attempts, gave evidence that the authorities would be equally successful at every point. The example of the first success of the rioters had encouraged the general uprising, so now their failure would naturally have a corresponding effect. Besides, the general government was firm, and the press to a man advocated vigorous, prompt action. Even those who sympathized with the laborers on the railroads, and thought they had been unjustly treated, felt it was no time to express that sympathy. Law must first be vindicated and anarchy cease before they would consent to consider the case at all. But though the riots were suppressed, a great evil was imminent, nay, was already present. If order was restored in one place, the trains were obstructed at so many different points that through trains to the east could not be run. It is true, mail trains were not stopped, but the companies refused to run any trains unless a safe passage was guaranteed to all. If the government protected its own mails, it must protect the road that carried them. Besides this, all internal commerce was stopped between the great West and our seaboard. Nearly all the meat and flour that feed our large cities comes from the West, and this was suddenly stopped on the way. The great thoroughfares must not only be cleared up, but

speedily, or a sort of famine would prevail. Therefore no delay must be allowed, and troops were accordingly hurried to the threatened points with all possible
speed, and in the middle of the week the following
summed up the alarming situation :

No through freight is arriving at New York, Philadelphia, Boston, or Baltimore.

On the Baltimore and Ohio Railroad, where the
strike began, the blockade continues at Cumberland,
Keysers, and Grafton.

On the Pennsylvania Central the blockade is complete.

On the Lake Shore no trains are running.   No
trains leave Cleveland or Toledo.

On the Erie road the blockade at Hornellsville is
perfect, way trains only running on the branches.

On the Central and Hudson trains are running to
Buffalo, but a strike is expected.

On the Ohio and Mississippi the road is blockaded
at Vincennes.

The Central Pacific, Union Pacific, Louisville and
Lexington, Cincinnati and Muskingum, St. Louis, Iron
Mountain and Southern, St. Louis, Kansas City and
Northern have acceded to the demands of the strikers.

To alter this state of things, and reopen traffic, the
following dispatch shows what vigorous steps the general government were taking independent of the efforts
put forth by the separate States and local authorities.

WASHINGTON, July 23d.—In the War Department
this morning there was a scene of unusual activity, and
numerous dispatches were under transmission between

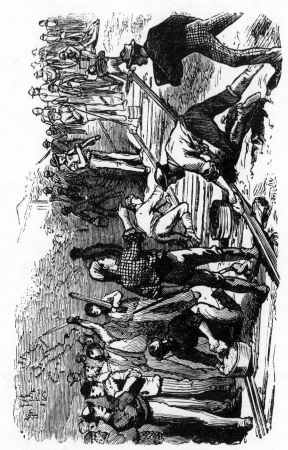

NEW YORK—RIOTERS SOAPING THE TRACK AT HORNELLSVILLE.

the department and various military commanders, especially General Pope, commanding the Department of the Missouri, and General Hancock, commanding the Military Division of the Atlantic, in regard to the movements of troops for the protection of public property. Adjutant-General Townsend, with a corps of assistants, was at the department throughout the night, but all the officers are very reticent as to the plans and course of the authorities. The President, accompanied by his son, Webb Hayes, visited both the War and Navy departments this afternoon. The President was in consultation with Secretaries McCrary and Thompson.

General Hancock has been ordered to assume personal command of the troops in Pennsylvania, and General Schofield, who arrived here this morning and called on the President, has been requested to proceed to Philadelphia to confer with General Hancock.

The United States steamer Swatara arrived here this morning from Norfolk with one hundred and fifty-seven sailors and marines on board, all armed and equipped for active service. The Plymouth soon after arrived with an additional number, and the Essex is now on the way to the city with about two hundred sailors and marines; making a force of more than five hundred on the three vessels. The Powhatan was originally ordered here, but it was found that she drew too much water, and the Plymouth was directed to come here in her place.

The force on the United States steamer Tallapoosa and the receiving ship Wyoming at the Navy-Yard here, is kept in readiness for actual service, and can be sent to any point upon brief notice. The Secretary of the Navy has also given orders to have the force and vessels of the Philadelphia Navy-Yard in readiness for service to protect public property in that city and aid the civil authorities in the maintenance of law and order.

Orders have been issued from the War Department

17*

directing General Pope, commanding the Department of the Missouri, who has his headquarters at Fort Leavenworth, Kan., to send all the available force from that place to St. Louis for the protection of public property there, and go to that city himself if he deems it necessary.

General Ruger, commanding the Department of the South, has been ordered to send three companies of infantry to Louisville, Ky., and Jeffersonville, Ind. The six companies of the Twenty-second Infantry *en route* from the Sioux country to the Department of the Lakes have been ordered to stop at Chicago and are now at or near that city.

Orders were issued from the Navy Department to-day to have the various iron-clads at Washington, Philadelphia, and elsewhere prepared for service immediately, and engineer officers have been ordered to report on board, to move them without delay, should it be necessary to do so.

Governor Van Zandt has telegraphed to the President, giving assurance of Rhode Island's readiness to aid him in the preservation of law and order, and offering the support of military.

PROVIDENCE, R. I., July 23d.—Troops from Fort Adams for Baltimore started at 7 o'clock this morning by way of Wickford.

PORTLAND, Me., July 23d.—The artillery company garrisoning Fort Preble started for Pittsburg this morning.

WATERTOWN, N. Y., July 23d.—Battery H, United States Artillery, from Madison Barracks, Sackett's Harbor, passed through this city to-day, *en route* for Baltimore *via* New York.

FORTRESS MONROE, Va., July 23d.—General Geo. W. Getty, commandant of the Artillery School, has received orders from General Hancock to join him at Baltimore and take command of the troops on the Baltimore and Ohio Railroad. Captain Ward, Aide-de-Camp on General Hancock's staff who is here on an inspection tour, also leaves to-night for Baltimore.

BOSTON, Mass., July 23d.—At 11 o'clock this morning United States troops, consisting of Company L, First Artillery, twenty-nine men, Company D, First Artillery, twenty-four men, and Companies I and A, First Artillery, fifty-nine men, left here for Baltimore, *via* the Baltimore and Ohio Railroad.

POUGHKEEPSIE, N. Y., July 23d.—Battery F, Third Artillery, from Fort Ontario, passed through here to-night *en route* to Baltimore.

While in Maryland and in the southern portion of Pennsylvania, in Harrisburg, Reading, Pittsburg, and Altoona the riots were suppressed, more serious trouble was anticipated at Philadelphia.

# CHAPTER XXVIII.

## THE RAILROAD RIOT.——PENNSYLVANIA.

Philadelphia in the Riots.—The Fears respecting Her.—The Mayor's Proclamation.—The Mob.—Trains Stopped.—The Police.—Scranton Miners and Strikers Join.—Wilkesbarre.—Governor Hartranft.—His Energy, Skill, and Promptness.—New Jersey in the Strikes.—Her Conservative Position.

PHILADELPHIA being the centre to which so many railroads run, much anxiety was felt respecting what course would be taken there by the employés. That the terrible news, coming in such rapid, startling succession, from Martinsburg, Baltimore, and Pittsburg, should stir the city profoundly was to be expected. She was surrounded by fire ; her own soldiers had been killed in putting down riots elsewhere ; and no one could tell how interlinked all these places were in a general conspiracy.

The depots became crowded with eager multitudes, and on the afternoon of the 22d more than 3,000 people assembled at the Pennsylvania depot, where Colonel Scott and Mayor Stokely were in consultation. At the arrival of any train the crowd would rush hither and thither to obtain the news. By five o'clock the throng had become so vast that Mayor Stokely called out the reserve police and cleared the place, and then himself rode round the city to ascertain the state of things, and sent a messenger to the Bridesburg Arsenal to inquire what force they had there, in case the mob should attempt to seize the arms.   The reply came in a request to have an armed tug sent up from the navy-yard, which was done.

At the depot in the evening Col. Scott received a dispatch as follows :

" Gov. Hartranft is *en route* for Pennsylvania, and has telegraphed ahead ordering out every militia regiment in the State.   He has also telegraphed to the President of the United States calling for troops, and suggesting the propriety of a call for volunteers."

The mayor issued the following proclamation :

MAYOR'S OFFICE, }
PHILADELPHIA, July 22d. }

*To whom it may concern :*

*Whereas,* violence, tumult and riot exist in various portions of this Commonwealth, to the great injury of domestic industry and trade, and to the discredit of American institutions and form of government, the perfection of which was last year celebrated in this the city of the Republic's birth ; and

*Whereas,* It is of the highest importance that the great name which Philadelphia has made for herself among the nations of the earth during the Centennial year shall be preserved, and she shall be spared the horrible scenes enacted in our sister cities ;

*Now, therefore,* I, William S. Stokely, in the name of the Commonwealth of Pennsylvania, and by virtue of the authority vested in me by law, do hereby appeal to all citizens of every occupation and calling to render it unnecessary that in the performance of my duty I should be called upon to suppress any outbreak and violence, which I assuredly will do if the occasion requires it, and hand over the offenders to condign punishment; and I make this appeal in the firm belief that the citizens of Philadelphia appreciate, as I do, the importance of maintaining peace and good will among all classes of society, and I hereby pledge myself to give a patient hearing, and do impartial justice, as I best know how, to all persons who desire it. Let all the people resume and continue their lawful occupations, and avoid assembling and organizing together for discussion, or otherwise, at the present time. This is the surest and best means of preserving the honor and fair name of the City of Brotherly Love.

WM. S. STOKELY.

At six o'clock the strike began by the men in the Pennsylvania depot leaving their places, and it was with some difficulty an engineer could be obtained for the Cincinnati express, which was to start at 9.10. The first open resistance was exhibited when a loaded oil train, standing on the track above Callowhill Street, was ordered to be moved. The strikers interfered, when the police marched up. The train men then asked that it be left to stand where it was, and that no trains should be moved that night. To this Col. Scott, President of the road, consented.

The night passed without further disturbance, but the morning showed by the gathering crowd and serious faces that the excitement and danger were not over; and especially in the extensive yards of the railway company things looked ominous. But the police kept driving back the crowds a couple of blocks or more, thus keeping them clear. At five o'clock the police held all the bridges connecting with West Philadelphia, and let only residents and the horse-cars pass. To distract the attention of the authorities an oil train had been set on fire, which destroyed several cars on the Junction road, and two firemen were injured by the explosion of a tank. The strikers held several meetings during the day, in which there was much excited speech-making. Col. Scott wisely prevented any violence by resolving not to attempt to move any freight trains over the road for the present. A committee of strikers waited on him, and requested him to restore the ten per cent. taken off the engineers' wages on the 1st of June, but he firmly refused. Mayor Stokely called a meeting of the citizens, who took steps to aid in putting down the riot should one be attempted. The arrival of a hundred marines, commanded by Lieut. Hayward, who took a position where they could sweep the yard if trouble occurred, had a disheartening effect on the strikers.

Gen. Hancock also arrived with a few regulars and relieved some of the policemen, who had been on duty for five successive days, not sleeping more than an hour each day during the whole time.

By the 24th appearances indicated that no serious disturbance would take place in Philadelphia. It was evident that the mob element of the city that cares only to destroy and plunder had combined to rise the moment the strikers came in open conflict with the authorities. The latter being prevented, the desperadoes kept quiet. Just before noon, Col. Scott, after a consultation with the military officers, determined to start three freight trains and test at once the temper and reveal the intentions of the strikers. The fires were started in the locomotives, and at half-past three the first train was sent out, though not without much misgivings as to its fate before reaching New York.

A large crowd had assembled on the bluffs, at the head of Thirty-sixth Street, ostensibly for the purpose of playing ball; but their intention being suspected Capt. Chaztean, with his men, was ordered to disperse them. Some of the railroad men told them not to stir, when the Captain addressed them, telling them he was acting under the order of the mayor, which required him to clear the bluffs; that he should not attempt to make any arrests, but should obey that order at all hazards; and they would resist him at their peril.

At this point the Captain was interrupted by one of the railroad men, who asked him: "Have railroad men no rights any more?" The Captain replied: " If I know anything about President Scott he does not permit his engineers to leave their locomotives on the track under steam and go up on high bluffs to play base-ball." As the guards were well armed, the crowd, which numbered some four hundred or five hundred, deemed retreat wise, and sullenly moved off.

In the afternoon the mayor issued a proclamation congratulating the citizens on the maintenance of peace. He also gave orders to increase the police force, temporarily, to two thousand four hundred men, to relieve the one thousand two hundred men that had been on duty since Sunday. At night the strikers endeavored to hold a meeting at Kelly Hall, but at the request of the mayor the hall was refused them. They then attempted to hold it on the sidewalks, but the police dispersed them. The riot was dead in Philadelphia.

### THE RIOT AT SCRANTON.

But while the State was becoming quiet in other sections, trouble broke out in her northern boundary. On

PENN. R. R.—VIEW OF TRENTON, N. J., AND R. R. BRIDGE.

the very day the Mayor of Philadelphia was issuing his congratulatory address to the citizens on the peaceful state of affairs, the employés of the Lackawanna and Iron Coal Company struck, and marching to the steel works and machine-shops were joined by the men at work there. The firemen of the Lackawanna & Western Railroad Company having received an unfavorable answer to their request for a restoration of the ten per cent. reduction, also struck at six o'clock. There was no disorder; the engines were quietly taken from the round-house to the yard, the fires drawn, and then left standing in good order. At the same time the firemen in the employ of the Delaware & Hudson Canal Company struck for the same reason. All the trains on the two roads were stopped, but the strikers telegraphed to the State authorities that the company refused to run the mail, and that they would run it if necessary, and furnish a fireman and engineer. The Fourth Regiment, arriving at Allentown, dispersed the rioters there, but at Easton the hands on the New Jersey Central quit work. On the same day (the 25th), the brakemen on the Lehigh & Susquehanna Division struck, and also the railroad men and miners at Wilkesbarre.

At Scranton, on the 27th, matters became very much complicated by the vast number of miners in that region—an army in themselves—making common cause with the railroad men. They met in the road to the number of 10,000—a host of unarmed, yet angry men.

The answer of the President, stating that the company could not grant the demand of twenty-five per cent. advance, was read amid profound silence, and resolutions were adopted to the effect that the men would die before returning to work at what they called

starvation wages. The mine engineers and pump hands
struck at night. They drew the fires, and the mines
began to flood. If allowed to become flooded it would
take a year to prepare them for work again. A meeting of prominent citizens was held at the call of the
mayor, and to meet twice daily until further notice.
The citizens began to organize for protection.

In two or three days the railroad strike was over,
and a large portion of the employés returned to their
work, the only conditions required being that the
leaders in the strike should not be discharged. The
starting of the trains exasperated the striking miners, who declared that they had been sold by the
railroad men. They had not only made common
cause with them, but, like Cortez, had burned their
ships behind them, for by flooding the mines they
put it out of their power to return to work for a
long time. Attention was now turned to them, for
thousands of them were on the brink of starvation,
yet they declared they would hold out till winter
unless their wages were restored. A similar state of
things existed at Wilkesbarre and in other mining districts, but as these have really nothing to do with the
great railroad strike, they being of almost yearly occur-
rence in some part of the coal region, we shall not attempt to follow them up. Governor Hartranft is equal
to the emergency. And here, by the way, it should be
recorded that Governor Hartranft deserves the highest
praise for the promptness, energy, and indefatigable
activity he has displayed in stamping out the flames
of incipient revolution in Pennsylvania. Stopped at
Omaha on his way to San Francisco by the news of the
riots in his State, he hurried back fast as steam could

carry him, and going from place to place collected, massed, and moved troops with the celerity of a veteran commander. He did not argue with the rioters; he struck first and listened afterward. With such a Governor Pennsylvania may be sure that violence cannot long triumph within her borders.

# CHAPTER XXIX.

NEW JERSEY, though connected so intimately with Philadelphia and Pennsylvania by railroad, showed her true spirit in this wide-spread panic, and thus escaped the bloodshed that disfigured other States. There was, of course, great excitement among the railroad men, and a general strike was expected, and to a certain extent prevailed. Excited meetings were held at Hoboken and elsewhere, and the demand made as in Pennsylvania for a restoration of the ten per cent. reduction. The refusal to grant it exasperated the men, and some 400 or 500 engineers quit their work, but yet without showing any hostility to the road. They cleaned and fixed their engines, and quietly left. There was an interruption of the trains at Newark and other places, but no violence or force used. At the Pennsylvania depot the men refused to strike, although the same refusal to restore the wages was made to them as to the others, and they in a meeting bitterly denounced the company for their unjust and suicidal policy. In Newark a meeting was held, in which resolutions were passed upholding the strikers, denouncing the railroad companies and the military, who aided them in maintaining oppression; but throughout the State order was maintained, and no property destroyed.

The Governor issued a proclamation, and the military was held in readiness to act, but there is no evidence that fear had anything to do with the conduct of the strikers. It resulted rather from sound calculation, that although their wages were too small, and the action of the companies unwise and oppressive, a strike would not pay, but make matters worse. They were very moderate in their demands, the engineers agreeing to take the reduced wages if an additional fireman were allowed them to help them in their labors, which were too exacting. The strike caused heavy loss to many of the manufactories in Newark by loss of business, but the rights of property were respected.

# CHAPTER XXX.

## THE RAILROAD RIOTS—NEW YORK.

The Two Great Trunk Roads.—Table of Wages Given.—How to Decide What Are Fair Wages.—Strike at Hornellsville.—A Bold Engineer.—Arrest of Donohue.—Governor's Proclamation.—Arrival of Troops.—The Military Powerless.—Brooklyn Troops.— Terms Agreed On.—Strike over the Central Road.—Strike at Albany.—Arrival of the Ninth Regiment.—Strike at Syracuse.— Riot at Buffalo.—Mr. Vanderbilt's Views.—The Great Meeting in New York.

It was natural that public attention should be turned to the great State of New York, to see what effect this widespread railroad revolution would have on her. With her two great trunk roads tapping the far West, and concentering in the commercial emporium of the nation, and employing, as they did, such an army of men, it was a serious matter whether she responded in her might to this call of the strikers, or maintained her integrity. Perhaps, before entering on the history of the strike in her borders, it would be better to give an elaborate statement of the wages formerly paid and afterwards reduced on these two great roads. In this way the reader can form an intelligent opinion as to the justice of the complaints of the employee, better than by any argument. Not that it has anything to do with the right of men to obstruct trains—drive men off who wish to work in their places, and much less to destroy property. It is taken from the *New York Times:*

"On the New York Central and Hudson River Railroad a ten per cent. reduction was made in the wages of employees on the first of the present month. The following table gives the former and the present wages on the road:

|  | Old Rate. | New Rate. |
|---|---|---|
| Engineers, per day........ | $3 50 | $3 15 |
| Firemen, per day.......... | 1 75 | 1 58 |
| Brakemen, per day........ | 1 75 | 1 58 |
| Switchmen, per month..... | 40 | 36 |
| Yard hands per month..... | 40 to $55 | 36 to $49 50 |
| Shop hands, per month..... | 45 to 125 | 38 50 to $112 50 |

"On account of the evenness of the grade on this road, a run of 100 miles constitutes a day's work for engineers on all sections of the line. But, whether the engineers run 100 miles or but 10, they get $3 15 a day. For all miles run in a day over 100, they get at the rate of 3.15 cents per mile; and every engineer on the road who wishes gets 150 miles a day, twenty-six days out of the month, thus earning $4 72 a day, or $122 85 a month, if they take all their Sundays off. Under the old rate engineers got $3 50 a day, at the same rate for extra mileage, and $136 50 a month. Contrary to general opinion, the managers of the New York and Hudson River Railroad assert that the present reduction is the first one made among their employees since war times, with the exception of a 2½ per cent. reduction made against the switchmen and yard hands, two years ago. The managers also informed the reporter that previous to the war engineers earned only from $65 to $80 per month, and firemen, yard hands, and switchmen only $30 to $35 when roads were rough and dangerous, when machinery was very imperfect and hard to handle, and when boilers used frequently burst, and the real expenses of living were greater than they are now. The railroad officials seem to be of the opinion that their employees and the employees of all corporations have no conception of the difficulty to be found in managing affairs so that business can be run at all, and employment given in these dull times; and insist that laboring men have had decidedly the best of the bargain for the past four years. The officials think that the laborers should be kept better informed and should be advised of the selfishness of their conduct in striking and crippling what little business there is left in the country, merely because the profits on labor, which has no risks, happens by necessity to be cut down ten per cent., while its employers have conducted business for a long time at a loss, without shutting off labor at all.

"At the Erie Railroad affairs were found in an almost similar condition. Although the employees and the company have of late had frequent disputes about wages, still the managers assert that the present reduction is the first one made on that road since the war, and they claim that at the reduced rates their men are not only the best paid of all laborers of equal skill in the country, but that they are, considering the prices of living and the relative values of the currency now and then, far better paid than they were during the flush times of the war. The following is a table of the wages paid on the Erie now and before the reduction:

|  | Old rate. | Reduced 10 per cent. |
|---|---|---|
| Engineers, per day................... | $4 00 | $3 60 |
| Firemen, per day.................... | 2 36 | 2 13 |
| Conductors, per month.............. | 100 00 | 90 00 |
| Brakemen, per day.................. | 2 00 | 1 80 |
| Baggage-masters, per month........ | 55 00 | 49 50 |
| Track foremen, per month.......... | 50 00 | 45 00 |
| Track laborers, per day............ | 1 25 | 1 12½ |
| Switchmen, per day................ | 1 50 | 1 35 |
| Laborers in yards, per day.......... | 1 50 | 1 35 |

"It should be borne in mind that these men all get work at least twenty-six days in the month, and that the engineers and firemen get paid pro rata for every

SEE THE HOTLY CONTESTED TRAGEDY OF WAR AT THE BRIDGE AT EULER

NEW YORK—RIOTERS TEARING UP RAILS AT THE BRIDGE AT
CORNING.

extra mile they run (the number of miles making a day's run on this road varies on each section according to the ease or difficulty of the grade), and that the engineer and firemen all have an opportunity of earning a half day's extra wages every day they choose to do so. Before the war men were paid on the Erie the same wages as on the New York Central."

From this table of rates one may easily see how much reason there was for complaint, especially when it is considered that almost every citizen has to reduce his rate of living more than these workmen were called upon to do. The rates of wages before the war are the proper ones now, for the simple reason that the whole country has got to come down to the standard of those times before it can recover its prosperity. It is absurd to say that everything must come down but labor, for that also must yield to the general pressure and obey the general law. Men may yield to it willingly, or not; yield they must, or go without work. There must be a certain relation between labor and the prices its products bring in the market. If the price of labor is fair when the article it produces brings a high price, when the time comes that the price falls ten per cent., labor must fall in proportion, or the industry cease. If men expect houses to be cheaper, the labor must be cheaper that constructs them. If certain manufactured articles fall in price, the labor that fabricates them must be cheaper also, or the manufactory must stop. This reciprocal law underlies all our industries. If a railroad does less freighting business, and at reduced rates, the labor that moves it forward must come down in price also. This whole talk about keeping up or returning to old rates of wages, when

18

all the industries of the country are paralyzed, is the absurdest folly that was ever conceived. The very men who insist on the old standard of labor, demand that everything else should be cheaper on account of hard times. Why, the laboring men, who for the last few years have had steady employment, have received more for their work than the average salary of the clergy of the country outside of the great cities amounts to, and to-day there are thousands of hard-laboring ministers, who have spent years and money in fitting themselves for their profession, who would be glad to accept the price for their services that many of those men received who strike for higher wages. Before the war, before everything went up like a kite, a dollar a day was all a man asked for his services; but now he feels insulted if offered any such sum. But why should not wages come down to the old standard, if everything else does? It may be said it is hard for the poor man to be deprived of those comforts and luxuries he has so long enjoyed. So it is. It is hard also for a man to live on an income of $1,500 a year, who has been accustomed to live on $3,000. It is hard for the man to find land he paid $200 per acre for worth but $150; or for him who paid $10,000 for a house to see it bring but $5,000; or the builder to find where he built ten houses he now builds but five; or the merchant to find where he sold $100,000 worth of goods, he now sells but $50,000 worth. All this is hard, but it is going on all over the country—nay, worse than this, men are constantly losing all the earnings of years, and, at the end of life, instead of finding their incomes reduced 10 per cent., see them swept away entirely. Now, is the laboring man not to share in these hardships? Must his high wages go on just the same? They *will* not, that is certain, and he must submit to the change, or do far worse. In the general depression, almost paralysis of all the industries and business of the country, only a few of enormous ·wealth are exempt, and they solely because the reduction of their incomes does not rob them of any of the comforts, nor even luxuries of life —at least none that a reasonable man should desire.

### THE ERIE RAILROAD STRIKE.

It was natural that this great trunk road of New York State, lying as it does on the borders of Pennsylvania, and connected with so many of its roads and industries, should be the first, as it was, to feel the disturbance that occurred there. Why the strike should commence at Hornellsville instead of at either end is not so plain, except that at the former place there happened to be more able or reckless leaders to inflame the passions of the men. As early as the 20th of July, firemen, brakemen, and trackmen at Hornellsville had a meeting at midnight, at which they resolved to strike next day, and sent a committee to the superintendent to apprise him of their intentions. This was immediately telegraphed to headquarters at New York, when word was sent back along the line to have all trains approaching Hornellsville stopped. It was not desirable to bring any more of the employees on to help swell the strike. Train men who were aware of what was passing in Hornellsville were thus disappointed in getting on, though some of them seized hand-cars and reached it in that way. But the timely stopping of the trains prevented a large accumulation of disaffected men at this point, as well as a great jam of cars. Several conferences were held between the men and two of the superintendents that had come on. At 2 o'clock the former made known their demand, which was that the pay of firemen should be made the same as it was previous to July 1, 1877; that brakemen should receive $2 a day; switchmen, $2 ; head switchmen, $2 25 ; yard track-men, $1 50, and section workmen, $1 40 ; that monthly passes should be continued as before, and passes issued to trackmen and switchmen, and that no rent should be paid for company ground occupied by them, except according to agreement. A large majority of the trackmen here live in houses built on land belonging to the company. These terms the company decline to comply with.

The passage of trains was then at once stopped. A lightning express train, however, got on by coolness and strategy. It was stopped at Elmira by the strikers, the cars uncoupled, and Dan Chapman, who was one of the oldest engineers on the road, was notified that he could take his cars no farther. He told them he should go on, and getting the cars coupled up, he started. At Olean the strikers stopped it again, and held it thirteen hours. When it got under way once more, the engineer determined it should reach Horn-ellsville without any more stoppage. He knew, when he reached the freight-trains stretched along the sid-ings, that the men, if aware of his approach, would stop the train, and he directed his fireman not to ring the bell at stations, while he refused to whistle down brakes, although there were some heavy grades ; but with a full head of steam on, went dashing on through the darkness like some demon of the night—the thundering of the train as with its blazing headlight it swept by, alone announcing its approach and departure. The brave engineer said that he could hear their howls of defiance and rage, over the deep rumble of the train as he sped on. It was near midnight when in dashed into the place, the strikers guarding the switches outside made aware of its approach only when they saw the flaming headlight almost upon them.

In a conference held in the office of the railroad company on the 23d, Donahue, the leader of the strikers, asked Mr. Bowen, the general superintendent, if he would reinstate the men who had been discharged. He replied that he certainly would not. This was at the close of the conference in which the strikers had stated the terms on which they would come back. That evening, while at supper in the Nicols House, the astonished Donahue was arrested on a warrant sworn out by Receiver Jewett, and issued from the Supreme Court of New York by Judge Donahue, on the charge of contempt of court. The rioter forgot that the road was in the hands of a receiver, and that he was responsible to some one else than the officers of the company. In the mean time the Governor had been called on for troops from this and various other quarters to put down the strikers and help to open the road. He was at his home in Elmira, and hastening to Albany, sent the following telegram to Adjutant-General Townsend: "I am on my way to Albany. You will direct the Major-General of each division in the State to hold his command in readiness for service at a moment's notice, subject to my orders." General Townsend immediately

put the telegraph at work and soon all was excitement
and bustle at the different armories of the State, and
by next day more than 3,000 men were ready to move
wherever directed. It recalled the war times of a few
years ago. Two days after his arrival at Albany, Governor Robinson issued the following proclamation. He
had three days before issued a general one from
Elmira:

STATE OF NEW YORK, EXECUTIVE CHAMBER, ⎱
ALBANY, July 25, 1877.    ⎰

I deem it my duty to invite the special attention of
all the citizens of this State, and especially of such
persons as are now attempting to interfere by unlawful
means with the running of railway trains, to the following act passed by the Legislature at its last session:

*Chapter* 261—*An Act to Punish Trespassing on
Railroads, passed May* 10, 1877.

The people of the State of New York, represented
in Senate and Assembly, do enact as follows:

SECTION 1. Any person who shall wilfully place any
obstruction upon any railroad, or loosen, tear up, or remove any part of a railroad, or displace, transfer, or in
any way interfere with the switches, frogs, rail, track,
or other part of any railroad, so as to endanger the
safety of any train, or who shall wilfully throw any
stone or other missile at any train on any railroad, shall,
upon conviction thereof, be punished by imprisonment
in a State prison not exceeding ten years, or liable to a
fine not exceeding $1,000, or by both such fine and im-
prisonment.

SEC. 2. This act shall take effect immediately.

I warn all persons engaged in the violation of the
above law to desist therefrom, and I call upon all

sheriffs, magistrates, district attorneys and other civil officers, and upon all good citizens, to aid in the enforcement of the said law, and of punishment of all who are guilty of its violation; and I hereby offer a reward of $500, to be paid upon the arrest and conviction of each and every person who shall be guilty of a violation of the said act.

The failure or omission of any sheriff, district attorney or other civil officer to take the most active steps in his power to enforce the provisions of this act will be considered sufficient cause for his removal.

L. ROBINSON.

By the Governor:

D. C. Robinson, Private Secretary.

There was something more in this than the empty call on the rioters to lay down their arms and disperse. He first calls their attention to a law, of which he had no doubt they were ignorant, and clinches the whole by a reward of $500 for the arrest and conviction of any one guilty of violating that law. This reward was a masterly move and doubtless did more to make the ringleaders cautious than even the presence of the military. It was like having a price set on one's head, and tempting the very men he would incite to violence to betray him.

In the meantime, troops had arrived at Hornellsville. The 54th Regiment of New York State militia from Rochester reached there on the night of the 21st, and soon after the 110th from Elmira with a battery. The latter were formed in line and marched through the yard, driving out the crowd, while the Rochester troops guarded the approaches. The strikers called a meeting, and resolved to be firm in spite of the military, and were encourged in their course by telegrams from all along the line, promising aid.   On the 22d it was resolved to start a train, which the strikers swore should not leave.   Forty soldiers of the 110th Battalion were placed on the train, five being on the locomotives, two on each car platform, and the rest inside the cars.   The rioters had assembled at West street, having previously soaped the rails to prevent the train from getting headway.

When the engine struck the soapy rails, no amount of sand the engineer could let down in front of the drivers could overcome the slippery surface sufficiently to maintain any degree of speed, and the train approached the boisterous assemblage not faster than eight miles an hour.   The strikers, yelling like a pack of Indians, crowded on the track, waved a red flag, and demanded the engineer to stop the train, with threats of violence.   Engineer Carey was firm, and kept right on against the great disadvantages that beset his progress.   As the train pulled into the midst of the crowd they made a dash for the engine and the cars.   The soldiers made confused and feeble attempts to keep the howling strikers back, one burly fellow, meanwhile, gaining the front platform of the car next the baggage-car.   The guard was pushed aside and the brake seized.   By this time every platform had two or three strikers upon it, the brakes were put on, and the passenger cars stopped and cut loose.   The engine and the mail and baggage cars went on a little way, when the engine stopped.   Instantly a strong gang of the strikers surrounded and climbed upon the engine.   They threatened the engineer with violence if he did not proceed, but he replied firmly, if there was any chance for his getting possession of his passenger cars,

NEW YORK.—THE STAIRWAY DEFENDED BY ARTILLERY.

NEWARK, O.—AN ENGINEER LIFTED FROM HIS TRAIN.

he would run the risk of their threats. He saw, however, that the effort would be useless, and pulled on up the grade. The whole force of the strikers then swarmed upon the cars that had stopped. The soldiers came out of them, followed by the passengers. The strikers then began disabling the cars. They tore the brake-rods loose and bent them out of shape with axes; they smashed the brake-wheels to pieces and broke everything necessary to be used on the cars, with wild yells, then starting them down the grade towards the station. The train dashed into the yard at a high rate of speed, threatening destruction to everything that might be in the way, but the cars were turned off upon a switch in time to save a collision with a locomotive and train that stood on the main track near the depot.

The crowd then marched savagely jubilant to the guard limits of the yard, where they were soon approached by train No. 7, which the company had started out on the way to Buffalo, guarded by soldiers. They threw open a switch ahead of the locomotive, bringing the train to a stop, and then did considerable damage to the engine. They pulled the fireman from the cab and forced from him a promise not to go out again. The train was then brought back into the yard by the engineer.

Soon after this a gang of strikers boarded an engine and some cars that were being switched in the Susquehanna Division yard, preparatory to starting a train east. Besides the engineer, there were several deputy sheriffs on board, who were all driven off, and the engine and cars run to the bridge, some distance east of this station, where the steam was blown off, the fire

18*

extinguished, and the engine crippled. The attack was made from localities•where the men seemed to have been hiding.

The troops seemed to be paralyzed with fear, or indifferent to the actions of the strikers, for the latter were allowed to have their own way without molestation.

The next day the first detachment of the 23d Regiment of Brooklyn, which had been ordered on, arrived. They were insulted all the way at the different stations. Some 1,500 troops were soon under orders at this point. The strikers saw at once that they were in a net, from which there was no escape, and immediately agreed to go to work on the following terms :

The firemen and brakemen to go to work at the reduction of 10 per cent. ; no men engaged in the strike are to be proceeded against or discharged, except those who have destroyed the company's property ; the reinstatement of the committee who were discharged is left to the superintendent of the divisions in which the dismissals occurred, and the brakemen are to go to work at the wages they received before July 1 ; the case of Donahue, in the settlement, is left to the counsel of the Erie and that of the strikers to arrange.

It is not necessary to speak of the minor strikes along the line of the road, except at Corning, where the strikers, not satisfied with stopping trains, commenced to tear up the track and to overturn locomotives, enlivening their work by shouts and oaths. But the construction gang soon put everything in order, and the excitement soon subsided. The one at Hornellsville was the backbone of all, the rest were mere offshoots ; with the breaking down of that the trouble was over.

### THE CENTRAL ROAD.

Right on the heels of the strike at Hornellsville on the 20th, there was a meeting of the New York and Hudson River Railroad men in the Capitol Park, at Albany, on the 23d, at which a resolution was passed demanding a general increase of 25 per cent. on their wages. A committee was appointed to wait on Mr. Vanderbilt to present this resolution, and if the demand was not complied with, to inform him that they should strike on the following morning at 8 o'clock. They met next morning, but there was no life in the meeting, and after some consultation the crowd started for West Albany, where the shops of the New York Central & Hudson River Railroad are located. Here some 300 or 400 men were persuaded to quit work, whether from fear of a fight or from sympathy, or partly from both, does not appear. After the shops were closed, the following letter from Mr. Vanderbilt to a committee of employees on the road, was read :

" The public interest should not suffer from any differences between the road and its employees. Keep at work till the excitement is over and a fair conference can be had.

"WILLIAM H. VANDERBILT."

This dispatch was received with shouts of derision by a portion of the crowd. They then resolved to hold another meeting in the park in the afternoon. In the meantime they compelled the switch and track-men to quit work, and posted them where they could stop all freight trains. Two freight trains coming in, and one bound out, were both stopped. They had hardly accomplished this when a western bound train was seen approaching. At the sight a great shout was raised, and a rush made for it, and the cars were uncoupled. At two o'clock, the mob, made up of railroad strikers and vagabonds, again began to assemble in the Capitol Park. A meeting was organized, and a brakeman made an inflammatory speech. Another young man followed, denouncing the outside element, and declaring the company's property should not be destroyed. About 1,000 men then started for Greenbush and East Albany, and, taking the freight-house in their way, compelled the workmen to stop, as well as some of the switchmen. But about half-past nine the Ninth Regiment from New York arrived, and their appearance excited the admiration of the citizens, who crowded around the depot to see them as they marched out with fixed bayonets and took up their quarters at the Delavan House. It was feared that an outbreak might occur at West Albany, and so the next morning the Ninth was carried thither. General Carr made his headquarters at the railway station. The workmen who stopped work the day before, feeling themselves safe under the protection of the military, cheerfully resumed it. The Tenth Regiment of Albany arrived soon after, Colonel Amasa J. Parker, Jr., and the track was well guarded. Early in the afternoon, the pickets south came in and reported disturbances in that direction. The Ninth instantly formed into line and moved down the track, and cleared the bridge and roadway. Soon the trains were again moving, and it was evident that what threatened to be a dangerous riot at Albany was quelled.

## SYRACUSE.

At Syracuse the railroad men blockaded the road, allowing no trains to pass, and the 54th Regiment was ordered out for duty. The next day they struck, together with the machinists of East Syracuse, 100 in number. Six hundred freight cars, seventy engines, and forty trains were stopped there, but the strikers detailed a guard of their own men to guard the property of the company. No violence was attempted, except so far as was necessary to stop the trains. The next evening a live-stock train ran past the yard and proceeded towards Albany. The strikers were astonished to find that the train was not going to stop. They seized an engine and started in pursuit of the stock train. They overtook it about six miles east of Syracuse and ordered the fireman to leave the engine. He did so, and the strikers brought him back to Syracuse.

The 8th New York Regiment, bound for Buffalo, was stopped by orders of the adjutant-general, in order to quell the mob. The excitement gradually allayed, and, as the news from various quarters came in announcing the steady collapse of the strike, the confidence and boldness of the misguided men sensibly decreased.

## BUFFALO.

At Buffalo, the western terminus of the Central road, occurred the most serious riot on the whole length of the line. On the 22d of July the men struck, and by midnight numbered over 1,500, with constant accessions to their strength. In the morning they took the firemen and brakemen from the New York Central trains, unloaded the stock, and forbade the employés to do any further work.

The mob, reinforced by large numbers, called at the car-shops of the Lake Shore and Erie companies and ordered all the workmen there to quit, which they did forthwith. About four o'clock in the afternoon, a Buffalo and Jamestown train, which leaves the Erie depot, on arriving at Compromise Crossing, two miles from the depot, had a passenger coach detached and shoved on the Central track, and the fireman was forcibly taken from the engine. Superintendent Doyle, who was on the train, remonstrated with the strikers, stating there had been no reduction of wages on their road, nor had there been any since its inauguration. The effect of this statement was the bringing back of the coach by the strikers, who coupled it on, and assured the Superintendent that nothing should be done in any way to interfere with the working of his road.

"Early in the afternoon an assault was made by nearly 2,000 rioters on about 200 soldiers who were guarding the Lake Shore round-house. The military were obliged to leave the building, which was then barricaded by the mob, who placed cars in position as defense against an attack. Col. Flach, of the 65th Regiment, with about thirty men and three officers, proceeded to the round-house to retake it from the mob. They were met with yells of derision from the crowd, and, under a shower of stones were obliged to retreat at the double-quick and force their way through the yelling crowd at the point of the bayonet, many of the soldiers being badly cut on the hands with knives, and also clubbed. Four of the soldiers lost their muskets, which, however, were afterwards recovered. Col. Flach was badly clubbed, twice knocked down, forced across the canal, and obliged to take refuge in the Lake Shore paint-shop."

A public meeting was held that night, called by the mayor, but was composed mostly of strikers, and those who sympathized with them. Committees were appointed, and resolutions offered, and speeches made, chiefly by the mob. If any one attempted to pour oil on the troubled waters, and advocated peaceful measure and mutual forbearance, he was hissed down. It was a disorderly meeting, and never should have been called. At any rate, the moment the rioters assumed a bold and insolent bearing, they should have been told very plainly that if they persisted in committing acts of violence, they would be shot down without mercy—that they had got to conquer the troops of their own State, and then of the General Government, before they could succeed. As it was, the meeting broke up, leaving a worse state of feeling than when it began.

The train coming from Westfield, on the Lake Shore Road, with a company of militia belonging to the Eighth Division, was stopped by the strikers about nine o'clock in the evening above Tifft's Station, on the outskirts of the city. The mob entered the cars and took from some of the soldiers their muskets, when a general fight ensued, with firing of guns on both sides, and the throwing of stones by the assailants.

This did not seem to confirm Mr. Vanderbilt's theory, which from the outset he had maintained, that the employés of the road were loyal, and would re-

main so.  He was frequently sending despatches like
the following or expressing similar sentiments :

" SARATOGA, N. Y., July 22.
" *To J. W. Tillinghast, Buffalo :*

" Your despatch received.  I have every confidence
in the good sense and stability of a large majority of
our employés.  The whole country is now looking
most anxiously on them, and I feel confident that they
will sustain their reputation and that of the road, by
making common cause, having the fullest assurance
that when the business of the country will justify it,
they will receive compensation accordingly.

" W. H. VANDERBILT."

Now, there is no evidence that the men of this road
were any more loyal than those of other roads.
Doubtless a large majority of those who had destroyed
property and openly resisted the military, elsewhere as
well as here, were not railroad men.  It is true also
that all over the country a majority of the employés
were afraid of the result of a strike—that it would
make matters worse, although not a few might be truly
loyal.  But in every case like this, much depends on
momentary excitement, the influence of leaders, and external circumstances.  Here, at Buffalo, there was no
reason why the men should not be as loyal as in Utica.
The circumstances happened to be different.  A man
like Donohue of Hornellsville, at Albany, would soon
have shown how little difference of feeling there was
among the men on the various railroads.  A general
dissatisfaction prevailed against the way they were
treated.  One and all believed that they were oppressed
by powerful companies, and if success could have been

CHICAGO—THE FIGHT AT TURNER HALL, ARRIVAL OF U. S. ARTILLERY.

surely promised in a general strike, Mr. Vanderbilt
would soon have seen how few loyal men he had on
the Central Road.   To talk of loyalty either as a feeling of love or obligation on the part of the employés
of our railroads at the present day is a farce.   It does
not exist.   All the loyalty on the Central or other
railroads grew out of the fear of not succeeding and
faring worse.   Poverty and suffering in the future,
and bayonets at their bosoms at the time, wrung from
them all the loyalty they exhibited.   There is a bitter
antagonism between those who own and those who
run the railroads which ought not to exist, and is
fraught with evil.

Mr. Vanderbilt afterwards presented the men of the
Central Road $100,000.

## THE GREAT COMMUNIST MEETING IN NEW YORK CITY.

But while things were in this chaotic state, not only
in New York, but all over the country, an event occurred that diverted the general attention, from the
mere possibilities that might result from it.   New
York city is not only the largest in the union, but is
composed of a dangerous population, exceeding in
number that of any other city in the country.   Consequently, the most extensive and dangerous riots have
occurred there.   Hence, anything like a convulsion there
would naturally be regarded with special anxiety.   It
caused, therefore, serious alarm, especially throughout
the State, when it was announced that a public meeting was called to be held in Tompkins Square on the
25th—just as we seemed to be getting out of our
troubles, and in a fair way to have the traffic of the
country flow in its usual channels—in order to sympa-

thize with the strikers, which of course meant to encourage them to hold in and resist to the last.  It is
not necessary to go into all the preliminaries of this
meeting.  The object was plain—to sympathize with
and encourage the strikers to fight it out.  What we
have to do is with the propriety of the city authorities granting as they did the permission to hold the
meeting.  That permission was wrong and the fact
that no evil resulted has nothing to do with the other
fact that it should not have been allowed.  We have
seen but two reasons advanced by the city authorities
for granting it.  Whether these reasons were the real
ones or not, we do not know; we only know they are
the only ones that could be given.

These were, first, the city had no constitutional right
to prevent the meeting.  In the first place, no such
right of prohibition was involved.  The very simple
question was whether the city authorities had the power
and right to postpone it for four or five days.  This
does not admit of a doubt.  If the meeting were called
on a Sabbath or in the midst of a general conflagration,
no one doubts it could be postponed for a day or two.
But, more than this, we assert that the city authorities
had the power and the right not only to adjourn, but
prohibit the meeting altogether, so long as the object it
had in view was not only understood but confessed.
A meeting whose object is to help violators of the law
succeed in their attempts to overcome both civil and
military authority, and destroy property and murder
innocent citizens, is never legal, and to grant it is to be
accessory to crime.  Discussion of questions that divide
and agitate the public, and are more or less dangerous
according to the views of individuals, is one thing, but

quite another to encourage men with arms in their hands who are violating law and resisting the legal authorities. Now, this meeting was called for the express and only purpose of extending sympathy to such violators of law, and encourage them in the destruction of property and in shooting down men while in the discharge of their duty. The right to prevent such a meeting lies back of all written constitutions, in the eternal law of self-protection that God, not man, made for the preservation of human government and the well-being of society.

The second is quite as untenable as the first reason —that the city was well prepared—that was as good a time as ever to test the question whether a mob could rule New York. The time to test such a question is when it arises, not before. It is the duty of those in power to be prepared for an event, not force it. Slaughter and death are serious enough when they are inevitable, without being provoked. The doctrine that doing evil that good may come has no place in the Christian code. It was the simplest, easiest thing in the world to postpone this meeting a week, when it would probably never have taken place. But it might not have been so easy as the Police Commissioners supposed, to prevent a slaughter when a collision had once taken place, and still harder to clear the conscience of the guilt of having caused the death of even one man unnecessarily. Precaution in all governments, whether general or municipal, is one of the first duties of those representing them. Certainly the granting of a permission to hold this meeting was something quite the reverse of that. No man can foretell the extent or results of an outbreak when it has once commenced ; hence, no wise man should ever provoke one.

Freedom of speech is one thing. Freedom to stop public conveyances, destroy property, and throw everything into chaos, is quite another. To give rope to a mad dog just to show how easily you can master him, may do in sporting circles, but not in the government of a great municipality.

But the meeting was a total failure, and the strike in New York was virtually over.

# CHAPTER XXXI.

## THE RAILROAD RIOTS—OHIO.

Cincinnati, Zanesville, Newark, Toledo, and Fort Wayne.—Military at Newark Sympathize with the Mob.—The Latter Entertain Them.—The Governor Orders Troops from Cincinnati.—Commands in Person.—Issues a Proclamation.—Raiding in Cincinnati.—Public Meeting at Toledo.—Strikers Draw up a Tariff of Wages, and Protect Railroad Property.—Men Driven from their Work at Fort Wayne.

THE strike on the Baltimore and Ohio Road spread with the rapidity of lightning, and on the very day of the riot in Baltimore a meeting of firemen and brakemen was held at Columbus to consider the situation. Cincinnati was also alarmed, and very naturally, for the reduction of the wages ten per cent. took place only the day before on some of the roads, and on that very day on one; while it was clear that the strike on the Pan-Handle Road was rapidly working westward. Two days after the firemen and brakemen of the Lake Shore Road struck at Cleveland, and a vigilance committee was formed at Zanesville. At Newark the strikers were masters of the situation. On the evening of the 21st four companies of militia arrived, and at noon next day marched into the freight yard, and the officer in command advised the strikers to withdraw. They refused, declaring they had committed no act of violence, and appealed to the soldiers' sympathies by relating their wrongs.  It was evident that the appeal was not in vain, for the troops soon quietly returned to their quarters.  Governor Young then ordered on four companies from Cincinnati, and two from Dayton.  The militia in the meantime mingled freely with the strikers, who, hearing that the County Commissioners, then in session, refused to make any arrangements by which the troops could be fed, sent a committee around to raise money to buy food for them.  The business men subscribed freely, and provisions were purchased, and the militia became the guests of those whom they were sent to disperse.  The sympathy of the citizens was generally with them, and it was very evident, if the railroad companies depended on the State militia to open their roads for them, they would remain closed for a long time.  In the evening a meeting of the Brotherhood of Locomotive Engineers was held, in which it was resolved to take no part in the strike of the firemen and brakemen, but to wait awhile.  Governor Young issued a short proclamation on the 21st, calling on all the citizens of Newark to keep away from the yard. He tried every way to make the strikers see the hopelessness of the movement, but in vain, and so ordered parts of the First, Second, and Third Regiments to report at Newark.

Two days after a mob patrolled a portion of Cincinnati, raiding private establishments and closing up nearly all the rolling-mills, machine-shops, and factories on the west side of the river.  But few railroad men were in the raid, however, the main part being tramps, roughs, and miners.  Warrants were issued for the arrest of some of the leaders.  Several hundred special policemen were enrolled, and a call made for a vigilance committee to be organized. The people of Newark in the meanwhile were thrown into great excitement by a report that a body of 1,000 miners were on the way to join the strikers there.

## TOLEDO.

At Toledo also there was much excitement, and on the 25th a large crowd of laboring men of all occupations appointed a committee to draw up a tariff of wages. They also appointed a committee to see that no injury was done to property. Mayor Jones was present, and made a conciliatory speech.

At the conclusion of the mayor's remarks, the crowd formed a line, it being announced that they would first go the whole length of Water Street to the Pennsylvania Depot, and then through the manufacturing districts, notifying all the establishments to stop work at once. This plan was followed out, and the crowd proceeded from place to place, gaining strength as it proceeded, ordering the employés of lumber yards, mills, foundries, etc., to stop work. Most of the day was consumed in this manner, and in many, if not quite every instance, their demands were complied with, though not without protest in some cases on the part of the workmen. The Milburn Wagon Works, employing 300 hands, closed at two o'clock, before the arrival of the procession. Every large manufacturing establishment in the city was closed. A call for a mass meeting of citizens at eight o'clock in the evening was issued by the mayor early in the day, and in pursuance thereof an immense crowd assembled in the market space at that hour. Mayor Jones presided, and after addresses by several citizens, a resolution was adopted calling on the mayor to appoint a committee to consist of twenty persons from each ward, to take measures for the preservation of peace and protection of property. The meeting was composed largely of the discontented element, representatives of which took possession of the stand and proceeded to address the crowd, and the meeting finally broke up in confusion and disorder. But the strike collapsed here when it seemed most threatening.

Governor Young having returned from Newark, where he had in person commanded the troops, issued another proclamation at the capital, and it soon became apparent that tranquillity would be restored without any bloodshed or destruction of property. It is not necessary to mention all the strikes in the State—they were all alike, while those given above were the principal ones. The great evil they accomplished was stopping for a while the transmission of freight between the West and the East.

## INDIANA.

A similar state of things occurred in Indiana. At Fort Wayne the trainmen assembled on the 23d, and compelled the closing of the Pittsburg, Fort Wayne and Chicago shops, employing 1,000 men. The trackmen and switchmen on this division of the same road also refused to work, and flocked to the city, where they joined the strikers. The situation looked very critical at noon, when threats were made that every railway shop and manufactory in the city would be forced to shut down. The mayor, therefore, called the City Council together in special session, and they passed resolutions ordering the strikers to disperse, compelling

CHICAGO—DEPOT OF THE CHICAGO AND NORTH WESTERN RAILROAD.

all saloons to close up, and providing for the employment of 200 extra policemen to preserve order and guard railroad property.

The strikers assembled in the afternoon and passed resolutions respecting wages, etc., like those we have heretofore given. The same obstruction of trains occurred at Terre Haute and Indianapolis. In short, Indiana shoved another block across the great railroads, although the strikers refrained from destroying property and from coming in collision with the military.

19

# CHAPTER XXXII.

## THE RAILROAD RIOTS—ILLINOIS.

BLOODY RIOT IN CHICAGO.—Character of its Population—Commencement of the Mob—Shops and Factories forced to shut up—Mobs in various Sections of the City—A Communist Editor taught a Lesson—Mob on the Lake Front—United States Troops sent for—A Mass-Meeting in the Tabernacle- A Night Attack—The Second Day's Struggle—A Fight between the Military and Mob—The Latter shot down—Severe Fight near Canalport Avenue—A Brave Boy—The Regulars—Battle of the Last Night—General View of the Design of the Strikers.

PERSONS acquainted with the population of Chicago feared that when the riots broke out there, blood would be shed. Foreigners, especially Germans, constitute a very considerable portion of the inhabitants. These, if not communists, as the papers call them, believe in a democracy closely akin to their doctrines. Fleeing from the oppressions of the Old World, they bring with them all the hatred toward the upper classes which has grown up with their growth. It is not difficult to make them believe that men here possessed of wealth, though born of the people, belong in some way to that upper class at home which they so cordially hated. Especially is this true the moment the poor cry out that they are oppressed or treated unjustly. These men, whether injured or not, are sure to take sides in any conflict of the poor against the rich, or rich companies. Hence, a strike of railroad men there would be certain to rouse up this large population so that a formidable mob would be quickly collected and be characterized by more than usual ferocity. The strikers, beginning east, travelled westward steadily, and by the time they assumed any formidable appearance in Illinois, were virtually over east of the Alleghanies. It was not till the 25th that any serious demonstration was made in Chicago.

On Tuesday a mob had entered the planing-mills and lumber yards in the south-west part of the city, and compelled the men to stop work. Encouraged by their success, they assembled again on Thursday to finish their diabolical work. They began to gather as early as seven in the morning, in or about 22d Street bridge, near which are some of the larger mills and yards. It was composed of a motley set, only a portion of it being railroad men. All were armed with pieces of wood some four or five feet in length, and the pockets of nearly all were bulged out and weighted down with stones. When ready, they moved slowly out Twenty-second street in a westerly direction, stopping at all the mills and yards along the route, and investigating for themselves as to whether all labor had ceased or not. The first lively demonstration made was at the Chicago Planing-Mill Company, and an adjoining distillery. The mill had fired up, and seemed all ready for work, which seemed to enrage the mob. Threats were freely made to fire the structure, but the mob suddenly proceeded onward without doing any damage. Pond & Soper's mill, in which the men were at work, closed down suddenly as the mob advanced.

Lieut. Vesey, of the Hinman Street Station, saw the rabble advancing, and bethought himself of a way to baffle them.  Telegraphing the state of affairs to Madison and Twelfth Street Stations, Lieut. Callahan and the Twelfth Street police, and Lieut. Blettner with fifty police from Madison Street, came down to aid him.  Vesey, nothing daunted by the overpowering number of the mob, massed his men on the corner of Blue Island Avenue and Twenty-second Street.  They had no muskets out, as they expected no more trouble than upon the day previous.  Finding his position a poor one for dispersing a mob, and ascertaining that the crowd were heading for the works of the United States Rolling Stock Company, McCormick's mammoth factory, and similar large establishments in the neighborhood, Vesey marched his men down Blue Island Avenue, or the Black Road, as that part of it is called, and, taking up position at the gates of the Rolling-Stock Works, awaited the arrival of the strikers.  The crisis came soon enough.  Just about 10.30 o'clock the mob hove in sight, and, nothing daunted by the sight of the police, approached on the double-quick.  Several of the leaders made a surly demand upon the police to stand aside and let them in at the gates. Lieut. Vesey addressed them, exhorting them to return to their homes and do no violence, as under no consideration would the police allow them to proceed further.  He also cautioned them that any violence would be repulsed by the police with slaughter, as they were heavily armed.

The mob jeered and derided him throughout, and one of the leaders became so furious that Vesey and and his able Sergeant, McCabe, placed him under arrest.  This infuriated the mob, and they rushed upon the fence and torn some 100 feet of it down, and then,

turning in with their companions, made a desperate
sortie upon the police with stones and sticks. The
police retaliated with their batons, until, finding several of their number stricken down, they drew their
revolvers and fired, several men firing as many as a
dozen shots each. "Presumably they fired over the
crowd or under them, but several have since averred
that they were so enraged at the violence of the mob
that they fired their shots where they thought to do
the most injury. At this summary treatment the mob
fled, slowly and sullenly enough, however, and fighting
back bitterly." The police advanced and the crowd
scattered north, east, and west, the main body coming directly along Blue Island Avenue. Reaching
Lincoln street, Lieut. Callahan and his Twelfth street
men completely surprised them, and greatly encouraged Vesey and his men. By their combined efforts
the mob was routed completely, and chased out on to
the prairie. After skirmishing about for some time
the policemen returned to the station, and found that
in this encounter six of their number were wounded.
It was said that the rioters were going to McCormick's reaper factory to make the workmen there
stop work; but this onslaught arrested them, and
the mill kept running, the men all being satisfied.
The routed mob gathered together on the prairie and
discussed matters in a savage spirit. The Bohemians,
as they were called, said they had two independent
military companies, armed and equipped, and that
they would get them out to protect them from the
military; proposed to tear down Bridewell, so that
no more bricks could be made by contract, and declared they would have eight hours labor a day's

work, and an advance of 20 per cent. on present wages, or they would tear down and destroy, etc., and then dispersed.

The mob in the lumber yard was very large. At nine o'clock nearly 2,000 men assembled in the vicinity of 22d and Loomis streets. Adjacent mills were stopped, and the workmen driven away. Foreman Frese, of the Kirby Carpenter Company, was beaten unmercifully. They went to the gas company, but after a little parley concluded to let it continue the manufacture of gas that day, but swore that on the morrow they would close it up.

Early in the morning another crowd collected near Eighteenth Street bridge almost at the commencement of the day's work. This proceeded westward, sending off detachments now and then into side streets to close up the factories. They met with little resistance at first. At the Garden City Distillery and Rectifying Company, corner of Canalport Avenue and Twenty-Second Street, the mob tried to force the employés to leave, but they were told by a Government officer that that institution was in the hands of Uncle Sam, and that if they interfered in any way they would be summarily squelched.

In the west division, along Canal, Clinton, Jefferson, and other streets, a mob of 100 or more appeared at about ten o'clock, and descending upon the lumber yard of C. J. L. Meyers, compelled the men in it to quit work. Other lumber yards were visited in succession and work in them stopped. They made the driver of Noble's lumber wagon unhitch his horse and put him in the stable—waiting till it was done. They then visited the shot tower on Clinton Street, but the place was closed before they reached it, and they vented their spite in smashing in the windows with stones. After this achievement they proceeded to the Vulcan Iron Works, and stopped the work there. They attempted the same thing at Carlisle Mason's, but were driven off. Hooting and yelling, they then broke on a run into a passenger depot at the North-western Railroad, and endeavored to stop the passenger train, but a squad of police suddenly arriving they were taken by surprise, and one of their chief leaders, Sattal, was arrested and borne off to the police station, followed by the crowd, which yet dared not attempt to rescue him.

On the north side was another crowd of working men, roaming about, perhaps 300 in number, closing all the manufacturing establishments, brick-kilns, the Chicago Furniture Company, cooper-shops, etc., many of which resisted this tyrannical way of making them cease working. Some twenty-five tanneries which lined the river on both sides came next under the supervision of the mob, and had to shut up. Coming to the Phenix Distillery, they met with a good deal of opposition. As the crowd pushed its way into the building where some 6,000 bushels of grain were in a state of fermentation, the proprietors begged to be allowed to go on for the present and thus prevent the loss which would result from stopping work just then. But the mob would listen to no reason, and threatened to burn the building if their demands were not complied with, and everything was stopped. The mob now began to thin out, but a villainous-looking man put himself at the head of about 150 men and boys, and went to a tailor's shop where some twenty-five sewing girls were at work, and in spite of all remonstrances achieved the great victory of making them stop.

But there seemed no end now to the mobs that had taken possession of Chicago, for while this high-handed action was carried out in other parts of the city, a drunken German gathered a crowd around him at the corner of Division and Halstead streets, which, armed with clubs and iron bars, soon frightened all the stores, shops and saloons in the vicinity to shut up, and a stone-yard near by to stop work.

The mob had now swelled to thousands, and started for Goose Island to stop the work in the tanneries there. They then made their way towards the gas-works, but, met unexpectedly by the police, which had been sent for, fled in every direction.

Mobs this morning seemed everywhere, for, while the various quarters of the city were being inundated by these lawless gangs, a mob sprang up, no one knew from where, in the North Division, south part of Chicago Avenue. There were not, perhaps, over a hundred and fifty of these thieves and ragamuffins and boys in all, yet they succeeded in stopping work in the lumber-yards and factories in the vicinity; but in the midst of their success a squad of fifty policemen, under Lieut. Hathaway, came up, and charging on them, scattered them like sheep. In another direction a gang of a hundred or so visited David Woodville's wire screen factory, in Ohio Street, and compelled it to close up, and keeping on, made all the shops on their route stop work. It was a mere gang of rowdies, having their brief holiday of power in the utter helplessness of men who were weak simply because they were

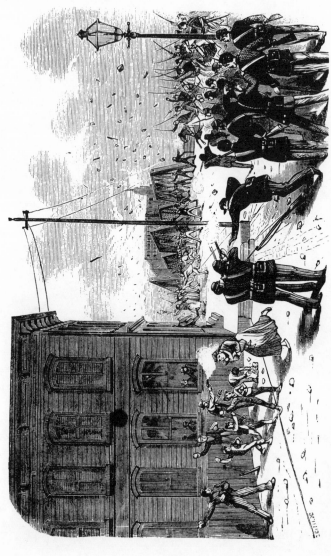

CHICAGO—CHARGE OF THE CAVALRY AND 2D REGIMENT UPON THE MOB AT HALSTEAD ST.

anticipating no such high-handed robbery. The editor of the *New World*, a Scandinavian Socialist, went into the North Side planing-mill and told the men to quit. There were several hundred of them, and they obeyed. Then he went down into the engine-room and told the engineer to do likewise until more wages were paid. He was followed by the proprietor, John O'Neil, who told him that he didn't know what wages the men were getting; that the best way for the strikers to do was to appoint committees to visit the different shops and find out the rates, and then they could tell which were paying fair wages, and which were not; that all his men were getting good pay, and were perfectly satisfied to work. Calling to one of his men, Mr. O'Neil said, "Jim, how much do you get?" "Three dollars a day," was the reply. Then Mr. O'Neil seized the Communist's hands and held them up for the workmen to look at. They were like a woman's— soft and white; the fellow had never done manual labor in his life. This fact made Mr. O'Neil angry, and he said to him: "Here, I'll set you to work and give you three dollars a day." But the fraud said "Not now."

Mr. O'Neil then told him that he never did an honest day's work in his life—that he would rather steal than work, and drove him out of the shop. One of the other men who went in—there were only three or four of them—was a workingman; his hands showed he was a toiler. The crowd, which, when it reached the corner, numbered perhaps 200, was doubled in half an hour after it arrived there, men, women, and children coming from all directions to see the "fun." Threats being made against the brass works, the police

19*

were notified, and Lieut. Hathaway, with fifty men, responded, and coming suddenly upon them, scattered them, and gave the socialist editor matter for a new leader in his paper. It is useless to follow the course of all the mobs in various sections of the city. It was the same story over—factories and shops were visited and closed under threats of violence. There was a little variation in the incidents which relieved the monotony, as for instance, on the lake front from the south side.

A mob of about 150 of the roughest kind of loafers marched to the lake front in the morning, and went through the lumber-yard of Ludington, Wells & Co., compelling the men at work there to quit and join them. Thus augmented, they went to the Central Elevator, compelling the men there to stop work. They then visited the Michigan Central Elevator, but found no one at work there. Finally they reached Goodrich's dock, where they committed sundry excesses, kicking boxes open, and forcing the men to leave their work. After leaving this point, they went to Waldron, Niblock & Co.'s place, where they found some men at work on boilers, and some others who unloaded stoves. These were driven off unceremoniously and the fires in the boiler-shops extinguished. Amid yells and hoots they marched back to the Michigan Central freight-house, back of Goodrich's office. Here the leader of the mob, a rough, dirty loafer, mounted a flat car and commenced to harangue the crowd. "The first words he uttered were that he must have three glasses of beer, and by the eternal he was going to have them, though blood should be spilled in the attempt. If they had nothing to do in the summer, they would have nothing to eat in the winter. 'Look at me,' he continued, casting around ferocious glances; 'do I look like a loafer or a laborer?' The crowd yelled and cheered, and assured him that he was one of them. 'Of course I am,' he said; 'I am as honest a workingman as ever worked in a shop. Look at my hands,' holding out a pair of paws the color of which cannot be described in words, the same being a mixture between black and yellow. 'These hands show what I am. We know what we are fighting for, and what we are doing. We are fighting those God d—d capitalists. That is what we are doing. Ain't we?' The crowd hurrahed and yelled, and a number of them shouted, 'Let us kill those d—d aristocrats.' He had been a railroad man himself once, he said, and knew what he was talking about. They had the thing started and they were going to keep it going until all these big-bugs had been put down. He was a boat-hand now, and was getting but $12 a month, and he just wanted enough to keep him from starvation." * That's what they wanted, and nothing else. They were going to make the aristocrats sick, and they were not going to stop until the work was accomplished. He was ready to die for the workingmen, and so were they all. The crowd again hooted and yelled, and assured the orator that they were in sympathy with him, and that they would turn out and fix things in the evening. After completing this harangue he descended from the car and marched his mob around the freight-houses. Of a sudden there was a great commotion, and some one shouted, " The peelers are coming ! " The

---

* Chicago *Tribune.*

bravado of the mob, which but a moment before vowed to annihilate every aristocrat in town, suddenly gave way, and the crowd became panic-stricken and tried to escape. But the valiant peelers pounced upon them from all sides, making great havoc among the heads of about a dozen of them, whose feet were not fleet enough to carry them away in time. Among this number was the leader and orator of the mob. One special policeman took hold of him by the ears, lifted him up, shook him as a dog shakes a rat, and then rapped him a few times over the head with his club. A whole wagon-load of wounded were conveyed to the station after the affray. The squad of police then marched through all the neighboring streets, clearing them of suspicious characters. The treatment which the mob received was so efficient, though radical, that no more mobs visited or molested that part of the city further during the day.*

The uprising had now become so universal that Governor Cullom thought the city had got beyond the control of the police, and before noon sent to Washington for the aid of the regular troops, and received the following answers.

WASHINGTON, July 25, 1877.

*Colonel R. C. Drum, Assistant Adjutant-General Chicago Ill. :*

The President directs that you use United States troops in case of emergency in suppressing the riot at Chicago, under orders of the Governor of the State.

E. D. TOWNSEND, Adjutant-General.

---

* Chicago *Tribune.*

CHICAGO, ILL., July 26.

*To Hon. S. M. Cullom, Governor of Illinois :*

I have the honor to report that I am authorized by the President of the United States to use, under your orders, national troops in this city in suppressing the riots.                              R. C. DRUM,
                         Assistant Adjutant-General.

SPRINGFIELD, ILL., July 26, 1877.

*Colonel R. C. Drum, U. S. A. :*

You will please report to the Mayor of Chicago, and act in concert with him in putting down the mobs and riots, and in keeping the peace and protecting the property of the people.     S. M. CULLOM, Governor.

Immediately on the receipt of the Governor's order the national forces in the city were placed at his disposal. A mass meeting was held in the afternoon in the Tabernacle, in which were gathered a more anxious crowd than ever came together there to hear the famous preacher Moody. Speeches were made by distinguished citizens, and a proclamation of the Mayor was read, calling on five thousand citizens to report at police headquarters for duty ; and various other precautions were taken to meet the coming storm.

At evening the strikers gathered in the railroad yards, all the way from Canal street to Halsted. One portion moved towards the Round House, others broke in the windows of the freight-house and attempted to enter the building. In the meantime a body of police sixteen strong, under Lieutenant Callahan, came tearing down the street in a stage to the scene of disorder. Before reaching it, however, they were met by a mob led by a man named Miles Clynch, who attacked the stage with stones and sticks, and, cutting the harness of the team, sent them dashing up the street. The driver was knocked from his seat and badly cut, and the squad of police was pressed so close by the yelling crowd that they at last drew their revolvers and fired into it from the stage windows. They then dashed out and scattered those nearest them, and drove the whole crowd before them till they reached the Viaduct, when they halted. The police then ran through an opening into Fifteenth Street, and gaining the approach to it, fired down on the mob. The latter at once fell back and attacked the police with such a shower of stones that they were compelled to retreat to their station to find out why they had not been re-enforced. A detachment had been sent to their aid, but missing them, came on the mob after they had left, and were also badly beaten, and retreated to the station, where each recriminated the other for being left to fight the crowd alone.

During all this time the mob had been carrying things at their will. The first street-car that attempted to cross the Viaduct was pelted with a shower of stones, the conductor and driver both driven from their positions, the horses lashed into madness until they ran away, and finally the car was overturned at the junction of Halsted and Evans streets, where it was pulled to pieces by a pack of howling young wretches not older than fourteen years. Respectable citizens stood in their doorways, and quietly deprecated all such destruction, but were powerless to prevent it. The other cars that came to the Viaduct were stopped, the conductors rifled of the contents of their pockets, and the passengers compelled to flee under serious threats. Farther up the street, the crowd, advancing towards Twelfth Street, entered the gun-store of M. J. Pribyl, No. 522 Halsted Street. Pribyl and family were scared out of their wits, and offered no resistance to the pillagers. The mob cleaned the store out, taking thirty-five guns, as many revolvers, and as many more pistols of the powder-and-shot kind, and a quantity of ammunition.* This was done, not by the workingmen, but by those who made off with their plunder. The street-lights were put out. The mob now went to the hardware store of Mr. E. H. Lott, and wrenching off the iron bars, they broke in the windows, and entering the building carried off what plunder they wished. The street-cars were again attacked, and howls and yells made night hideous. Soon after a battalion of police came up and cleared the streets.

On the next day, the 26th, the trouble began early in the morning. A meeting of workingmen had been called at 9 o'clock, and before that hour a large crowd had gathered at Turner Hall, and surged up and down the street, boasting what they would do. About 10 o'clock a squad of police hove in sight, when the mob began to hoot, yell, and pelt them with stones. The police charged on them with their clubs. While hitting right and left, another squad of police arrived and took them in rear and soon settled them. They then entered the building, when a fight began. Many jumped from the windows, and several received wounds more or less severe. A passenger train coming in was attacked and switched off the track. At the Viaduct a street-car was stopped. Twenty-five policemen were sent down to disperse the crowd, but

---

* Chicago paper.

were attacked with such violence that they drew their revolvers and fired into it. But the mob increased so rapidly, and from under cover, and from the tops of houses hurled stones so fiercely, that the police slowly retired, followed by the hooting, yelling rioters. Seeing that in all probability the territory between Canalport Avenue and the Viaduct would be the spot on which most of the rioting would take place, the military were ordered there. Two cavalry companies soon came rattling down the street, followed by the Second Regiment, Col. Funk, 700 strong, with two ten-pound guns. By half-past ten it was estimated that nearly 10,000 people were gathered here, though not all open rioters. Through this immense throng the police would march, the crowd fleeing down the cross streets as they advanced, but rushing up again as they retired. Arrests were made and the prisoners hurried off in express wagons to the stations. A little after noon things became quiet. But about three o'clock a company of cavalrymen, some twenty strong, that had been out patrolling the country, came in, but getting separated from the police and militia, they were set upon by the crowd with stones and revolvers. The former returned the fire, and several were hit when the police came to their rescue and ended the fight. Seeing that the mob at the Halsted Street Viaduct was meditating an assault, Captain Learey of the west side was ordered to hurry all the men at his command to the spot. Laying aside their clubs, they had armed themselves with Springfield muskets and were ordered to fire at the first assault of the mob. At Fourteenth Street they were joined by a body of cavalry under Captain Anderson. They marched down the street,

IOWA—RAILWAY BRIDGE OVER THE MISSISSIPPI AT CLINTON.

clearing the mob, and effected a junction with those
at the Viaduct and charged up and down the streets,
dispersing the crowd.  Joined by Col. Daly's cavalry,
they then marched south to clear the rioters near the
river.  Reaching the bridge, they were fiercely attacked with stones and revolvers.  A detachment was
ordered across to clear the mob there.  They did so,
and were soon lost to sight as they charged into the
crowd.

At this critical moment some one swung the bridge
and cut them off from all succor.  A mere handful,
it now seemed that they must perish, enveloped
as they were in such a mass of maddened men.  At
this juncture, when all seemed up with the brave fellows, a lad named James O'Neill, residing on Twenty-
fifth street, certainly no older than ten years, came to
their rescue.  "This gallant little hero, of whom too
much cannot be said in praise, jumped into the river,
and, swimming to the pier, mounted the structure, and
swung it around, thus opening communication between
the beleaguered squad and the main forces.  As soon
as the bridge swung to, the cavalry charged across,
while the gun of the Second Regiment was unlimbered,
and aimed so as to sweep the street.  Two companies
of the second also wheeled into position, ready to support both the artillery and cavalry."  The crossing
being effected, firing commenced, and several were shot
down, when the mob gave way and fled in every direction.  But while a mob disappeared in one quarter of
the city, another would suddenly be announced in another.

"Rumors of fighting kept coming in, and consequently, at 12.30, two companies of the regulars were

ordered forward ; and as the veteran Indian fighters, all bronzed and rugged, filed out of headquarters, and marched down La Salle Street towards Twelfth Street, a cheer went up from the assembled crowd that fairly shook the building. Their soldierly appearance, their total lack of excitement, the clock-like regularity of their step, and the determination depicted on the countenances of the commanding officers, and more than all, the appearance of those ounce-bore Spencer rifles, that shoot sixteen times without loading, indicated that when they got on the scene something would have to give way. They proceeded immediately to Twelfth Street to support the battery where it had been stationed."

In the afternoon a troop of cavalry, some fifty in number, with two companies and a howitzer, and with the police on both flanks, started from a point south of the Viaduct, and marched to Twelfth Street. Rioters were seized, and then would follow a shower of stones, while pistol-shots and the sound of clubs falling on human heads were heard in every direction. Joined by more of the police, the force moved on amid hooting and yells of rage, the police making arrests till soon there were three wagon-loads of them. A rioter fired point blank at an officer, just missing him. The latter leaped from his horse, knocked him down and handed him over to the police. It was a terrible scene along the route of this force. Broken heads were everywhere visible. The police would charge right and left in the face of stones and pistol-shots, while screaming women helped to swell the Babel. The windows of the houses were closed ; the heat poured down without mercy, and Chicago seemed reeling in a hurricane of excitement that swept not onward, but round and round through the devoted city. At Canal Street a body of police, fifty strong, held the Viaduct— one portion armed with rifles—and as fast as the mob congregated it was dispersed. Captain Agramonte's squad of horsemen here joined the force. Shots being fired from a house, No. 23, in Canal street, the doors were burst open, and Learey's men made their way through a dozen infuriated women and seized the inmates. Lieutenant Frese, commanding another squad of mounted men, was shot at from an alley, and instantly emptied the seven barrels of his revolver into the crowd. In taking the prisoners to the station the force was frequently assailed, and at Fourteenth Street a shot was fired from the crowd. Instantly Learey's men charged on it with fixed bayonets, wounding several.

At headquarters all was commotion from the coming and departing of those engaged in putting down the riots, and the arrival of prisoners. News came in incessantly—often contradictory, but on the whole it was plain the authorities were getting the rioters under control.

One of the worst mobs was started in the morning at the stock yard, but it had to give way before the police and military. There was a severe fight in the rear and vicinity of Neill & Co.'s elevator. The mob had taken possession of several loaded coal-cars, the coal being used for missiles with which to attack the police. The mob was defiant, the cavalry and police determined, and the support back of them, in the shape of the battery and the Second Regiment, fully prepared.

Just previous to this there had been only a slight sortie, a portion of the mob having been driven south of the river, which rallied with the other portion immediately after from Bridgeport.

The rioters were armed with long, ugly-looking knives, and revolvers, pistols, guns, and stones. They fired several volleys without effect upon the cavalry and police, when the latter jointly fired their revolvers with terrible effect. Three of the rioters fell mortally wounded, and how many were more or less seriously injured, it was impossible to ascertain. It was said in this attack fourteen were wounded.

The wild and stormy day at last wore away and night came down. What would these maddened men attempt to do under cover of darkness, was a question asked by many with anxious hearts.

About eight o'clock the mob began to assemble, but the police charged and scattered them. In the meantime the Second Regiment was ordered to march towards the Halsted Street Viaduct, where the mob were assuming a threatening aspect. They were supplied with blankets, expecting to make a night of it. As they marched steadily on they were greeted with yells and curses. Col. Quirk cleared sidewalks, door-steps, etc. It was soon ascertained that the Communists were in force at the Viaduct, and were preparing to march towards the Twelfth Street station-house. The regiment at the time was at parade rest; but in an instant the orders, "Attention, shoulder arms," brought every man in position. Several companies were left in reserve, and the rest marched towards the Viaduct. Soon after a volley of musketry rang out on the night air in the direction they had taken, followed by sounds of a heavy fight. The reserve was quickly put in motion, their bayonets gleaming in the moonlight. Advancing in dead silence, save their steady, measured tramp over the pavement, they could hear the shouts and yells in advance. As they approached the mob, Col. Quirk gave the order to fire, and a quick, sharp volley rang out, and the mob scattered. The troops returned to their position, and thinking the trouble was over, were preparing to take a nap, when word was brought that the mob had congregated on Col. Quirk's front at a coal-heap near the Chicago, Burlington and Quincy coal track. Soon the coal began to fall in a shower upon the troops. The order to fire was at once given, and the reserve was called up. The rioters held their ground doggedly till two volleys were poured into them, lighting up the shadows with their blaze, when they turned and fled. This substantially closed the riot and there was no more serious disturbance that night, and in the morning only the wrecks remained. Arrests were now the order of the day. Business soon resumed its ordinary course, and preparations were made to set the trains in motion again. This was not so difficult, as only a small portion of the rioters were railroad men, the main part being Communists and the offscouring of the city. It is not necessary to mention the minor strikes in the State—at Springfield, Peoria, and smaller places—they were all interlocked with the strike at Chicago. At Braidwood they attempted to drive 200 colored miners out of the town, but the arrival of two regiments put an end to this fanatical outrage and quelled the rioters.

# CHAPTER XXXIII.

## THE STRIKERS AT ST. LOUIS AND LOUISVILLE.

The Mob overcome the Police at Carondelet.—Citizens enrolling themselves.—Workingmen's Party.—Their Arrogance and Assumption.—A Steamer Boarded, and the Captain compelled to Raise the Wages of his Hands.—The Mob confront the Police and Citizens.—The Citizens of Louisville Join the Military.—The Mob put down.

MISSOURI fell into line with the other States and began to move as the Eastern ones were becoming tranquil.

"July 25.—The workingmen held an excited meeting in Lucas Market last night, in which they denounced capitalists. One speaker said they had 7,000 stand of arms in their possession, at which cries of "Let us have them and we will use them!" Another speaker charged the responsibility of bloodshed on the President of the United States. The meeting recommended a general strike for eight hours as a day's labor."

The Mayor issued a proclamation, warning the people against violence and announcing a Committee of Safety.

At nine o'clock on the 25th a crowd assembled again in Lucas Market Place, around a stand erected by the Workingmen's Party, 1,500 strong, while 2,000 or 3,000 spectators gathered in the vicinity. The crowd was made up mostly of wire-workers, who had struck, and strikers from other manufacturing establishments. At ten o'clock they formed in column and marched past the City Hall to Turner Hall, where the executive committee of the Workingmen's Party was in session. Half an hour later a body of 500, made up chiefly of negroes, was sent to the levee, and marched its length for the purpose of inducing the roustabouts to join them. The steamer Centennial was boarded just as she was pushing out for New Orleans. They stopped the boat, and demanded that the captain should sign an agreement to pay a specified increase of wages. He did so, and the boat was allowed to depart.

The disturbance spread on every side, embracing machine-shops and factories of every kind. At Carondelet the police, endeavoring to defend the workmen at the Martindale Zinc Works, were driven off, and all coal trains stopped—in short, the strikers brought everything to a standstill. The next day the citizens, having waked up to the dangerous crisis, began to enroll themselves as a Citizens' Guard, which soon swelled to thousands. The vast mob marched up to the headquarters of the citizen militia and the police, at Four Courts Building, and boldly confronted them, but were compelled to retire without force being used.

The railroad strikers almost entirely passed out of sight in the city in view of the magnitude of the movement inaugurated by the Workingmen's Party, and the high hand with which they conducted it in closing mills, factories, etc., and compelled mechanics and laborers to cease work. The water-works in the northern part of the city, and the distributing reservoirs, were placed under guard by soldiers. The levee laborers, who compelled the granting of an extortionate advance in wages of all steamboat employees, boarded every boat that arrived and exacted accession to their terms.

The Workingmen's Party assumed to dictate all kinds of terms to the mayor, passed resolutions asking the legislature to be convened to take up the labor question, arranging beforehand what that legislature should be. But the military and cannon soon brought down their arrogant spirits, and order was restored. The numerous strikes in various smaller localities in the State need not be mentioned here. A strike at the same time took place at Louisville and Kansas. The scenes at each were a repetition of those already described, while to make the chain across the continent complete, a terrible riot broke out in San Francisco, aimed at the poor Chinese instead of the rich railroad companies.

At Louisville there would doubtless have been serious trouble but for the prompt action of the citizens, who took the matter in their own hands, and were determined to make quick work if the strikers resorted to violence.

---

\* Ninety-six pages are here added to correct the omission in paging the illustrations.

IOWA—RAILROAD DEPOT AT COUNCIL BLUFFS.

# CHAPTER XXXIV.

## LESSONS OF THE STRIKE.

FOR more than a week the country had now lain in a sort of paralysis from this unexpected, unparalleled strike, running as it did the length and breath of the land. The strikers doubtless thought this would work in their favor, and public opinion would compel the railroad companies to yield to their terms and relieve the pressure. They forgot that those whose interests are suffering by the detention of peaceful men look to the bold robber who tells the latter to stand and deliver, for redress. The strikers said to the entire East and West, " You have got to suffer, and, if necessary, starve, until we get ten or twenty-five per cent. advance on our wages. Now, if railroad employés ever think of repeating this experiment, let them lay to heart this one fact : that utter indifference of the authorities and the non-interference of the military, both of which they desired in this strike, would be the greatest calamity that could overtake them. If they suppose they are going to sever the West from the East, strike down with impunity, at one blow, all the interests—nay, the very life itself of the great West, they are sadly mistaken. They may want an increase of wages, but the West want and will have an outlet to the flour and grain and provisions they raise. These

they will not let rot on their hands, to their own im-
poverishment, for anybody's wages.   Hence, the more
complete sway the strikers are allowed, the more terrible their doom will be when a suffering people arises.
Non-interference of the authorities would only let the
destruction of property for the time be greater, to
make that punishment more terrible, for when the people of the West arose, as arise they would be compelled
to or starve, that punishment would be swift and decisive.   Those who had attempted to impoverish them,
and imperiously told them, "you shall take no more of
the products of your industry to market until *we* grant
permission," would be shot down like dogs and hung
like felons.   The *people*, from self-preservation alone,
would be compelled to take the matter in hand, and
then it would be mob against mob; and who would go
to the wall in such a conflict admits of no doubt.   Men
may cripple a single railroad company with impunity,
but they cannot cut a continent in two and ruin both
portions, as such a strike as the recent one would do if
prolonged.   This is a truth which railroad employés
of all grades should well consider before they undertake another such experiment.   It turns out hard
enough for them to be put down speedily by the strong
arm of law, but it will be infinitely worse if the time
ever comes when the people, East and West, for their
own preservation, shall be compelled to crush them.
When that day comes they will find that they " who
sow the wind shall reap the whirlwind."   They will
find that whether their demands are just and right will
have nothing to do with the settlement of the question.
That will be, whether a slight wrong is going to justify
a great one—whether the right of 100,000 men to

to an increase of ten per cent. on their wages is to override the well-being—nay, almost the preservation of a whole continent.

Of course the unparalleled scenes through which we had passed awakened the attention of the entire country to the possibilities of similar ones in the future, and consequently filled the press with suggestions and methods of preventing them. Some endeavor to show what lessons they had taught the railroad companies; the burden of which was the imprudence of irritating and maddening men by oppressing them and compelling them to work at starvation prices. Others dwelt on the importance of putting an end to the fallacy that there was any real antagonism between capital and labor. Now it is one thing to suggest a remedy against such a strike as the one we had just put down, and another to provide some method of settling ordinary disputes and differences between railroad companies and their employees. The former, aiming as it did at the ruin of the country for the attainment of selfish ends, allows of but one remedy—the bullet, and teaches but one lesson, the sooner and more unsparingly it is used the better. When men conspire in such a diabolical plan as that, arbitration and commissions and appeals are worthless —point-blank volleys are the only resources. To provide against the latter is most desirable if it can be done.

It is suggested by one portion that the Government should own the railroads and thus be able to fix a fair and just remuneration for those who are employed on them. But this is simply an impossibility. If Government had constructed the roads in the first place and built those only that the country needed, the plan might have worked well. But to buy up all the railroads now built at cost, and be compelled to run them by paying wages higher than those now paid, would be a losing business, and the country would have to be taxed to make up the loss sure to occur.   With the exception of a few extravagant salaries paid to officers, they are run more cheaply than the Government could run them ; yet a large portion are insolvent, and those which are not pay no dividend on their stock.   That the people of the country will ever consent to be taxed to make up any deficiencies in the earnings of railroads, few will believe. Others propose that Congress shall fix the wages of employees.   Many think that all evils can be cured by the passage of right laws.   The trouble is, some laws are totally inconsistent with republican institutions and, hence, cannot be enforced.   Congress can no more fix the wages of railroad men than of those engaged in manufactures, or of household servants.   Such interference is the purest despotism, and the laws passed to that end would be declared unconstitutional by the courts, just as the eight hour system was.

Again, it is suggested that Congress fix the tariff on freight.  Perhaps as it has power to regulate internal commerce it might do this.   But if it were regulated according to the distance freight was carried, the longer roads must be abandoned and the more direct lines enjoy the monopoly of the carrying business. Perhaps this would be desirable, as we have too many railroads, but what would the West say, if told, " You can no longer make your own bargains, but let Congress make them for you."   It is evident that this plan would be beset with great difficulties, though, perhaps, not insurmountable.

A third proposition is to have commissioners of

arbitration, to which all difficulties between the rail-road companies and their employees shall be referred. It is said that such a plan has worked well in England. A great many things may work well in the monarchies of Europe, that would fail disastrously here. If the difficulty be one of wages, the matter might as well be referred to Congress at once, and if such commissions are proper for railroads, why not for manufactories, farmers, builders—nay families. Such arbitrary commissions would not do in a republic like ours. The last method —viz. to cause the antagonism between capital and labor to cease, and harmony of feeling to take its place, is most excellent, and if carried out will solve the difficulty. But the great trouble is, how to bring about this desira-ble state of things. There seems no way except that proposed by the communists, to have all things in common, which is just what cannot be effected until the world is wholly changed, and the long looked-for millennium takes place.

The antagonism between capital and labor is but an-other form of saying that the poor envy the rich, and are discontented that their lot is so different. " The rich oppress you," is not merely a scriptural utterance, it is an historical truth—not so much as applied to in-dividuals as a simple statement that the accumula-tion of wealth is necessarily secured, more or less, at the expense of the lower classes. The feeling of contempt on the one side, and restlessness or hatred on the other, are old as civilization, but, as stated in a former article, is more strongly developed in a republican government than in a despotic monarchy. In the latter men are born to a certain rank or condition in life, out of which they cannot escape and which from childhood they are taught to consider irremediable.   More than this, they are told by the priests of religion that this is a divine arrangement; hence to rebel against it is to rebel against God.   It is plain, therefore, that to a people born into such a social state and made to accept it as a divine institution, that nothing but the most maddening oppression or intolerable suffering can make them rebel against it   It was on this account that Macaulay's memorable saying was based, that the more violent a revolution was, only showed the greater necessity for it.   But in a republic the reverse of this, both in politics and religion, is taught.   The State says that all men are born free and equal, and religious teachers reiterate the same truth while the poor and suffering class say that both are a lie, if it is right for them to accept their condition and be contented with it.   Hence, while some strikes are based on particular grievances, and all may be referred to some wrong which should be righted, as the immediate cause, the real trouble has a deeper foundation—it rests on the belief that the inequality in the good things of this world is unjust, and the worst of it is that the more enlightened and intelligent the lower classes become, the stronger is this feeling in them.   If this is true, the question naturally arises— What then is to be the end of it all?   That is just the problem that man has been trying to solve for a thousand years, and we are no nearer its solution to-day than at the outset.   It is the very difficulty which surrounds it that has given birth to that universal belief in some sort of millennium in the far future, more than from the dim hints of it in the sacred Scriptures.   All feel that the Creator of man can alone solve it.   To one occupying a distant point of observation, this poor planet of ours seems like a ship on a lee shore, forever struggling towards the desired haven, yet ever baffled in its efforts, and the failure of every experiment, the overthrow of every government sounds a signal-gun of distress fired through the gloom, saying, We cannot help ourselves.

Now, this general philosophical fact has been dwelt upon because it lies at the bottom of all this antagonism between the rich and poor, and, call it by what name you will, which none of the proposed remedies reach. This is abundantly proved in the recent strike. The more terrible features that accompanied it—nay, gave it its real strength—owed their origin not to the disaffection of laborers, but to this hostile feeling of one class against another. As long as this distinction exists, the only transient security is in the liberality, kindness, and justice of the rich. If the hovel stands under the shadow of the palace, the latter must ameliorate the condition of the former. If the wealthy flaunt their wealth, and exhibit their prodigality in the presence of the suffering, and wretched, and starving, that prodigality must be directed on other objects than themselves. The sounds of mirth and revelry are discordant in the ears of the inmates of sordid tenements and filthy cellars, and no amount of sophistry can change it. On the other hand, the working classes must submit patiently to the law of demand and supply, in labor, or do worse. The problem which the ages have tried to solve, cannot be solved by the torch and the bludgeon. They only make matters worse. Love thy neighbor as thyself, is the only remedy for the evils we suffer, and all amelioration of our condition can be measured by an approximation to it. We may pile tome on tome on political economy, write philosophical treatises without end, form organizations and make laws, so long as they represent mere human sagacity they can only alleviate the symptoms—they do not reach the disease. We see great results brought about by material means, but they are useless to eradicate the evil we wish to reach, except as they are based on that elementary principle, "LOVE THY NEIGHBOR AS THYSELF."